"Paul Tyson is an authentic lover of wisdom. We are in desperate need of sane and straight-talking philosophers like him because the most basic commonsense realities of human sexuality have now been abandoned by many academic elites. In this book Tyson provides an accessible and illuminating unpacking of why obvious truths about the facts of life have become invisible to our elites. He walks us through the long and surprising story of how we got to this very strange sex-and-gender-fluid place. Then, after making sure we understand what makes gender theory seem credible, he goes on to show why it is wrong. And dangerous. This book is an important read for anyone struggling to understand what gender theory is and why anyone believes it."
—DERRICK JENSEN, author of *A Language Older Than Words*

"In this immensely erudite book, Paul Tyson argues for basic commonsense biological sex, without denying the fact that biological sex can be lived out in many ways. His core goal is to persuade policymakers and academics to stop persecuting people who insist on the fact that a man cannot become a woman and vice versa. A society built upon the notion that biological sex is false or at least radically fungible will, indeed, be one that produces far more injustices than were endured by non–sexually conforming persons in past societies. Tyson provides an ample genealogy for the current academic, cultural, and political understanding of the transgender cause. He identifies roots as far back as Peter Abelard's and William of Ockham's nominalism, continuing on through the anti-realist epistemologies of Kant and his praxis- and will-focused heirs, joined to left-wing Hegelian understandings of the march of history. Nietzsche, Marx, critical theory, postmodernism, and Judith Butler, among many others, play their part here. Calling for a return to rationality grounded in realist metaphysics, Tyson shows that the result could paradoxically assist modern liberalism in being properly liberal."
—MATTHEW LEVERING, James N. Jr. and Mary D. Perry Chair of Theology, Mundelein Seminary

"A fascinating look at the deep philosophical background to gender theory and the basis of its superficial intellectual appeal. Essential reading for anyone interested in this vital contemporary debate."
—KATHLEEN STOCK, author of *Material Girls*

"Paul Tyson has the critical academic credentials in the relevant areas of philosophy, theology, sociology, science, and politics to address this challenging area of gender theory. He also writes directly and lucidly. For too long the debate about gender theory has been hampered by obscure and dense verbiage designed to mystify its readers. It leads many to surrender to a range of powers aiming to take away their agency. Tyson clears away the undergrowth to empower those open to his and the great philosophical and scientific realist tradition of a 'meaningful understanding of natural facts.' I found light-globes going off regularly as Tyson's genealogy clearly linked movement to movement, finally opening a door through the dark. Having shown how our 'knowledge elites' frolicked along in their performative meaning-making games, Tyson takes seriously what they do not—people's lives, especially young people's lives, are at stake. He draws on a range of practical and radical arguments to show not only that, but how gender theory is wrong. It has taken a Kantian and linguistic wrong turn away from reality. But by 'recovering a lifeworld without gender theory,' Tyson provides a patch for rebooting the Enlightenment and the natural meaning of sex, in all its goodness and familial importance. As law and medicine, the courts and upholders of the Hippocratic Oath slowly seek to recover some sense of scientific sexual sanity, for the sake of a whole generation, this brilliant and courageous book is well placed to best help so many sufferers from their seemingly never-ending gender nightmare, to recover a route back to a semblance of reality."
—GORDON PREECE, Director of Ethos Centre for Christianity and Society, Melbourne

"A tour de force through centuries of intellectual thought on sex, gender, and politics, Tyson situates contemporary debates within a long philosophical genealogy, inviting readers to consider how formerly unthinkable ideas about truth, biology, and identity have come to be taken for granted and enshrined in our institutions."
PETER BOGHOSSIAN, Founding Faculty Advisor, University of Austin

Gender Theory Is Wrong

Gender Theory Is Wrong

A Genealogy of Sex-Irrealism, Why It Fails, and How We Can Restore a Meaningful Understanding of Natural Facts

PAUL TYSON

CASCADE *Books* • Eugene, Oregon

GENDER THEORY IS WRONG
A Genealogy of Sex-Irrealism, Why It Fails, and How We Can Restore a Meaningful Understanding of Natural Facts

Copyright © 2026 Paul Tyson. All rights reserved. Except for brief quotations in critical publications or reviews, no part of this book may be reproduced in any manner without prior written permission from the publisher. Write: Permissions, Wipf and Stock Publishers, 199 W. 8th Ave., Suite 3, Eugene, OR 97401.

Cascade Books
An Imprint of Wipf and Stock Publishers
199 W. 8th Ave., Suite 3
Eugene, OR 97401

www.wipfandstock.com

PAPERBACK ISBN: 979-8-3852-6440-7
HARDCOVER ISBN: 979-8-3852-6441-4
EBOOK ISBN: 979-8-3852-6442-1

Cataloguing-in-Publication data:

Names: Tyson, Paul [author].

Title: Gender theory is wrong : a genealogy of sex-irrealism, why it fails, and how we can restore a meaningful understanding of natural facts / Paul Tyson.

Description: Eugene, OR: Cascade Books, 2026 | Includes bibliographical references.

Identifiers: ISBN 979-8-3852-6440-7 (paperback) | ISBN 979-8-3852-6441-4 (hardcover) | ISBN 979-8-3852-6442-1 (ebook)

Subjects: LCSH: Gender identity—Philosophy. | Sex-realism. | Transgender nonconformity. | Gender. | Transsexualism. | Philosophy—History. | Faith and reason. | Queer theory. | Sex.

Classification: HQ18.55 T976 2026 (paperback) | HQ18.55 (ebook)

01/28/26

Contents

Introduction | vii

1. Is Gender Theory Not Even Wrong? | 1
2. What Is Gender Theory? | 8

A GENEALOGY OF GENDER THEORY | 15

3. The Enlightenment Roots of Queer Gender Theory | 17
4. Nineteenth-Century Continental Thought | 27
5. Positivism | 40
6. Linguistic Deflation and Analytic Formalism | 57
7. Postmodernism | 75
8. Gender Theory Makes Sense to Our Knowledge Elites and to Our Lifeworld | 98

WHY GENDER THEORY IS WRONG | 111

9. Gender Theory Is Wrong: Practical Arguments | 115
10. Gender Theory Is Wrong: Radical Arguments | 149
11. Recovering a Lifeworld Without Gender Theory | 170

Bibliography | 177

Introduction

IF GENDER THEORY WAS only a matter of academic interest it would be entirely sensible for most people to ignore it. For let us be blunt: What science-respecting person really and honestly believes that if you are male, but you feel like a woman, then you are in fact female? Even though non-queer people may not believe gender theory to be true, most of us are not going to object to queer people performing whatever imaginative gender identity they like among themselves, and good luck to them. But why should non-queer people even know about gender theory, let alone comply with its aspiration to make sex and gender queer for everyone?

The answer to the above question is that through legislative means a gender-identity reformation is now being imposed on us all by a well-organized and strategically influential cohort of deeply committed gender-theory advocates. Further, this reformation is decidedly *not* liberal or democratic. Whether the large majority likes it or not, we are all now required to accept that single-sex spaces, sex-defined sporting categories, and factual sex-identity categories in any context are no longer permitted. Breastfeeding associations, maternity wards, and gynecologists, for example, must adopt inclusive language that no longer uses "exclusionary" words like "woman," "breast," and "mother," and under no circumstances are they to exclude any XY sex-chromosomed person who wants to be included. We are—it seems—legally required to meekly comply with this rainbow revolution, even though it turns the clock back on sex-defined women's rights, is unfair and can be dangerous in sporting contexts, and creates entirely new domains of women's and children's sexual safety and wellbeing risks. We now live in a world where you can set up a lavender soccer league that is *only* for "queer women, nonbinary, and transpeople" (an excellent idea), but you cannot have a woman's soccer league for females only.[1]

The fact is, gender theory has really caught on in the circles of knowledge and power. Complex arguments promoted by respected academics that nobody seems to really understand are now being accepted as authoritative. Well resourced gender-identity advocates have been remarkably successful in achieving a sweeping range of significant legislative and institutional captures. Our intellectual and governing elites have largely come to accept that the queer reform of all society is a moral imperative. Thus, long-established linguistic and social conventions around sex-linked gender, for everyone, are now being frowned on and even outlawed. Even more disturbingly for concerned parents, the gender-identity reformation has deeply penetrated the online world in which our children and young adults now seem to live and move and have their being.[2]

There indeed are academic reasons why gender theory has caught on in our high intellectual culture, but this is now no merely academic matter. Our knowledge and power classes are imposing a queer sex and gender reformation on us all. Through legislation, media, corporate culture, and education, the gender-theory reform movement surges forward at speed. Gender theory is no longer only of academic interest.

But what if gender theory really is wrong? What if the normal commonsense and science-respecting assumptions of people who are not

---

1. Barker, "Lavender League." Interestingly, in another of Barker's articles about the aborted Oxford Union debate with Imane Khelif (Barker, "Did Mara Yamauchi's Question") there is a link to a YouTube story examining the 2016 Olympics where first-, second-, and third-place winners in the women's 800-meter track event were all 46 XY DSD males. When I clicked on the link (here in Australia) I was informed that this video was unavailable in my country. It seems that in Australia our disinformation filtering authorities will not let me see this piece, presumably because it would be bigoted hate speech to even ask if excluding biological females from any place on a women's elite sporting podium is fair.

2. See Haidt, *Anxious Generation*. Haidt here explains how the world our children and young people now inhabit has inbuilt reality-excluding features in it that make normal human development, and a normal relationship with human and natural reality, increasingly hard for them to know and experience. The online world encourages reality-disconnected (magical) thinking. This has very serious mental-illness implications for the young. And as Hannah Barnes points out, there is strong anecdotal evidence from parents of mentally unwell children spending large amounts of time online, that their children are easily influenced by transgender activists into embracing a transgender identity as a solution to their anomia, depression, and social isolation. See Barnes, *Time to Think*, 83–89.

INTRODUCTION

deeply invested in the gender-identity reformation are not backward and bigoted? What if it is simply *true* that there are only two sexes, no matter who says it, or who refuses to say it?

This book will argue that while there indeed are demanding intellectual justifications for gender theory, those justifications are not ultimately persuasive, and there are good reasons to believe that gender theory indeed is wrong. I will argue that gender theory arises as a symptom of larger pathologies in Western intellectual development over the past two or three centuries, thus gender theory cannot be adequately understood in isolation from the big sweep of ideas. If we are to understand the intellectual justifications for gender theory, then we need to understand why the modern West suffers from a lack of confidence in the truth-revealing powers of science, and why we suffer from a lack of confidence in our ability to discern any real natural meanings in the world. But the appeal of gender theory is not only caused by the failure of modern realism, for there are things we really like about making up knowledge and meaning to suit ourselves. Indeed, the main reason gender theory seems to "work" is because we *want* it to work rather than because it is true. So at the core of this matter there is a conflict between power and interest on the one hand and truth and natural meaning on the other hand. At present, scientific truth and commonsense natural meanings are getting a very serious hammering. This is because our knowledge and power elites have largely embraced the background intellectual assumptions of our times, where reality is unknowable, so only power and interest really define knowledge and meaning.

In this book I wish to take you on a journey out of gender theory's intellectual captivity to unreality. This is going to be demanding, though I am not writing for academic specialists. This book is for anyone who finds themselves unwillingly swept along by the rainbow reformation but they do not know how to critically engage with the world of gender theory that justifies this reformation.

OUTLINE

The first chapter addresses the question of whether it even makes sense to ask if gender theory is right or wrong. On the one hand, the linguistically slippery and reality-denying nature of gender theory makes one uninclined to take it seriously. On the other hand, people—intelligent people, boards of directors, and legislators—do take gender theory seriously, which is why it has gotten itself embedded in power. Hence, we must engage with it.

Chapter 2 aims to provide the reader with a workable conceptual handle outlining what the phrase "gender theory" at least functionally means.

After these opening chapters we leap into the genealogical core of the book.

A genealogy is a family history. You have to know someone's family history to really understand them. We cannot understand what gender theory is, let alone why it has been such a fabulous recent success, unless we know its generative history. My argument about that history concerns the way in which some of the defining signatures of Enlightenment thinking have produced gender theory. Specifically, it is Immanuel Kant's determination to purify knowledge from faith and reason from metaphysics that eventually produces gender theory. The sequence goes something like this. The Enlightenment purging of science and reason from anything religious or speculative begat nineteenth- and twentieth-century anti-realism, positivism, linguistic deflation, and rational formalism, which all in different ways begat late twentieth-century postmodernism, which in turn begat the gender theory of today.

The central theoretical argument in this book is that the purifying methodology of the Enlightenment ends up killing its noble aim. The noble aim of the Enlightenment is liberation from ignorance and inhumanity by means of science and reason. I think the aim of the Enlightenment is excellent, but it now also seems undeniably clear that Kant's purifying methodology crashes the Enlightenment's noble aim. Intractable difficulties in trying to make science and reason spotlessly pure (i.e., rigorously self-justifying) produced a spiral into madness. For one must have *faith* in the truth-revealing powers of science if one is to uphold the sacred epistemic responsibility of being rigorously transparent and truth-concerned, otherwise science collapses into a tool of manipulative power. Philosophically, pure positivism fails to justify itself, and the move to treat science as an entirely phenomenological construction of human power and interest destroys the philosophical-truth integrity of science. Likewise reason degrades into a meaningless logical formalism where arguments for the most preposterous fantasies cannot be distinguished from arguments that connect with the obvious and real meanings of natural reality. One must have some *metaphysical* conception of a meaningful natural world if reason is not to descend into madness. Hence, I argue, attempting to purify

INTRODUCTION

knowledge from faith and reason from metaphysics has crashed the noble Enlightenment aim. The anti-science and linguistic constructivism of gender theory is, alas, the natural outcome of that crash.

Chapter 4 continues the developmental story of where Kantian purity takes us. We trace a reactive chain of ideas expressed in two key nineteenth-century Continental thinkers, Hegel and Marx. Marx, inverting Hegel, plays a significant role in the materialist progressive background assumptions of gender theory. Other Continental thinkers from this time of formative relevance to postmodernism will come up in chapter 7.

Chapter 5 looks at positivism. This is the idea that science without any traditional religious warrants gives us truth. Modern positivism, however, has always been at least quasi-religious, as it starts out as a form of atheist yet explicitly religious rationalism in revolutionary France. This is a fascinating aspect of our genealogy as it is the inevitable failure of positivism to deliver truth, under the conditions of Enlightenment purity, that is a signature formation influence on gender theory.

Chapter 6 takes a far-ranging look at the long history of linguistic deflation and analytical formalism in the West. Linguistic deflation is the art of purifying words from any high meaning. Analytic formalism is the art of purifying logic from any cosmic significance and making it just about the grammar of arguments. Both of these trends are very prominent in twentieth-century modern philosophy, but the surprising fact is, they both have roots in the twelfth century. Playing games with language and logic to do tricky things with common sense and to attack metaphysical meaning is a very old Western intellectual craft, and it is integral to gender theory.

Chapter 7 looks at postmodernism. This movement did not start in the 1970s. The counter-Enlightenment had been steadily evolving since the eighteenth century. We briefly examine the Christian counter-Enlightenment with Hamann and Kierkegaard, though this was largely a road not taken. We then briefly examine the anti-Christian counter-Enlightenment with Nietzsche and Schopenhauer, who take us firmly in the direction of the complete destruction of the Enlightenment aim. These latter two thinkers are radical nihilist advocates of mythopoetic perspectivism and creatively asserted will and power, and their impact on postmodernism is very strong. An appreciation of the counter-Enlightenment leads naturally into a quick description of recent and contemporary postmodern thinkers, such as Derrida and Butler.

INTRODUCTION

There are significant features of postmodernism that should be taken very seriously, as the "pure" modernity that Kant bequeathed to us indeed does not fly. But this does not mean that the postmodern dismissal of any true knowledge of reality, and the devolution of philosophy into sophistry, are actually justified. So we work our way up to the 1970s and beyond and look at how this movement shapes gender theory.

At chapter 8 we arrive at the present, and at gender theory. This signals the completion of our genealogy. At this point we are in a position to appreciate just how well gender theory fits in with the present times. Now that we understand these reasons we can seriously ask, is gender theory wrong?

Chapter 9 gives practical and commonsense arguments for thinking gender theory indeed is wrong.

Chapter 10 gives more radical attention not only to why gender theory is wrong, but how the Enlightenment aim of liberation through science and reason can be retrieved. It is not enough to just say that gender theory is practically wrong; we must show how science and reason can be recovered, as truth-revealing, so that gender theory will no longer seem persuasive to our intellectual elites.

Chapter 11 concludes the book in a summary way, and points toward what sort of work needs to be done if we are to free ourselves from the bane of gender theory.

DEFINING "SEX-IRREALISM" AND "SEX-REALISM"

Before we take off I should outline the meaning of a word that appears in the subtitle of this book—"sex-irrealism"—and its nemesis, "sex-realism."

An irrealist thinks the question of whether something is real or not does not apply. Simply put, sex-irrealists think "sex" is a term that is far too complex in its shades of use and meaning to be pinned down to any crude factual definition. In contrast, sex-realists think we can have a true knowledge of what the sex of any given person is, which is not difficult to objectively determine. This needs a bit more unpacking.

To a sex-irrealist there are no obvious and objective meanings for the words "man," "woman," "male," and "female." These four words do have meanings, but they are always meanings in use. Further, their use is always situated within ever-shifting and interactive matrixes of identity, power, nature, and culture. Hence, to a sex-irrealist anyone who thinks there is an

INTRODUCTION

objective meaning to those four words is not only hopelessly naïve, but they are also oppressive bigots. Sex-irrealists boldly uphold the complexity and diversity of the uncontainable meanings of sex and gender, and the right to freedom of sex-identity and gender-identity expression. They are reformers fighting against the out-of-date sex-realist prejudices of the uneducated, the oppressive, and the bigoted. A righteous and crusading ethos is common among committed sex-irrealists.

Trans-rights activists (TRAs) are sex-irrealists who do not well tolerate or engage with their primary opponents, who are sex-realists. TRAs are often disruptively opposed not only to the views of sex-realists but also to sex-realists expressing their stance publicly. TRAs are often convinced that any public statement of a sex-realist understanding of the world is "hate speech" displaying the same sort of bigotry and genocidal intention as a Nazi swastika. The moralized framing of TRA opposition toward sex-realists is often at a very shrill level, and it usually has legislative and institutional support. As a result, sex-realists typically experience concerted and often vitriolic opposition to their attempts to present reasons for rejecting sex-irrealism in any public context. But sex-realism is by no means indefensible, as we shall see.

A sex-realist believes that there are uncontroversial scientific ways of separating the entire human race into two sexes: male and female.[3] Upholding a commitment to the validity of scientific truth, sex-realists maintain that it is the case that in clearly observable objective reality there are *only* two reproductive human sexes. Sex-realists hold that the human reproductive sex binary is a matter of objective fact; it is not a matter of bigoted or any other value-inflected opinion. It is also a matter of demonstrable and incontrovertible fact that humans have no natural or artificial means of changing from being one reproductively functional sex to being the other reproductively functional sex. It follows, then, that to a sex-realist there is no such thing as a male who really is a woman. Transwomen, as males who

---

3. Sex-realists fully appreciate that a very small proportion of the human race are people with genetic disorders of sexual development (DSDs). However, people with DSDs are *unlike* non-DSD transpeople, for such transpeople have a medically unambiguous male or female sex and then undergo hormonal and surgical treatments to reconfigure their sex appearance, often at the cost of making themselves sexually infertile. Genetic abnormalities of sexual development in no manner invalidate the full humanity of the person who suffers with such a natural abnormality (they are often infertile; if having children is a blessing then infertility is a suffering), but neither do they render the normal male/female reproductive sex binary for the vast majority of people in any way complex or obsolete.

gender-identify as women, certainly exist, but they are not, and never will be, real reproductive females.

Sex-realists often understand "man" and "woman" to be more primarily sex-defined terms than they are gender-defined terms.[4] Even so, there are highly diverse ways in which people express their sexuality. To the sex-realist, males, for example, can express their sexuality as heterosexuals, homosexuals, bisexuals, drag-queens, transwomen, any performative fantasy category you can think of, autogynephilia, sado-masochistic eunuchs, or whatever, but they remain males and they remain men; they do not in reality *become* females or women, even if they can effectively "pass" as a woman. Being female is not a performance, it is not a cultural construction, it is not a cross-sex hormonal or cosmetic surgical construction, it is a natural fact. A real woman is a natural female. Thus, anyone who is performing being a woman but who is not a natural female is a man.[5]

In sum, the sex-irrealist denies any fixed and objective meaning to male and female sex and insists that the gender-identity categories of "man" and "woman" must be defined only by the free choice of each individual. The sex-realist affirms the objective and knowable reality of the human reproductive biological sex binary and insists that no male can be a woman, and female-only spaces, contests, and forums should not include males.

THE ACADEMIC EXPERTISE THIS BOOK DRAWS ON

Finally, as regards introductory matters, I wish to make some quick disclosures about what sort of scholarship informs the arguments of this book.

My doctorate was in the sociology of knowledge, and I have other post-graduate qualifications in philosophy and theology as well as an

---

4. To be more nuanced, Simone de Beauvoir famously noted that one is not born but rather becomes a woman. A sex-realist would say, one is born female though, and only a female can become a woman. A person who is born male cannot become a woman, as cultural and social formation are not the only reasons why a person becomes a woman; the most significant and indeed physically defining reason why anyone becomes a woman is that they are, from conception and until death, female.

5. The fact that there is a very small population of people who are born with medically identifiable disorders of sexual development, and at some point, such people may undergo surgical interventions should they or their parents decide to remove sex-presentation ambiguity, is the exception to the above comment, but it is in no manner a meaningful rule applicable to people who are unambiguously born either male or female.

INTRODUCTION

undergraduate social science degree majoring in politics. All four of these domains are useful in understanding gender theory.

Significantly, gender theory is not a *scientific* theory; it arises out of literary criticism, postmodernism, and the queer movement, so mainstream biology is not relevant to understanding gender theory.[6] Even so, sexologists, such as Debra Soh, and biologists, such as Richard Dawkins, are astonished at how unwelcome their knowledge expertise is to the domain of gender theory.[7]

On science, in recent years I have done considerable work with my colleague at the University of Queensland, the renowned historian of science Professor Peter Harrison.[8] Understanding the nature of modern scientific facts is an important area of my research, which is also highly relevant to understanding gender theory. For one of the most prominent features of gender theory is its distinctive way of culturally constructing all knowledge claims, including scientific claims. Gender theory's fabulous dexterity in being linguistically tricky with factual knowledge claims is the central engine of its ideological power.

In what follows you can expect me to draw on all areas of my academic expertise, but I am explicitly endeavoring to write a trade book rather than a book for scholars. So I will not presume the reader has a specialist philosophical knowledge background. However, I do presume the reader is intelligent, curious, and interested in doing some serious thinking.

Because the problematic theory (gender theory) has philosophical roots, the reader will need to be prepared to be philosophically educated. This will be conceptually demanding in places. But I do believe the picture will come into focus as we go, even if you may be learning more about the past 250 years of Western philosophy than you thought you ever wanted to know.

---

6. Gender theorists have been working on re-constructing biology itself so as to make it compatible with a fluid, performative, spectral, and culturally interpreted account of what sex "is." Anne Fausto-Sterling is a lead figure in this innovative domain. See Fausto-Sterling, *Sexing the Body*. "Gender Politics and the Construction of Sexuality" is the subtitle of this book. Overtly, "politics" and "construction" are key features of her approach to "sexuality." This is not the broadly mainstream conception of science, which most practicing scientists assume, where science is understood as a non-political and objective, truth concerned knowledge enterprise.

7. See Soh, *End of Gender*; Dawkins, "Race Is a Spectrum. Sex Is Pretty Damn Binary."

8. See Harrison and Tyson, *New Directions in Theology and Science*; Harrison and Milbank, *After Science and Religion*; Tyson, *Astonishment and Science*.

1

Is Gender Theory Not Even Wrong?

IS SEX TRICKY OR OBVIOUS?

Is it almost always socially obvious whether a person is male or female? Is a person's male or female sex an objective, natural, and scientific fact about who they are? Are there only two sexes? Is a person's natural sex, as identified at birth, unchangeable? Gender theory says "no" to all these questions. Further, the *way* gender theory says "no" is tricky.

The Council of Europe (COE) is compliant with the European Union's Gender Equality Commission, and hence the COE is up to date with the latest academic trends in gender theory. Here are the three definitions of the term "sex" used by the COE:

1. Sex refers to biological differences between males and females (e.g., gonads, sexual organs, chromosomes, hormones).
2. Sex is usually assigned at birth (there are examples when it is assigned later . . .).
3. Sex can be changed: in cases of transsexual people, who are born with the sex characteristics of one sex and the gender identity of the other, sex reassignment surgeries are performed. This includes a change of sex organs and the administration of hormones.[1]

---

1. Council of Europe, "Sex and Gender."

Taken on its own (1) seems to imply that "sex refers to" the objective and identifiable physiological, reproductive, and genetic facts that differentiate human males (formerly known as boys and men) from human females (formerly known as girls and women). However (2) asserts that sex is an *assignment* that, it seems, only arbitrarily or conventionally *refers* to the observable external sex characteristics of most babies. Being born with normal male genitals, and without female genitals, does not, apparently, objectively *define* your sex as male. Should a baby with normal male genitals discover—as a child, youth, or adult—that they have a female gender identity, then their *sex* can be surgically, hormonally, and legally (or just declaratively) reassigned, and they can transition from having an assigned at birth male sex to having a reassigned female sex. As sex itself *is* an assignment, there is no material difference between a so-called "cis" female, who has only ever had natural female reproductive sex characteristics, and an "assigned male at birth" transgender female, who has transitioned their sex from male to female (with or without surgery, etc.). Further, (3) makes it clear that a person's assigned sex should align with each individual's subjectively determined gender identity, such that cosmetic surgeries and cross-sex hormone treatments are deemed to not only reassign but to actually *change* a person's sex. Gender identity, it seems, actually *determines* appropriately assigned sex, but natural physiology does not.

Point (3) above is carefully formulated in a linguistically tricky manner. Even though the COE is not claiming the undeniable falsehood that sex reassignment treatments change a person's sex chromosomes, or change the size of the gametes that a reassigned transsexual person produces (should they still be fertile after their reassignment), the COE does assert that sex reassignment surgeries produce "a change of sex organs" and hence a change of sex. This is tricky language.

It seems that should I have my penis and testicles surgically removed, and then have a body cavity artificially inserted in place of my removed natural genitals, this prosthetic cavity (though unconnected to a uterus and entirely non-reproductive) would, I suppose, be "a change of [my] sex organs." By such means, it seems, the COE believes I would have really changed my sex (from assigned male to assigned female). And it seems that they are genuinely determined to police the mandatory belief in this astonishingly anti-scientific view in Europe. As I write in early 2025, the French gynecologist Dr. Victor Acharian has been suspended from medical practice for claiming he was only qualified to treat "real women" and then refusing to inspect and treat the prosthetic body cavity of a genetically male transwoman.[2]

In short, gender theory really does maintain that a person's male or female sex is *not* an objective, scientifically demonstrable, and unchangeable natural reality.

The argument of this book is that contrary to what gender theory asserts, a person's male or female sex indeed can be objectively and demonstrably known, and cannot, in reality, be changed. But, do objective and scientifically demonstrable facts about natural reality even matter anymore? It seems that the answer to this question—when it comes to sex and gender—is "apparently not."

The first difficulty one faces in seeking to refute gender theory is having to engage with the manner in which it deliberately problematizes rational and evidence-based arguments about natural truths. The Bible counsels against engaging with people who are determinedly at odds with commonsense reality with the sage advice that we should not answer fools according to their folly, or else we become like them (Proverbs 26:4). But unfortunately we have gone past the point where simply ignoring reality-denying folly is the best strategy, and so we are forced to move on to Proverbs 26:5: "Answer a fool according to his folly, lest he be wise in his own eyes." So we must engage. But what an opponent! One of the very few things you can unproblematically know about gender theory is that it rejects objectively demonstrable bivalent truth claims when it comes to both the gender and the sex of any given person. It is very hard to know how one might meaningfully reason about natural truths with such an opponent.

But what, you may be wondering, is a bivalent truth claim?

DENYING BIVALENT TRUTH CLAIMS ABOUT NATURAL FACTS

The categories of "true" and "false" are what philosophers call bivalent truth categories. In any traditional bivalent truth claim about the natural world, some proposed fact, event, or state of affairs in the world can be identified as being *either* true *or* false. In traditional philosophy the principle of bivalence is also expressed in logic as the law of the excluded middle. Which is to say that if a logical proposition is valid, it cannot also be invalid. True

---

2. The incident in question happened in 2023, but the suspension was put in place in early 2025. As regards the incident, see Llach and Bodinier, "Cavity Is Not a Vagina."

or false, valid *or* invalid, right *or* wrong; bivalence is defined by an "*or*" between two options, only one of which (at the most)[3] is true/valid/right. And if a bivalent truth claim is true/valid/right, then its contrary claim is false/invalid/wrong. A bivalent truth claim is a matter of "either/or"; it is *not* defined by "both/and" or by undecidable indeterminacy.

For example, it is *either* true *or* it is false that I have two legs. Assuming the validity of bivalent truth claims about natural facts, I cannot arrive at the conclusion that I have both only one leg and two legs at the same time. To ask a bivalent question about something, it must be of the nature of the thing that there is a demonstrably true answer to the question of, for example, how many legs I really have. As normal humans are bipedal, and I am within the usual range of natural physical norms characteristics of the species homo sapiens (I do not have, say, six legs), it is reasonable to assume that the question of how many legs I have can be demonstrably determined by the normal means of sensory-based observation. This assumption is valid, even if I have had a terrible accident and now have no legs. Here the fact that I unnaturally have no legs would not be an indeterminate answer, as my lack of having legs would also be a bivalent fact about how many legs I have—that is, none. None here is not an indeterminate term that could mean any or no number of legs. None here means precisely and only zero number of legs.

Does assuming that there are bivalent truths about the normal physical attributes of humans seem sensible and reasonable to you?

Until very recently the male and female human sexes were understood as bivalent truth categories. Whatever has gone on in the linguistically tricky domain of gender theory, this old-fashioned outlook still seems, well . . . true. Outside of rare genetic abnormalities, it is still the case that one is bivalently *either* a male *or* a female human, and this can be objectively determined without any scientific difficulty. For chromosomal determinants of the normal natural sex binary are scientifically known to be present from conception, and these genetic determinates are also scientifically known to be unalterable until death. One can undergo cosmetic surgery and take

---

3. Of course, if I live in Australia and I think I am fifteen hours ahead of New York, but I am not sure about whether daylight savings applies on the other side of the world, I might make the bivalent claim that the time in New York is either 6 a.m. or 7 a.m., when both of these possibilities might be false (depending on what Australian time zone I am in, for example, I might be fifteen and a half or seventeen hours ahead of New York). However it cannot be true that it is *both* 6 a.m. *and* 7 a.m., at the same time, in New York. Bivalence works on the principle that a true claim excludes the truth of a directly contradictory claim.

cross-sex hormones in order to change one's socially projected sexual *appearance*, one can change one's *legal* sex assignment, but this does not mean a small-gamete-producing male person with normal XY sex-determining chromosomes in every cell of their body can actually become a large-gamete-producing XX chromosomed human female (which used to be called "a woman"). And whatever advocates of mosaic or spectral "sex fluidity" may claim, it remains an irrefutable fact that when it comes to successful human sexual reproduction—the biological point of sex, after all—this can only occur because of the totally unambiguous male/female sex binary. That is, 100 percent of all people alive today have a male biological father and a female biological mother.

Until recently it was assumed that one could not be both male *and* female, excepting in the case of very rare genetic abnormalities. It was assumed that one could not ignore the natural reality of one's sex, and it was assumed that one could not be whatever sex one subjectively identified as, and one could not simply decide to be sexually non-binary. We also used to assume that one could not change one's sex from male to female or female to male, as this is a medical impossibility. But as we now know, queer ideological activism and gender-identity legislation have swept all the above commonsense and scientific assumptions aside.

Gender theory asserts that human sex is no longer (and never really was) a binary and bivalent truth category. As we shall eventually get to, this is because gender theory is a linguistic theory that asserts that natural reality has no actual meaning and we simply *impose* meaning on cultural and social reality via our words. So, in effect, the word "sex" can mean whatever we decide it means, although—apparently—it can no longer mean an actual objective fact describing a human as either male or female.

Because gender theory rejects bivalence as regards natural reality, gender theory is simply not interested in whether its claims about "sex" are true or false. This puts my attempt to argue that gender theory is wrong—and in particular, wrong about the reality of the natural sex binary—in a difficult place. I am presupposing that the question of whether a person is of the male or female sex admits of a bivalent true or false answer. Gender theory finds my assumption inadmissible and will not engage with me, but will instead insist that I do not understand how complex "sex" is, even by COE's first definition. Gender theory also maintains that I do not appreciate the (ironically) true nature of how all meanings are assigned to words, such that objectivist natural truth categories are themselves inherently immoral and oppressive, particularly as regards "sex" and gender. So how are we going to resolve this presuppositional impasse?

THE "NOT EVEN WRONG" OPTION

If we simply stick with old-fashioned bivalent scientific truth as an appropriate means of defining what sex objectively is, then it is not exactly appropriate to descry gender theory as false; it is more accurate to describe it as not even wrong.

When it comes to evaluating any given theory as "not even wrong," this turn of phrase is credited to the twentieth-century physicist Wolfgang Pauli. What this theoretical scientist is here implying is that for a theory about how the natural world actually is to be shown to be either right or wrong, it would need to have some at least functionally viable relation to objectively testable reality. One would need to be able to understand what reality would look like if the theory was right, and then test the theory against reality to see if it is at least partially correct. For even though gender theory makes "sex" definable by (or co-constructed with) "gender" it cannot say what any objective reality about *gender* might really be, because to gender theory, "gender identity" is an entirely subjective and poetic performance. Whatever the amazingly amorphous category of "gender" actually is to gender theory, it is *not* an objectively verifiable and bivalent natural reality about which one might construct a testable scientific theory. Hence gender theory—if we are to treat it as a theory about objective reality—is not even wrong, because it is not capable of being bivalently right.

If a theory needs to be about objectively testable reality for you to take it seriously, then you need read no further. No one who is interested in natural reality as a scientifically demonstrable and objective truth need take gender theory seriously. However, often highly educated people *do* take it seriously, and understanding why they do not take ordinary bivalent natural facts about human sex seriously will need a long and involved explanation. If we want to understand why gender theory is believed (or at least accepted) by highly intelligent and well-educated people, we cannot rest with a "not even wrong" dismissal of gender theory.

SHOWING WHY A "NOT EVEN WRONG" THEORY IS ACTUALLY WRONG

In the final analysis, gender theorists are what they used to call sophists in ancient Greece.[4] The sophists of old—Protagoras, Gorgias, Antiphon, Thrasymachus, and so forth—like our contemporary sophists, held that there is no real meaning in the world, and you cannot know the truth about reality. Hence, both nature and culture are co-constructed linguistic fabrications, and words and arguments can be made to mean whatever a clever linguistic wizard can make other people believe. This stance holds that all human meanings are performative, imaginative constructions of power and interest. Ergo, truth is a fiction, and (ironically) fiction is the only real truth about human meaning. These are the people who now have our high intellectual culture in a truth-suffocating headlock, and these are the people who have managed to change our laws and the formation contexts of our children such that we are all now required to comply with the so-called morality of gender theory sophistry or face serious reprisals.

The birth of the Western academic tradition, which deeply shaped the Western intellectual landscape from the fourth century BC until—in some isolated intellectual asylums—today, is Plato's academy in Athens. The three great Greek sages—Socrates, Plato, and Aristotle—separated philosophy out from sophistry, defining philosophy as a good-faith truth-seeking enterprise in contrast to sophistry as a linguistically tricky and skeptical power-seeking enterprise. Plato's academy was effectively a revolt against sophistry. If we are to uphold truth over power today, then we will have to affect a similar revolt against sophistry as Plato did. For the past half century has seen the powerful rise of sophistry in our universities, and pragmatic, skeptical, and linguistically tricky sophistry is now firmly in the ascendancy of our very influential knowledge class.

To actually achieve my aim of showing why gender theory is wrong (even though it is not even wrong), I will need to show you why contemporary sophistry is wrong. Without going to that sort of space, we are just dealing with symptoms and not looking at causes. So, this is going to be quite an adventure!

---

4. Martha Nussbaum has pointed this out very effectively some time ago. See Nussbaum, "Professor of Parody."

2

What Is Gender Theory?

LET US GET UNDERWAY with an at least provisional attempt at a definition of what gender theory is. This is going to be harder than you might anticipate as gender theory is not actually "a" theory, and this "not a theory" is most centrally about what "gender" is *not*. Have you got that? Gender theory is the {not a theory} that is {not about gender}. Sounds queer, I know, but this is important to understand.

GENDER THEORY IS NOT "A" THEORY, AND "GENDER" IS UNDEFINED IN GENDER THEORY

Judith Butler is up front about the theoretical undecidability of gender theory. On the opening page of her 2024 book, she notes,

> Certain feminists have distinguished between ["sex" and "gender"], associating "sex" with either biology or legal assignment at birth, and "gender" with sociocultural forms of becoming. At the same time, feminists and other scholars in gender studies disagree among themselves about which definitions and distinctions are right. The myriad, continuing debates about the word show that no one approach to defining, or understanding, gender reigns.[1]

This brings to mind the following sage observation by Maurice Blondel: "There are no problems more insoluble than those that do not

---

1. Butler, *Who's Afraid*, 3.

exist."[2] Leaving to one side for the moment the possibility that discovering the truth about the meaning of what Butler calls "the word... gender" might be an insoluble problem, because gender does not exist, let us proceed.

"Scholars in gender studies" do not agree on the very basic question of what gender is. Put slightly differently, gender theorists do not agree on what it is that they are theorizing. Remarkably, this has not stopped government policies and laws being drafted and put into place inserting a conspicuously undefined notion of "gender identity" into the public domain. Major legal and policy "definitions" of gender in the UK and Australia, for example, are astonishingly unspecific. Most of them specify what gender *is not* defined by (which is sex, though it also can be sex-related), but they do not say what gender *is* defined by in any objective and scientifically determinate manner.

Significantly, this objective undecidability about gender is a feature rather than a bug. Only with such a "non-definition" can each individual specify what their gender is, and they can specify their own gender however they choose. Provided, that is, their gender is *not* objectively defined by their real and natural sex. One cannot have the gender identity of being a woman *because* one is female, for that would be immorally exclusionary toward transwomen. One is allowed to have a "cis woman" gender identity, which requires one to acknowledge that there is no *real* relationship between one's biological sex and one's gender, for a "cis woman" only acknowledges an accidental alignment of her (as Butler puts it) "sex" with her "gender." So one's gender identity is not really as inclusively undecidable as it might seem. Tough luck for the gender identity of "sex-realist women" (and tough luck to same-*sex* attracted lesbians who don't want to be hit on by male transwomen claiming to be lesbians).[3]

Butler thinks that her hyper-liberal, individualistic, and objectively indeterminate approach to "what gender is" is an intellectually valid and morally virtuous stance. Only unsophisticated and uneducated people will

---

2. Blondel, *Action*, 16.

3. Szego, "LGBTQ Is Really QTBGL." Investigative reporter Julie Szego has written a carefully documented piece on the failed attempt of the Lesbian Action Group to hold a Lesbians Born Female event at the publicly funded Victorian Pride Centre in October of 2023. The Lesbian Action Group applied to the Australian Human Rights Commission for a temporary exemption from anti-discrimination legislation so that they could hold an event for exclusively same-sex-attracted biological women. Opposing their application was Equality Australia, who successfully fought against the application, which the Commission denied.

hubristically think that they know better than "scholars in gender studies" and *can* objectively define gender, and only immoral and illiberal people will assert that any individual or society is entitled to foist their definition of gender onto any dissenting individual. In the final analysis gender theorists hold that there must be as many views of what gender is as there are individuals. For whatever else gender is not, gender theory maintains that gender is a personal and subjective identity that every individual is entitled to have as a moral right. According to this stance, to deny the validity of any person's self-designated gender identity (other than refusing to believe that they are "cis-gendered" if they adhere to binary sex-defined gender categories) is to perform *identity genocide* against that individual. Hence, "mis-gendering" someone is considered to be *hate speech*, which must not be permitted in any public or online forum. That is why in an increasing number of jurisdictions "mis-gendering" is a legally actionable hate crime.

The key "definitional" issue here is that there is no universally accepted theory of what gender is among the advocates of gender identity, and this absence of a definition is considered intellectually and morally virtuous by its advocates. But let us briefly home in on how exactly *not* defined gender must be to gender theorists, and what such a non-definition actually does in law.

(UNDEFINED) GENDER IS AS (LEGAL) GENDER DOES

In simple terms, there is no real definition of gender put forward by gender theorists to either defend or attack, as "gender" is only ever "defined" in a circular manner.

To say that a Jabberwocky is a creature defined as having the subjectively felt property of Jabberwockiness, or possessing an innate inner sense of its own Jabberwockery, tells us nothing about what a Jabberwocky actually is. (And it might even be entirely fictitious!) Self-referential definitions are no definition at all. Andrew Doyle, in his carefully researched investigative program on the scandal of the leaked WPATH files,[4] notes three clear examples of circular "definitions" of "gender identity" thus:[5]

From the World Professional Association for Transgender Health:

---

4. Hughes, "WPATH Files."
5. Doyle, "WPATH Files."

> Gender Identity refers to a person's deeply felt, internal, intrinsic sense of their own gender.

From Stonewall:

> [Gender Identity refers to] a person's innate sense of their own gender, whether male, female or something else (see non-binary below), which may or may not correspond to the sex assigned at birth.

From the National Health Service (UK):

> Gender Identity is a way to describe a person's innate sense of their own gender, whether male, female, or non-binary, which may not correspond to the sex registered at birth.

We see the same circularity in Australian law. Note this "definition" from Australia's Sex Discrimination Act (1984), as amended in 2013. See Part I, Section 4:

> Gender identity means the gender-related identity, appearance or mannerisms or other gender-related characteristics of a person (whether by way of medical intervention or not), with or without regard to the person's designated sex at birth.

Thanks to the "not a theory" of gender theory, gender itself is "defined" only in a circular and undefined manner, yet (and here at least we get some clarity) "gender" explicitly has no necessary relation (or, incoherently, non-relation) to sex. So gender theory is not *a* theory, and it is a theoretical stance that refuses to define gender. But—to steal from their own argument—let us look at what gender theory "does" rather than what it undecidably "is" (and at the same time "is not").[6]

Subjective personal gender-identity feelings now have strong anti-discrimination legal rights, even though they are entirely subjective and circular. Further, after 2013 in Australia, the actual biological sex-identity of women, as females, within a so-called Sex Discrimination Act, has *no* legally defined status. What an astonishing switch of the objectively real and definable for the subjectively intuited and the undefinable!

So the actual effect of inserting gender theory into Australian law is that sex-based rights for women now have no legal meaning. Indeed,

---

6. For a biological-reality-denying attempt to make a performative virtue out of the supposed indefinability of, as Judith Butler often puts it, "sex," see Currah, *Sex Is as Sex Does*.

sex-based rights for women have been revoked. This is what gender theory actually does for 50 percent of all Australians.

Ironically, the 2013 "amendments" to the Federal Sex Discrimination Act (1984) removing sex-based definitions for "man" and "woman" are in a piece of legislation whose central object remains compliance with the international convention known as CEDAR (Convention on the Elimination of All Forms of Discrimination Against *Women*). When CEDAR was drawn up in the 1980s, "woman" unequivocally meant a human adult of the female sex, and did not "include" males gender-identifying as females. Legislation that still has its objective as the promotion and protection of sex-based anti-discrimination rights for women is now the very means of ensuring that women have no sex-based rights.

While gender theory explicitly excludes itself from having any clear *theoretical* definition of gender, we can *practically* define it. "Gender" is the linguistic tool that is used by gender theorists to exclude women's sex-based rights from having any legal meaning. But we can also *stylistically* define it.

GENDER THEORY IS A STYLE OF DISCOURSE AND ACTIVISM

Gender theory is not "a" theory, and gender theorists do not agree on what gender itself is. For these reasons it is clear that "gender theory" actually means a rhetorical *style* of discussion promoted by, as Judith Butler puts it, "scholars in gender studies," and a rhetorical *style* of advocating the so-called progressive political and moral importance of the gender-identity inclusion of queer minorities, to the *exclusion* of sex-based rights for women (50 percent of the human race). As hard to believe as this really is, we must firmly grasp that to the gender theory *style*, there is no objective or theoretical agreement on what gender is or is not, but women's sex-based rights are held to be inherently oppressive.

One of the reasons gender theory has "worked" so well is that most people cannot actually take it seriously or understand what its unrealistic and radical revolt against sex, and against publicly accepted gender norms, could actually mean in practice. Gender theory is functionally incomprehensible to commonsense normal people. Usually, people will try to play along with a transperson, but not because they believe gender theory to be true, just because they feel they should try to be nice to people who are deluded about their own sex. A bit of game playing of this sort is not particularly problematic until your own son wants to emasculate himself or you are a female nurse required to share your changing room with a male transwoman.[7] Then both the unreality of gender theory and the violation of natural reality that it imposes become visible.

WHO BELIEVES IN GENDER THEORY?

You might think, how can gender identity be so important that its protection is now written into law, and yet central theorists in this domain cannot define what gender is with any scholarly or fact-based agreement? These are reasonable questions, but here, the "what" questions are less important than the "who" and "why" questions. The central question that drives the writing of this book is: Why does gender theory (meaning a certain rhetorical *style* of discourse and activism) have such a powerful influence on our law makers and policy setters?

The short answer to the above question is that gender theory is very mainstream in our high intellectual culture. How this came about, and why intelligent and highly educated people are far more likely than anyone else to accept that sex is now a fluid social construct, and a man can become female by undergoing hormonal treatments and cosmetic surgery, is the puzzle this book is hoping to solve.

---

7. In the UK the NHS now requires female nurses to accept transwomen (biological males) in their workplace changing rooms. See Baines, "Nurses Threaten to Sue Trust over Behaviour of Trans Colleague." At present, if female nurses complain about males in their changing rooms, they are treated as intolerant and expected to "broaden their mindset" and "be more inclusive" by their employers, if they are lucky. Suspension and dismissal for simply making a complaint are real possibilities. Sandie Peggie, a Scottish nurse, has been suspended from her job since 2023 when she complained about sharing the women's changing room with a transwoman, and she will have to go through a ten-day workplace tribunal (as I write) in February 2025 when her right (should she be found to have it) to be comfortable in her workplace changing room will be balanced against the transwoman's (legally valid) inclusiveness rights. So reality averse is gender theory as embedded in law that Peggie has had to fight for the right just to refer to the real sex of the transwoman that she is complaining about. For if the tribunal only recognizes gender identity, then Peggie has no case at all, as this is simply one woman complaining about another woman in the female change room. See Walker, "Nurse Wins Right to Call Female-Identifying Transgender Doctor a Man in Tribunal Case." These anti-realist, anti-normative, and anti-commonsense implications of gender theory in practice are not immediately apparent (or even imaginable) to average, commonsense people, until it is too late.

A Genealogy of Gender Theory

GENDER THEORY ARISES OUT of a series of five broadly identifiable interacting intellectual developments from the eighteenth century to the present. Most immediately, gender theory arises out of the postmodern intellectual scene of the late twentieth century. That postmodern scene arises out of the conspicuous philosophical failures of modern philosophy, particularly the failure of positivism. Positivism is the attempt to justify the objective truth of scientific facts without any reference to theology or metaphysics.[1]

Varieties of modern positivism, combined with linguistic deflation (cleansing words of all high meanings) and logical formalism (cleansing reason from any cosmic significance), were dominant in the Anglophone scene from the late nineteenth century right up until the 1980s. Modern positivism and analytical rationalism have their own drivers, but they are also something of an Anglo-American reaction to sophisticated nineteenth-century Continental philosophy. In the nineteenth century, counter-Enlightenment thinkers like Nietzsche, on the one hand, and the train of reactions where Hegel reacts to Kant and then Marx reacts to Hegel, make up a complex set of highly contested ideas. These trajectories are often in uncomfortable tension with Anglo-American philosophy. This

---

1. Metaphysics is the branch of philosophy that asks the question "what is reality?" Modern scientific positivism often seems to have an assumed metaphysics, which is that only material and observable things and forces are real, but actually, that is the metaphysics of materialism. Modern positivist philosophers, following Kant, typically think that metaphysical questions can only have speculative and indemonstrable "answers," which puts metaphysics itself beyond the scope of scientific positivism.

train of reaction was all started by Kant's Enlightenment thinking. So, the perhaps discouraging consequence of all this is that if one wants to understand just what gender theory is saying—let alone decide if it is persuasive or not—there is no getting around a fairly serious appreciation of some of the major thinkers in Western philosophy from the late eighteenth century to the present.

The genealogical core of this book aims to give you a serviceable appreciation of gender theory's intellectual roots. Chapter 3 looks at Kant and the Enlightenment, chapter 4 looks at nineteenth-century developments, chapter 5 looks at twentieth-century positivism, chapter 6 looks at linguistic deflation and logical formalism, and chapter 7 looks at postmodernism. None of these chapters aims to give a full explanation of intellectual developments in the periods under investigation, but they do aim to clarify what the intellectual origins of gender theory are. Chapter 8 will draw all the threads together by way of showing how gender theory is an entirely continuous development with the five philosophical trajectories that preceded it.

This genealogy will demonstrate—perhaps surprisingly—what a child of the Enlightenment Judith Butler's gender theory really is. This will also show us why the academy and our knowledge class in general—which is situated in the same 250-year intellectual heritage as gender theory—finds it so hard to sensibly critique the *prima facie* delusional assertions of gender theory. Bearing the above in mind, it should be clear why it is largely popularist rather than elite political actors who seem to have the capacity to push for common sense and continuity with traditional gender norms in our times. This in turn explains why gender-identity activists are so determined to paint their opponents as bigoted and morally backward ignoramuses. So there is much illumination to be had about the contemporary dynamics of gender theory politics by exploring the intellectual history outlined in the genealogy of this book.

We start, then, in Prussia, in the year 1784.

3

The Enlightenment Roots of Queer Gender Theory

WHAT IS ENLIGHTENMENT?

IMMANUEL KANT WAS BORN in Königsberg in 1724. Königsberg was then in Prussia, but it is now in Russia, as it was renamed Kaliningrad after Germany lost that part of the world to the former USSR after World War II. Kant never traveled outside of Prussia. He died in 1804.

In 1784 Kant wrote his famous essay "An Answer to the Question, 'What Is Enlightenment?'" Kant's essay describes a movement that was generating a new intellectual environment in Europe at the time. The heart of this venture was a casting off of scholastic metaphysical speculations, and firm rationalist distancing from both medieval Catholic and creedal Protestant theology. *Pure* empirical knowledge and *pure* natural reason were going to liberate humanity from superstition and ignorance.

According to Enlightenment enthusiasts, it was the unflinchingly bold and penetrating light of reason that was birthing a new era in human history: the Age of Reason. What could possibly go wrong? Of course, there would be bumps along the way, so the soon-to-come Reign of Terror in Paris and the horrors of the Industrial Revolution in England were surely but birth pains of the new and glorious cosmopolitan age of peace, reason, and liberty for all.

We are still enormously enamored by Kant's romantic and deeply optimistic vision of the liberations to be achieved by the anti-religious and anti-metaphysical scientific rationalism of the Enlightenment. His 1784 essay has aged well, and should you read it you will be surprised how much you will want to agree with Kant's vibe. Even today, Kant's intellectual fashion statement is a very attractive and desirable look. Us grown-up scientific rationalists are way too mature to take seriously anything our ignorant and superstitious religious forebears said. This is a look we not only like, but we simply assumed that all right-thinking people agree with it, and only backward, dogmatic nut-jobs who have not adapted to the times could have any problem with it. Showing how not-religious and how not-speculative we are is an intellectual groupie badge of honor that is still obviously sexy. For all Judith Butler's rejection of scientific positivism, she still has a decisively Enlightenment-framed "grown-up" disdain for religion and metaphysics.[1] But back to Kant.

Kant opined that humanity was now finally laying aside its ancient and the self-imposed immaturity and striding confidently forth into the properly adult freedom of Enlightened Man. (For inclusive language morality reasons I should note that "Man"—*des Menschen*—is Kant's gendered language throughout his essay, but its traditional meaning in German is the same as the traditional meaning of "mankind" in English, which is a sex-inclusive proper noun, meaning all the male and female individuals of the human race.)

To Kant, humanity was casting aside a servile conformism to ignorant, superstitious, and juvenile traditions. We were now, at last, mature enough to think and act for ourselves and rely on no venerable authority to tell us what we should do. The Enlightenment was thus a dare: Dare to understand, dare to act like a Man, dare to think and chose for yourself what you should believe and do.

There is a lot going on in Kant's highly influential essay, and a lot going on in the late eighteenth-century intellectual culture of Europe and its colonies. We shall not be concerned with all of that here.[2] All I wish to focus

---

1. In Butler, *Who's Afraid*, Judith Butler paints the Roman Catholic Church and the Religious Right as so obviously bigoted and regressive that no justification for rejecting their stance is needed. And the very idea that any natural category could have a real essential meaning (such as "male" and "female") is so preposterously "Platonist" that her disdain of sex-realism does not, again, warrant any justification.

2. For an excellent introduction to Kant's thought and the recent state of Kantian scholarship, see Scruton, *Kant*.

on at this point is the manner in which Enlightenment thinkers recast the nature and meaning of empirical and rational knowledge. This recasting is intimately tied up with a new attitude toward religious belief and religious authority, particularly in the intellectual domain of natural philosophy, which we now call science.

THE END OF THE SECULAR THEOLOGY OF MODERN NATURAL PHILOSOPHY

Amos Funkenstein notices a profound shift in Western European natural philosophy that happens with Kant. The early modern period prior to Kant was characterized by:

> a secular theology ... [which] emerged in the sixteenth and seventeenth centuries to a short career. It was secular in that it was conceived by laymen for laymen. Galileo and Descartes, Leibniz and Newton, Hobbes and Vico were either not clergymen at all or did not acquire an advanced degree in divinity. They were not professional theologians, and yet they treated theological issues at length. Their theology was secular also in the sense that it was oriented towards the world, *ad seculum*. The new sciences and scholarship, they believed, made the traditional modes of theologizing obsolete; a good many professional theologians agreed with them about that. Never before or after were science, philosophy, and theology seen as almost one and the same occupation.[3]

Even so, the "secular" theology of early modern science is strongly evolving away from the complex medieval embedding of nature in grace. To scholastic thinkers, the being and essential meaning of the natural world was always held within the divine embrace, and remained ever a sacred sign—as creation—pointing beyond itself to the Creator. At the same time, the scholastics of the Middle Ages well understood that nature ordinarily functioned naturalistically (that is, without special miraculous acts of God), which is why it is rationally comprehensible. But the relation of essential meaning and being itself to God was simply not interesting to the new secular theologians of what we now call the Scientific Revolution.[4]

---

3. Funkenstein, *Theology and the Scientific Imagination*, 3.

4. See pointed quotes from Galileo and Newton on the "modesty" of simply observing and mathematically modeling nature, as compared with the fabulous and indemonstrable metaphysical speculations of Aristotelian and scholastic thinking as regards what

Their theological interests lay elsewhere. Francis Bacon was theologically driven to exercise Man's God-given dominion over nature via instrumental natural knowledge, which was predictably mathematical, reductively experimental, and above all, useful.

In 1620 Bacon explains the theological driver motivating what we now call modern science by referencing the biblical story of humanity's creation and fall:

> For by the Fall man declined from the state of innocence and from his kingdom over the creatures. Both things can be repaired even in this life to some extent, the former by religion, the latter by the arts and sciences.[5]

And this repairing of our lost dominion over nature was primarily, to Bacon, the exercise of *power through knowledge*: "I am laboring to lay the foundation, not of any sect of doctrine, but of human utility and power."[6]

Understanding how nature *behaves* is what matters, for this is *useful* knowledge that unlocks our sovereign power *over* nature. Bacon was not interested in what any natural thing essentially is. Bacon's stance is embedded in his dominion theology, and it marks a firm break from medieval, scholastic natural philosophy. Come the Enlightenment, Kant's liberation of philosophy and science from metaphysics and theology indeed does end the "short career" of early modern natural theology, but Kant's move is continuous with Bacon's departure from scholastic natural theology.

A sharp break between theology and science is finally realized in Kant's famous *Critique of Pure Reason* (1781), even though the older integration of non-scholastic theology with natural philosophy is still clearly at play in Isaac Newton's occasionalism. The great mathematician thought of the laws of nature and gravity as the finger of God. Newton had a thoroughly supernatural view of natural operations, which is only flipped into anti-supernatural naturalism by Thomas Huxley in the late nineteenth century.[7]

---

natural beings essentially are, in Pasnau, *After Certainty*, "Trading Depth for Precision," 14–18.

5. Bacon, *New Organon*, 221.

6. Bacon, *New Atlantis and the Great Instauration*, 16.

7. Newton wrote much more about alchemy, biblical numerology, unitarian theology, and biblical interpretation than he did about mathematics and physics. Hence, John Maynard Keynes famously called Newton not the first man of the Age of Reason, but the last great magician. See Harrison, *Some New World*, 238, on the shift from Newton's supernatural naturalism to Thomas Huxley's anti-supernatural naturalism in the nineteenth century.

Funkenstein describes how this "short career" of natural philosophy as a secular theology (early modern science) comes to an end with Kant.[8] And it is the way that science is purged from theology and philosophy is purged from metaphysics that will eventually produce gender theory.

Getting a reasonably secure mental grip on the way Kant shapes Western thought thereafter is pretty hard work intellectually. Indeed, the next section may well be the hardest section in this book. Do not be discouraged if you find it a little heavy going. I shall do everything I can to help you pick up the central drift of Kant's brilliant intellectual moves, even if the details of how these moves are achieved may remain hazy. But this is very important. For it is Kant who lets go of any real knowledge of reality in the name of liberating science and reason from superstition and speculation. But this liberation is going to cause us serious trouble down the track. So hold on for a bit of a challenging ride as we take a quick dive into Kant's *Critique of Pure Reason*.

THE ENLIGHTENMENT REJECTION OF REALITY

As mentioned, trying to purge natural knowledge from metaphysical speculations and theological justifications was all the rage in the eighteenth century. Empirical knowledge had to be *just* empirical (i.e., *only* what the senses present to us) and rational knowledge had to be *just* rational (no superstitious or speculative metaphysics allowed). And for God's sake, keep theology out of philosophy and science! And if you want to do metaphysics, it must not be speculative, for you cannot appeal to transcendent mysteries, but you must *prove* your arguments about the transcendent from purely empirical and purely rational foundations. (This, by the way, assumes a totally daft concept of the transcendent, for if something is genuinely transcendent it is prior to and the grounds of any rational or empirical proof.) Hence, Kant's "transcendental" philosophy is exactly *not* concerned with the transcendent.

The long and short of the matter is that the only way Enlightenment faith-and-speculation-purged sense and reason could really get in the air was to dispense with any genuine knowledge of reality. Do pause here for a second to read that previous sentence again; it is quite a clanger! Kant is determined to preserve the Enlightened purity of sense and reason, so he

---

8. Funkenstein, *Theology and the Scientific Imagination*, "Kant and the De-Theologizing of Science," 346–56.

comes up with the idea of running a thought experiment where instead of making our ratio-empirical understanding conform with reality (the old-fashioned idea of truth) we make reality conform with our ratio-empirical understanding (the old-fashioned idea of insanity).

Near the start of Kant's *Critique of Pure Reason*,[9] he explains this move like this:

> It has hitherto been assumed that our knowledge must conform to the objects; but all attempts to ascertain anything about these objects *a priori*, by means of concepts, and thus to extend the range of our knowledge, have been rendered abortive by this assumption.

The old way (conforming our knowledge to reality) is abortive, in Kant's view, because no essential knowledge of reality can be demonstrated in the categories of pure Enlightenment reason or pure Enlightenment sensory knowledge. In traditional metaphysics one must—as Aristotle maintained—*assume* the divine truth of first principles, which are the grounds of essential knowledge, and then you can intelligibly and sensibly reason *from* these assumptions in order to gain a true knowledge of natural reality.[10] This is simply unacceptable to Kant's Enlightenment commitments where there must be *purely* reasonable and *purely* evidential—and irrefutable—demonstrations underpinning all claims to true knowledge.

Kant continues:

> Let us then make the experiment whether it may not be more successful in metaphysics, if we assume that the objects must conform to our knowledge.

---

9. Kant, *Critique of Pure Reason*, 15.

10. Aristotle, *Metaphysics*, book I, chapter 2 (982b, 1–5) "the first principles and the causes are most knowable {this is a Platonist outlook—insights of high mind are intrinsically revelational and concern essential knowledge in a way that modern categories of ratio-empirical knowledge can never obtain}; for by reason of these, and from these, all other things are known, {revelation is the grounds of empirical and rational knowledge} but these are not known by means of the things subordinate to them {empirical and rational "knowledge" cannot prove or justify revealed, primary and essential knowledge}." In *Metaphysics* book VI, chapter 1 (1026a, 10–33), Aristotle clearly identifies First Philosophy (which we now call metaphysics) with Theology. For (as per book I) first philosophy concerns the divine presuppositions of truth-seeking sense and reason. The traditional approach to presupposing the epistemic priority of objective truth about reality as primary and then conforming our understanding to it requires what Kant sees as a juvenile trust in a divinely intelligible reality, which the Enlightenment is simply too grown-up to do.

Did you notice the switch? If conforming our knowledge to reality does not give us a pure justification for valid knowledge and reason, then let us try "the experiment" of conforming reality to our knowledge and see if we can now get a pure rational justification that way.

In this switch, Kant is using the word "metaphysics" in a daring and cheeky manner. What he means here is that through his thought experiment we will be able to see what knowledge we can have that is *not* speculative and *not* superstitious, i.e., that does *not* require belief in divine meanings and transcendent first principles that surpass human sense and reason. That is, Kant is getting rid of metaphysics. So to Kant, "successful metaphysics" kills traditional metaphysics and produces rationally valid knowledge, even if Kant is too "modest" to presume to gain any knowledge of reality itself thereby.

The astonishing move here in Kant's mature philosophy is that his argument is entirely premised on the "experimental" switching of the order of knowledge from conforming our understanding to reality, to *reality conforming to our understanding*.

Kant goes on:

> This appears, at all events, to accord better with the possibility of our gaining the end we have in view, that is to say, of arriving at the knowledge of objects *a priori*, of determining something with respect to these objects, before they are given to us.

Kant—as the title of his Critique makes clear—is after *pure* reason. If we treat the rational and empirical structures of our own minds as the proper foundations of sense and reason, and simply lay aside the question of their relation to reality, then we can have what the Enlightenment is looking for; pure reason. Thus is reality laid aside, and properly reasoned knowledge becomes entirely subjective and anthropocentric. Do read that sentence again. Mark it well, this is the great intellectual advance of the Enlightenment! Who needs reality anyway?

Not meaning to be too modest about his stunning achievement in experimental thought, Kant goes on to say:

> We here propose to do just what Copernicus did in attempting to explain the celestial movements. When he found that he could make no progress by assuming that all the heavenly bodies revolved around the spectator, he reversed the process, and tried the experiment of assuming that the spectator revolved, while the stars remained at rest. We may make the same experiment with

regard to the intuition of objects. If the intuition must conform to the nature of the objects, I do not see how we can know anything about that nature *a priori*. If, on the other hand, the object (*qua* subject of the senses) conforms to the nature of our faculty of intuition, I can then easily conceive the possibility of such an *a priori* knowledge.

There you have it: Kant's Copernican revolution. Let reality revolve around my subjective knowledge. Are you picking up any resonances with gender identity yet?

WHY SUBORDINATING REALITY TO HUMAN RATIO-EMPIRICAL KNOWLEDGE WAS ATTRACTIVE TO THE ENLIGHTENMENT

Assuming you are unfamiliar with eighteenth-century philosophy, let me give you a quick explanation of what Kant means by *a priori*. This Latin phrase simply means "prior." *A priori* rational knowledge is the intuitive grasp of some universal principle—be it the laws of logic, of nature, of mathematics—which you know *before* (prior to) you experience an anticipated individual example or outworking of that universal truth. *A priori* knowledge is contrasted with empirical knowledge, which is *a posteriori*, meaning the knowledge that only comes *after* a sensory experience.

What we now tend to call eighteenth-century rationalism and empiricism were both in a difficult place in the 1780s because neither of them were able to justify their own truth claims by any *pure* warrants drawn from their own philosophical system. That is, empirical *truth* claims presuppose that there is a source to experience that is prior to experience, but one is unable to know that source using empirical means as empirical knowledge is always *a posteriori* knowledge. That is, there is no demonstrable empirical justification for there being any reality beyond my sensory experience, hence philosophically rigorous empirical knowledge cannot know if there is a real world causing empirical experience or not. David Hume was acutely aware of this, accepted it, and was a solipsist. A solipsist is someone who believes that their own immediate knowledge is the only knowledge they can ever know, so no assumptions can be made about reality beyond their own direct knowledge. A pure empiricist in the philosophically rigorous enlightened manner makes no truth claims about reality as such.

Rationalists had a similar philosophical problem to the empiricists, which Kant was very aware of. All rational knowledge is circular. 1 + 1 = 2, which can also be stated as 2 = 1 + 1. Reason is a system of mentally consistent circular logic, which is entirely valid for abstract intellectual constructs, but one cannot show that reason is anything other than an internal mind game by means of pure reason itself.

Kant's brilliant solution to both of these problems was to unify sense and reason, without reference to reality, but with reference to human experience alone. We know phenomena (reality *as it appears to us* in our experiences) but we do not know noumena (reality *as it is in itself*). This is Kant's famous phenomenological turn. And it works, if you are happy not to know reality. That is, the breakthrough achievement of Enlightenment philosophy—the purification of reason and sense experience from theology and speculative metaphysics—comes at a price.

If you just focus on how liberated you are from indemonstrable speculative high metaphysical truths and theological first-order beliefs (and religious authorities), then perhaps the price of pure Enlightenment knowledge seems worth it. This indeed was how many of the secularizing, then atheist nineteenth-century progeny of the Enlightenment saw matters. That you have lost any true knowledge of reality seems a small price to pay when you are trying to get the church off your back, grasp political and economic power, and fly forward in the great pragmatic age of scientific and commercial progress. Sacrificing reality was a small price to pay for freedom and power. Or so it was assumed.

AFTER KANT

Kant gave Western progressive enlightened modernity its ticket out of metaphysical and theological jail. Philosophy and science were thus purified from metaphysical speculation and religious faith. The very aspiration of a true knowledge of reality was laid aside in order to buy and then travel on this ticket. It is now a deep feature of what one might call the post-Enlightenment mythology of Western intellectual culture, that this was a ticket worth buying and a trip worth taking. Whether that will ultimately prove to be the case is another question. That question is the same question as to whether we can really do without an at least partially and commonsense true knowledge of reality (which must presuppose some metaphysical speculation and some ultimately religious/sacred faith). We will come back to this when we later look at what sort of philosophical and practical approach is really able to combat gender theory, but for the moment it is important to establish Kant's phenomenological turn away from a true knowledge of reality as the starting point of contemporary gender theory.

4

Nineteenth-Century Continental Thought

As we saw in chapter 3, isolating philosophy from metaphysics and science from theology were the central methodological features of Kant's "purity" approach. These isolations remained a core legacy of Enlightenment thinking in modern philosophy. Gender theory is deeply indebted to knowledge defined by anti-metaphysical and anti-faith commitments, and to an unknowable reality, so Kant's legacy is also alive and well in postmodern thinking today.

After Kant knowledge becomes an exclusively human construction. Here knowledge is always and *only* situated within *our* language, culture, power, and interests. Objective and sacred truth has become obsolete. The idea that human truth is in some sense overshadowed by an objective and partially knowable reality, and by high and essential meanings of value and purpose, is dropped. Truth is fully anthropomorphized and fully insulated within the human immanent horizon.[1] This is an astonishing break with the long traditions of the metaphysical and divine overshadowing of

---

1. See Taylor, *Secular Age*. This is Taylor's cumulative masterpiece of a long life of profound thinking. Taylor described the cultural and intellectual manner in which our vision of reality became locked down to the "immanent frame" and the manner in which the knowing individual became "buffered" and unable to really believe in meaning and reality outside of their own internalized world of self-construction. Objective truth and essential meaning have been squeezed out of our high culture, and perhaps we are all going mad as a result.

human knowledge in the Western life of the mind. This new, purely anthropocentric knowledge plays itself out in nineteenth-century intellectual developments in fascinating ways.

Many complex developments happen in nineteenth-century Continental thought, and I will only map what I take to be the key features of this story that are relevant to understanding gender theory. The first sequence of developments that we need to have a functional grasp of is the way Hegel reacts to Kant, and then the way that Marx inverts Hegel. We can have no appreciation of almost everything that happens in Western philosophy from the 1780s to the present without an at least serviceable grasp of the three Continental greats: Kant, Hegel, and Marx.

HEGEL AND THE HISTORICALLY SITUATED RETURN OF SPECULATIVE METAPHYSICS

Kant scholars to this day find the difficulties involved in interpreting the two versions of Kant's *Critique of Pure Reason* endlessly productive. Indeed, this domain is so productive that one can build an entire academic career exploring just this one text (in its two versions) by Kant. As profoundly influential as Kant really is, the ambition of his own aims is never fully realized, and he grapples with astonishing rigor with the difficulties of his own attempts at solutions. So it is no surprise that there are immediate reactions to Kant's work in the late eighteenth century and the early nineteenth century. No reaction is more significant than that of G. W. F. Hegel (1770–1831).

Hegel is not content to let go of reality, or metaphysics. And yet, Hegel is radically discontinuous with pre–nineteenth-century metaphysics, and his understanding of reality is explicitly historically, politically, and culturally situated. Hegel produces remarkable, seductive, insightful, and very demanding dialectical philosophy.

Whatever Kant may say about the unreachable knowledge of noumena, Hegel will not let go of the Absolute. To do so, Hegel "dialectically" breaks with the subject/object divide. ("Dialectic" here refers to Hegel's complex use of logic such that he consistently aims to synthesize opposites at a higher level.) By pointing out how the subjective (and the knowledge of phenomena) requires the objective (and the reality of noumena) to have any meaning, Hegel "overcomes" the unknowableness of noumena. The Absolute is thus integral to human consciousness. Though a rejector of traditional Christian doctrine (and yet a staunch self-professed Lutheran), spiritual reality is the high horizon of his philosophy. According to Hegel's younger rival Søren Kierkegaard (who was a doctrinally orthodox Lutheran), Hegel was profoundly intellectually seductive to many a Christian Continental theologian in the early nineteenth century. With Kierkegaard and William Desmond, I think a close reading of Hegel is anything but Christian, though his relation to Christian theology is complex and intimate, as all rationalist/idealist "heresies" are.[2]

In very simplified terms, it goes like this: God lives within human consciousness. God is evolving *through* human consciousness. Thus, through historical developments the Spirit comes to self-awareness. And here one cannot but help notice the Germanic philosophical tweak that you will also see in atheist thinkers like Heidegger. German art and philosophy are the pointy end of the advancement of Spirit through human culture and history. And it just so happens that Hegel is the pointy end of German philosophy. Effectively Hegel thinks of himself as, well ... the voice of God. Or to put this in more Hegelian terms, the consciousness of Spirit is always evolving (progressively!) and becoming self-aware, and this evolution is expressed through the most advanced creations of human culture (such as Hegel's dialectical philosophy). But this is not a hubristic individualist assertion to Hegel, as Spirit dialectically overcomes, without obliterating, the individual/collective dyad. Spirit effectively *is* the ethical community of the most advanced creative human culture, yet it is real individuals within that culture who embody and articulate Spirit. We are not quite done with Hegel yet, but before proceeding further, we must take a brief excursion into theology.

THEOLOGICAL DEVELOPMENTS

The science of God had an interesting career in the Germanic lands from the Enlightenment on. Late eighteenth-century rationalist deism was very embarrassed about superstitious religion, and had no interest in any credulous or literalist reading of the pre-modern myths and moralizing fairy tales of the Bible. At the same time as rationalist deism is very philosophically fashionable, Protestant biblical scholars were industriously developing what we now call historical textual criticism. The desire to interpret the Bible with the tools of modern science—and the assumptions of factual validity

2. Kierkegaard, *Philosophical Fragments*; Desmond, *Hegel's God*.

presupposing an interpretive frame of scientific naturalism—was going on apace from the late eighteenth century on. Unsurprisingly, rationalist philosophical theology combined with naturalistic scientific biblical scholarship seriously erodes orthodox Christian belief. Two trends in this period were eroding orthodox Christian faith. Firstly, a biblical-criticism model was developed that aimed at uncovering the *real* (i.e., non-miraculous) history of biblical developments by deconstructing and reconstructing the histories of biblical texts. This typically employed often highly speculative stylistic analysis which was then used to achieve the second trend in Enlightenment interpretation—hermeneutics. Biblical texts were now interpreted to suit the rationalist interpretive angle of the era so as to reveal the scripture's *real* (i.e., non-miraculous) meaning. The promotion of Christian unbelief by means of scientific biblical textual analysis and rationalist interpretation was becoming a fine art.

Roman Catholics back in the early Enlightenment era were horrified by these trends in Protestant Germany theology. I am not a Roman Catholic, but as a theologian myself I am inclined to think that such Protestant biblical scholarship indeed is liable to serious theological abuse,[3] facilitating the now fashionable malleability of scriptural analysis so as to make holy writ say whatever one wants it to say. But if one wants freedom *from* religion, one would have to say that liberal[4] Protestant theologians have done the West a big favor. Not surprisingly it is nineteenth-century liberal Protestant theologians—such as David Strauss—who are leading figures in

---

3. I accept that the sophisticated methods of textual analysis and inter-textual comparison that are integral with historical critical biblical scholarship can be genuinely illuminating of the meaning of Christian holy writ. There are fine, pious, and orthodox biblical scholars using such methods where appropriate. However, where there is a totally constructivist conception of human meaning itself, and where there is an anti-supernaturalist and anti-metaphysical interpretive lens, then hermeneutics becomes a tool of reframing any text in ultimately any direction one chooses. In what I have read, this is largely how queer theology works. Using sophisticated hermeneutic tools, presupposing total linguistic constructivism, queer evaluations of how oppressive certain scriptural passages are produce a reading against the text, which is then thrown against other scriptural passages deemed amenable to queer justice so as to subvert the validity of the "oppressive" biblical text. Being marginal itself seems to be the only criteria of Christian interpretive authenticity for queer theology.

4. The term "liberal" here means "free" from orthodox doctrinal rigidity, and it also means a strong commitment to a reductively scientific interpretive methodology (methodological naturalism) as regards interpreting the Christian Scriptures and traditional Christian doctrines.

the powerful rise of nineteenth-century atheism. We will come back to this when we look at Marx.

Liberal Protestant theology was very interested in both Kant and Hegel, and theology was a hugely important feature of nineteenth-century university life. For example, 40 percent of all graduates from German universities in the 1830s studied theology.[5]

Recovering a high frame of spiritual meaning, and meaning about reality, seemed needed after Kant's phenomenological turn away from reality. Theology's divine horizon of meaning seemed like the obvious way of keeping a high frame of meaning to Western thought. Yet the Enlightenment infatuation with pure reason, pure science, and with the phenomenological turn does not go away from the mainstream of Germanic intellectual life in the nineteenth century. The end result of all this is that Protestant liberal theology is deeply integral with Enlightenment framed philosophy in the nineteenth century, though how genuinely Christian it was is a significant question if measured by the ruler of credal orthodoxy. God as a kind of philosophical idea, and the kind that could be expressed culturally, historically, and politically, and that was ultimately a way of describing ourselves, was a very big deal in nineteenth-century Germanic lands. Back now to Hegel.

FROM HEGEL TO MARX

It is hard to convey how exciting, powerful, and attractive to the young and the radical the philosophical landscape was in the early nineteenth century. The same is true of the artistic, poetic, and musical worlds of that time. Hegel was a near exact contemporary of Beethoven. The Romantic cult of the creative genius was flourishing in Hegel's lifetime. Hegel was part of a cultural ethos that believed that our truly great men (they usually, but not exclusively, were men) imaginatively and artistically *create* meaning, real meaning, the meaning of reality even.

Hegel's immanentizing and humanizing of the divine was continuous with Kant's liberation of Western thought from traditional metaphysics and orthodox Christian theology. For, to the traditionalists, the Real is always above human creativity, and it is *not* produced by humans. To the traditionalists, reason and intelligible meaning (Logos) always transcend the human mind, and they are not functions *of* the human mind or human language.

---

5. Spencer, *Atheists*, 146.

To the traditionalist, natural reality is a creation that has divinely gifted essences, purposes, and moral flourishing, which we receive and discover rather than poetically create. Hegel has no interest in those traditionalist stances.[6] Gender theory is continuous with Hegel's divinizing of the human (we shall be our own creators); it is continuous with Hegel's enterprise in the human creation of meaning, and with Hegel's dialectical overcoming of all dyads, including the dyad of the natural as distinct from the cultural. There is something Romantic, liberationist, and self-creating about gender theory that is continuous with the nineteenth-century immanentizing of theology as done by Hegel. But gender theory is also deeply indebted to progressive Marxism, which is itself an intriguing reaction to and appropriation of Hegel. Famously, Marx claimed that his historical materialism was Hegel's dialectical philosophy turned on its head.

KARL MARX (1818–83)

Hegel idealistically appropriates and historically immanentizes Christian theology, but Marx sets out to critically destroy theology and cast aside the Christian religion, and religion as such.

John Calvin believed that the human heart is a perpetual idol factory.[7] Basically what he meant is that the impulse to replace God with constructions of our own making, that permit us to worship ourselves, is one of the most basic impulses of fallen humanity. When (to an orthodox Christian) Hegel undertakes his intellectual idol productions through high sounding theological philosophy, the result is neither orthodox faith nor decisive atheism. In this regard, when Marx simply throws God out and replaces God with Man as the first object of human worship, this has more, shall we say, theological integrity than does Hegel. And on this point Marx—in strange agreement with Calvin, but with a clear Enlightenment twist—is very direct. Marx says:

> The criticism of religion disillusions man so that he will think, act and fashion his reality as a man who has lost his illusions and regained his reason; so that he will revolve around himself as his

---

6. For excellent introductions to both Hegel and Marx see Peter Singer's following texts. Singer is a very able utilitarian ethicist and is well known for his animal welfare advocacy. He is also a fine scholar of Hegel and Marx. See Singer, *Hegel*; Singer, *Marx*.

7. Calvin, *Institutes* 1.11.8.

own true sun. Religion is only the illusory sun about which man revolves so long as he does not revolve about himself.[8]

The "Young Hegelians" of the 1830s and '40s—notably Ludwig Feuerbach, Bruno Baur, and Karl Marx—took Hegel's immanentizing of the divine a step further than Hegel. Here, the central idea of the Young Hegelian critique of religion is an uncovering of the real (that is, material) meaning of religion, which is that Man makes religion, Man makes God in his own image, and then wealthy ruling elites use religion to justify their power and privilege.

Significantly, it was the lead of a liberal Protestant theologian, David Strauss, that solidified the "Young Hegelian" critique of religion. For Strauss had fully embraced the idea that the real meaning of the Christian religion is mythological. He maintained that Christ did not miraculously rise from the dead, but rather the *mythic* Christ rises in the imagination of Christians, and Christ is then poetically embodied in the church, which perpetuates this myth.[9] But then, Feuerbach thinks, if the central Christian doctrines are just myths, and if myths are really a function of human poetic creativity and nothing else, then God is an imaginative construction of ourselves projected onto the universe.[10] Marx takes this train of thinking up and names religious belief itself as false consciousness, and a cover for the political and economic manipulation of the credulous masses by their wealthy and powerful masters. Contra Hegel, it is not that we ourselves are God, rather God is a poetic cultural alienation from our own truly material reality. Religion is not about the high spiritual domain of the Absolute (even if that is a divinization of humanity to Hegel). Rather, religion is really a mythic cloak for material and economic power. (Can you hear the resonance with Foucault's postmodern infatuation with all-defining power?) Thus does Marx invert Hegel and come up with dialectical materialism and, a little further down the track (1848), with *The Communist Manifesto*.

PROGRESSIVE MATERIALISM

Under the pen name of George Eliot, Mary Evans translated Strauss's *Life of Jesus* (in 1846) and Feuerbach's *Essence of Christianity* (in 1854) into

---

8. Marx, "Contribution to the Critique," 54.
9. Strauss, *Life of Jesus Critically Examined* (German original, 1836).
10. Feuerbach, *Essence of Christianity* (German original, 1841).

English. These two translations had an enormous impact, bringing the theological, economic, and political critiques of traditional Christianity on the Continent to the Anglophone world. The translations themselves are literary masterpieces, and the arguments and logic of these two powerful thinkers are gripping and persuasive. Thus was born what we now think of as socialist, communist, and often atheist progressivism in the Anglophone world.

Due to the influence of Marx in particular, materialism becomes a philosophical stance that eventually came to define radical progressivism. Considerable nuance is necessary here, though. There were plenty of nineteenth-century Christian progressives—Hannah Moore, William Wilberforce, Lord Shaftesbury, etc.—who worked tirelessly against slavery, against exploitation of the poor, against terrible conditions for women and children, for unionization, for education for the poor, who protected the natural environment, who promoted universal male suffrage and then suffrage for women, and who did all manner of things to progress the well-being of those who suffered most egregiously as a result of the Industrial Revolution. Through the latter half of the nineteenth century evangelicals, Anglicans, and Roman Catholics often worked side by side with radical atheist socialists in union movements seeking to improve the lot of workers. There were, for example, strong Methodist, Presbyterian, Anglican, and Roman Catholic activists at the heart of the late nineteenth-century formation of the Australian Labor Party.[11] However, the philosophical commitment of materialist atheism increasingly came to define a concertedly secularist and anti-Christian progressivism, and this linked up with scientific atheism in Thomas Huxley's circles of influence.[12] Progressivism was largely coopted by materialists among intellectual elites by the turn of the twentieth century. Scientific atheism in the universities became the central means of undermining Christian faith intellectually from the 1920s until its popular triumph in the 1960s.[13] Throwing off both Christian sexual morals and the historical embedding of institutions, education, and authority structures in Christian religious belief and practices became a central progressive aspiration through the twentieth century.

11. Pabst, *Story of Our Country*, 6.
12. See Stanley, *Huxley's Church and Maxwell's Demon*.
13. For a fascinating account of how atheist progressivism was promoted through a few lead radicals in philosophy departments at Australian universities through the twentieth century, see Franklin, *Corrupting the Youth*.

The materialism upheld by radical progressives maintained that there are no non-material spiritual or transcendent realities. This is in fact a metaphysical stance that claims continuity with the Enlightenment disdain of metaphysics. This contradiction—an anti-metaphysical metaphysical atheism—is produced by a philosophical sleight of hand.

To scientific atheism, material reality is thought of as the only thing that is practically real, so—following Marx's lead—practice (*praxis*) replaces metaphysics, and then only material power is real. This attempt to replace metaphysics does not work philosophically, as all you have really achieved is the replacing of one set of ultimately believed metaphysical understandings of reality with another set of ultimately believed metaphysical understandings—for it is *unavoidably metaphysical* to have any view of reality at all.

It is the nineteenth-century infatuation with science and technology that glosses over the need to do any serious metaphysical thinking about reality, and makes the material world seem simply real. That is: Because science works, scientific knowledge is practically true.[14] And what is practically true only works because it is real.[15] Ergo, only what science tells you is real.[16] This is all very philosophically naïve, but it certainly caught on. Fashion matters more than one might think in the illustrious halls of learning. A very significant figure promoting the nineteenth-century infatuation with science and progress through technological innovation was Thomas Huxley (1825–95).

Huxley was one of the great institutional and intellectual influencers of Late Victorian England. Huxley promoted scientific positivism, which holds that, for all practical and demonstrable purposes, only what science can identify is real. Being the consummate lobbyist and political strategist that he was, and being politically situated in a power and authority culture that was predominantly Christianity inflected, he was deliberately tricky about the metaphysical and theological implications of his stance. Huxley invented the word "agnosticism" to politely paint over the social reformation and educational implications of his anti-clericalism and his functional ignoring of God (methodological atheism). Claiming to only

14. This is a deflationary understanding of the traditional meaning of "true," which does not simply mean "it works."

15. This step does not directly follow, because, for instance, the fact that navigating by the stars works does not make Ptolemaic geocentrism true.

16. This does not necessarily follow. There may be other sources of real knowledge than science, and there may be types of real knowledge that are not scientific.

make comment on what he could demonstrate evidentially, he was often strategically silent about whether he believed there was or was not an immaterial and supernatural God. Other members of his circle, such as Herbert Spencer, and inheritors of his mantle, such as Bertrand Russell, were overt scientific atheists.

Materialism claims not just agnosticism as regards the immaterial, but positive disbelief in the immaterial. This makes it a metaphysical stance asserting that there is no God. This is a metaphysical claim because it is a claim about how reality really is, not just a claim about how things appear, and it is not itself a scientific claim. After all, if there is no scientific evidence that God is a material being, this is no sort of contradiction of the traditional theological view that God is indeed not a material being.

As an interesting aside, it is theologically orthodox to believe that God is no-thing; God as the extra-cosmic Creator and as the Ground of Being *for* creation, is not a being among other beings within the world. It has always struck me as strange that popularizing atheists do not seem to know that to traditional Christian theology, of course God does not exist in the normal categories of scientifically verifiable material existence. As regards the non-existence of God, I find it hard to understand what so-called scientific atheists and Christians are meant to disagree about.[17]

To tie this back to Marx, he makes a hyper-Enlightenment move where he believes he can see through the attempt by Hegel to recover theology (where Man and God are really one and the same) and metaphysics (where abstract dialectical reasoning achieves some sort of realization of the Absolute and the Infinite in the realm of mind, as a part of the historical forward movement of Spirit).[18] Philosophical ideas are, to Marx, *post hoc* imaginative glosses on material reality. To understand the real one needs to look at what is materially going on, rather than pre-interpret power relationships as good or natural based on religious or metaphysical theories. Marx believes he has replaced theoretical ideas with a focus on material realities and a critical unveiling of what the practical use of ideas and beliefs actually are. Famously, Marx claims the pressing concern is not to interpret

---

17. I share this perplexity with David Bentley Hart. See Hart, *Experience of God*, 13–18.

18. Kierkegaard is a relentless critic of Hegelian thinking. In contrast to the abstract mind-game of the Absolute/Ideal/Infinite, and an all-containing dialectical system of philosophical logic, Kierkegaard focuses on actual human existence and the always fragmentary and incomplete nature of our logical constructions. See Kierkegaard, *Philosophical Fragments*.

the world, but to change it. He thinks he has replaced theory with praxis. Being only concerned with the material as the real, he thus thinks of himself as entirely eliding metaphysical speculation (idealist philosophy) and entirely eliding theological false consciousness.

Marx is, in effect, a naïve positivist when it comes to material truths, and he is also a pragmatist when it comes to politics and economics. This doesn't really work, as his tacit theory of justice, where the workers *should not* be exploited, cannot be derived from any simply positivist reading of material reality, or from any simply pragmatic account of politics and economics.[19] Praxis does not really replace a tacit metaphysics of egalitarian justice in Marx, however much Marxists may wish to protest to the contrary. For inequality and exploitation are—to the pure positivist and the pure pragmatist—perfectly natural material realities; on what positivist and pragmatic grounds could they be *wrong*? Leaving such difficulties to one side, this sort of materialism became increasingly integral with both radical progressivism and atheist positivism.

TIE BACK TO GENDER THEORY

Gender theory has roots in nineteenth-century Romantic, atheist, materialist, and egalitarian progressivism. Gender theory's high poetic freedom, as well as its dazzling web of abstruse and sophisticated philosophical construction, has Hegel as its patron saint. The atheist, materialist, and radically egalitarian progressivism of gender theory has Marx as its patron saint. As regards Marx, gender theory's analysis of power and its amoral (yet moralistic) categories of radical egalitarianism need a little further unpacking.

When we look at postmodernism, the ties between Marx and Foucault—as regards power—will become very clear. But to indicate that briefly here, Marx (unlike, and yet strangely like Foucault) is a positivist in the nineteenth-century mechanistic manner, who looks at nature as a

---

19. Marx tries to get around his profoundly moral sense of the injustice of distributing wealth and power based on any other basis than non-alienated labor, by claiming Marxism is *not actually moral* at all, but has simply grasped an inevitable historical process. Historical materialism is seen by Marx as an inescapable process where the working class becomes aware of their power and casts off the exploitation of the ruling class. This is not "good"; it is simply inevitable. However, for the workers to realize their power, they must see their exploitation as bad and revolution as good. Things are *inescapably moral* in political reality, if Marx's historical necessity of the victory of the working class is to be realized.

web of causal physical chains determined by the necessity of force. Marx's economics, for example, is ridiculously mechanistic and deterministic by sophisticated contemporary standards.[20] Being a materialist, he sees nature as a set of mechanical power relations, which is also how he sees economics and politics. So human affairs—viewed with an eye to material reality and rejecting any view from ideology, moral philosophy, religion, metaphysics, and any other form of false consciousness—are ultimately *just about power*. Gender theory likewise presupposes an amoral and anti-metaphysical view of power (as force) mediated in human societies through an entirely constructivist understanding of norms, performative conventions, and language. We will explore this more closely when we look at Foucault and postmodernism, but this understanding of power comes to us in the atheist progressive tradition from Marx.

Something I did not draw attention to in my treatment of Kant is the manner in which freedom is central to the Enlightenment ethos. Freedom, to Kant, means rational autonomy. Because reason—to Kant—is universally valid, a rational person needs no external governance if they are acting in a genuinely rational manner. Freedom as freedom from external coercion is a central Enlightenment value embraced by gender theory. But this takes a strongly egalitarian trajectory with Marx. To Marx, all hierarchies and all nature-defined differences (say, between men and women) become obstacles to liberation. So what Mary Harrington calls "freedom feminism"[21] is a deep driver of gender theory, and it has Marxist egalitarian signatures (opposed to hierarchy), liberal individualist signatures (don't interfere with my autonomy), and progressive (materialist, anti-ideological) freedom-from-religion signatures.

---

20. The Marxist economist Yanis Varoufakis has written a fascinating book in economic theory: *Economic Indeterminacy*. Varoufakis admires Marx in a great many regards, but finds Marx's economic modeling hopelessly deterministic. And indeed, nineteenth-century deterministic naturalism remains integral with mainstream contemporary economic theory, according to Varoufakis. Yet, so Varoufakis argues, human agency and unforeseeable contingencies are integral with economic activity such that indeterminacy is an integral feature of the real economy. We now have mathematical models that can accommodate system indeterminacy to some extent, and these models are being used in economics. However, politics as a human activity is genuinely free, because economic structures are not natural, they are cultural and political, and we can create them differently to how they presently work if we choose.

21. Harrington, *Feminism Against Progress*, 16.

CODA

We now have a brief outline of how Kant, Hegel, and Marx are formative thinkers shaping the basic drivers of progressive Western philosophical, political, and cultural evolution. Gender theory is deeply integral with this evolution. We are about to see how things evolve further through a strongly positivist and pragmatic trajectory, then on to a postmodern trajectory. I will be endeavoring to show how gender theory is continuous with these two trajectories as well as the Enlightenment and Marxist trajectories, in an archaeological manner. That is, I shall be seeking to show how the new layers rest on the old layers even if they appear to be very different to that which they seemingly overcame and replaced. The end picture should enable us to see how deeply integral gender theory is with the big sweep of Western intellectual evolution, and for this reason—as deeply counterintuitive as gender theory really is—it is genuinely hard for our highly educated elites to treat it with the suspicion it deserves.

5

Positivism

IN THE END, IT is the complex and ultimately unworkable relationship between skeptical empiricism and atheist positivism that blows up the Age of Reason and ushers in postmodernism.

Empiricism—named after the late classical skeptic Sextus Empiricus—maintains that if one relies on sensory stimulation alone for knowledge, then one cannot justify any real knowledge of reality. This is so because all that a pure empiricist *can* know is their own sensorium. To Sextus Empiricus, this requires an openness to the world as it *appears* to us, while suspending all judgments as to what the world itself is (independent of my *experience* of phenomena), or even *if* it is.[1] In contrast, modern atheist positivism claims that sense-based scientific knowledge and mathematical models describing the physical laws of nature gives us the real practical *truth* about reality, and that nothing else (certainly not religion) gives us the truth about reality.[2] These two stances are philosophically incompatible, and yet modern scientific positivists typically think of their truth claims as grounded in empirical evidence. Philosophically this is trying to have your cake and eat it too. Either you are an empiricist who is rigorously skeptical

---

1. Empiricus, *Outline of Pyrrhonism*. This astonishing defense of sticking with appearances without making judgments about reality had an enormous reactive impact on Descartes and an enormous affirmative impact on Hume.

2. The positive assertion that God does not exist based on an atheism that its adherents believe is a function of scientific evidence is clearly evident in the "new atheism" of the first decade of the twenty-first century, most ably represented by Dawkins, *God Delusion*.

about all truth claims, or you are an atheist positivist who *believes*—for non-empirical reasons—that science is truth-revealing, and that religion is not truth-revealing.

The above has direct relevance to the "have your cake and eat it too"[3] orientation of gender theory, which is a postmodern stance. Looking at what modern positivism is, how it failed, and how that failure contributed to the rise to postmodernism is thus very significant for understanding gender theory.

NINETEENTH-CENTURY POSITIVIST RELIGIONS OF SCIENCE AND REASON

Positivism has a long backstory deeply embroiled in highly fascinating medieval innovations that we will briefly touch on later. These innovations were all theologically motivated and were integral with Christian natural philosophy. But modern positivism breaks not only with its medieval roots but equally with its early modern natural-philosophy roots, precisely by maintaining an innovative and essentially *religious* opposition to Christian theology. The modern positivism that we are now familiar with arises as a distinctly modern *alternative* to traditional religious belief in revolutionary France.

The manner in which the fabulously wealthy French aristocracy of the eighteenth century were integrated with the wealth and cultural authority of the Catholic Church tied the fate of the church in France to the fate of the aristocracy. Were it not for the impact of the Wesley brothers in the Christian conversion of large numbers of lower-class English men and women, and their upward transition into the middle class by the late nineteenth century, combined with the impact of Christian social reformers like William Wilberforce and the seventh Earl of Shaftesbury which enabled this upward mobility for the poor, the same fate may very well have met the nineteenth-century Anglican Church in England as met the post-revolutionary Catholic Church in France.

---

3. That is, gender theory wishes to claim that *all* conceptions of "sex" and "gender" are performative and imaginative co-constructions, at the same time as denying the *truth* of sex-realism. Logically, if one is reasoning as a genuine constructivist, if sex-realism is a construction then it is not false, for where everything is a construction then nothing is either-true-or-false. But gender theory wishes to denounce sex-realism *as false* in order to promote the (ironic) *truth* of the fictitious construction of all human meanings of "sex" and "gender."

Even though he did not live to see it, Voltaire's anti-clericalism, and his profound disdain for the Catholic Church, had a powerful impact on revolutionary France. Though the French Revolution proclaimed religious freedom as one of the liberal and universal "rights of Man" in 1789, anti-clerical violence, the confiscation and looting of church properties, and the suppression of Catholic religious practice was rampant in the first decade of the French Revolution. Between 1792 and 1794 the state-mandated atheist religion, the *Culte de la Raison*, was imposed on the French, which was in turn replaced (by violence) with Robespierre's deistic *Culte de l'Être suprême* in 1794.

Under the Cult of Reason, the altar (symbolizing Christ in Catholic theology) was dismantled in Paris's Cathedral of Notre Dame and replaced with an altar to Liberty, and *A LA PHILOSOPHIE* (to Philosophy) was inscribed in stone on the entrance to the cathedral. In the early period of the French Revolution thirty thousand Catholic priests were exiled from France and hundreds were executed. Revolutionary France, rejecting the old order and its authority structures, was teetered on the edge of internal implosion. Brutal reprisals against political opponents were the means by which the Jacobine Club (*Société des Jacobine, amis de la liberté et de l'égalité*) held and advanced their power. After Robespierre was beheaded in 1794, internal blood-letting and anti-Christian religious fanaticism bubbled down somewhat, with Napoleon's conquering prowess increasingly focusing violent revolutionary energy outside of France, and to his own political advantage within France.

As far as religion went, in 1801 the ever-pragmatic Napoleon made a strategic alliance with Pope Pius VII, recognizing Catholicism as the majority religion of France. From the outset Napoleon established the terms of the relationship between the Catholic Church and Napoleonic France firmly in his own favor. Allowing the Catholic Church back into France was no return to pre-revolutionary religion. Catholic bishops had to swear allegiance to the French state and its ruler, and the role of the Catholic Church was made firmly and discretely "religious" and rendered politically subservient to the state. In 1804 Napoleon effectively used the pope in a novel version of a traditional Christian coronation ceremony, wherein the Frenchman received the crown from the pope and then crowned himself emperor in the Cathedral of Notre Dame. In such manner religion was made firmly and overtly subservient to secular political power in revolutionary France.

The Enlightenment and atheist baptism of blood that characterized the French revolutionary period, followed by the pragmatic use of religion for political purposes, remained influential in France thereafter. Significantly, this baptism and pragmatism was a secularized religious movement. Religion—rituals, myths, festivals, special ceremonies, cosmic-meaning constructions, binding common doctrines, a priesthood, ethical frameworks, high oaths, pageantry, and so forth—is here understood as both a fundamental and politically useful human phenomena, both by Robespierre and then by Napoleon. For this reason one cannot simply *abolish* the aristocratic/Catholic *Ancien Régime*; one must *replace* it with the Cults of Reason, Leader, and Nationalism.

The interesting historical fact here is that modern French positivism—as established by Henri de Saint-Simon and Auguste Comte—is intimately tied up with a French revolutionary atheist, yet deeply religious, consciousness. Well after both the Cult of Reason and the Cult of the Supreme Being were disestablished, the most prominent French positivist—Auguste Comte—invented the "Religion of Humanity" (*Religion de l'Humanité*). Through Comte's close friendship with John Stuart Mill, Comte's positivism became well known in England. Progressive English intellectual elites, in a somewhat upper-class Anglican manner, were inclined to be largely derisive of religion, hence Thomas Huxley's dismissive description of Comte's Religion of Humanity as Catholicism minus God. At the same time, Huxley was working to replace the power and influence of the Church of England with the power and influence of science. More on Huxley later.

AUGUSTE COMTE

Treating science (pure sense) and mathematics and logic (pure reason) as *truth*-revealing, within an atheist and materialist set of interpretive commitments, is fully compatible with treating science as a religion,[4] an orientation later critics have called "scientism." Acknowledging an empirical philosophical understanding of sensory knowledge, Comte denies that any absolute truth can be known, but the *practical* truths of sense and logic are

---

4. Famously, in Francis Bacon's famous *New Atlantis*, the priest-caste who runs his utopian society are obviously what we would now call scientists. Religious scientism is by no means a discretely French social phenomenon. See Bacon, *New Atlantis and the Great Instauration*. And Auguste Comte's close personal ties with John Stuart Mill show a strong English utilitarian sympathy toward positivism, even though Mill is surely the more subtle philosophical thinker of the two men.

elevated to the status of the *only* truth we *can* have, and are thus held to be adequate to the metaphysical claim that only scientific and logical truths are really true, and hence traditional theistic claims are false.

Positivism is not simply a pragmatic philosophical stance; it first comes to us as a humanistic religious consciousness, quite compatible with aspects of Hegelian idealism, where the human Spirit (Mind) is the measure and locus of all real truth and meaning. In Hegel, this is Protagoras's ancient sophist dictum "Man is the measure of all things" with a post-Christian Germanic twist. Such a stance is compatible with the liberal and Romantic myth of human greatness, a myth Napoleon worked hard to performatively embody. As the French of the early nineteenth century take up the mantle of Protagoras, our own creative imagination combined with acts of power *produces* the reality we choose.

Philosophically, Comte's secular religious approach to science is quite understandable; indeed, it is arguably necessary. For one must have *faith* in human science and human logic as truth-revealing if one has abandoned religion and yet remains interested in truth. Prior to the Enlightenment such faith in science was religiously warranted, but after the French Revolution, an atheist religious sensibility simply asserts that no warrant beyond human science and logic is necessary for us to have faith in the truth-revealing powers of our own scientific and logical knowledge-constructions. In this manner the old religious and metaphysical warrants for the truths of sense and reason are replaced with a new atheist (which is, religious)—and a supposedly metaphysical load-bearing—science and logic. That we just make up all the religious features of this new outlook was seen as entirely unproblematic by its originators. For—and this is preemptively postmodern—is not all meaning and all truth usefully made up by us?

SAINT-SIMON, MARX, AND PROGRESSIVE SECULARISM

In Saint-Simon's first published work, *Lettres d'un habitant de Genève* (1802), he proposed the founding of a religion of science with Isaac Newton as a saint. A decade later, and as a teenager, Auguste Comte (born in 1798) was a student and secretary to Saint-Simon, which was no doubt a significant influence of Comte's religious interest in science. But this was by no means Saint-Simon's only interest. The central concern of Saint-Simon in later life was a scientific understanding of political economics. This was profoundly influential on Comte and, later, on Marx.

Saint-Simon was an uncommonly gifted and uncommonly unlucky man. Of aristocratic birth, he was an enthusiastic anti-Catholic atheist and strongly supported the French Revolution. He had hoped to strip and sell the building materials of the Cathedral of Notre Dame as an act of revolutionary fervor. However, he was imprisoned under suspicion of being anti-revolutionary by the Jacobines, and was at no small risk of execution. In a turn of good luck, the Reign of Terror ended before he was executed. His marriage in 1801 only lasted one year, and as a result of this failed marriage and other mishaps, he lived in penury from 1802 until his death in 1825. Not making the impact on the world that his considerable gifts and astonishing ambitions desired, he shot himself in the head six times in his suicide attempt of 1823, but unluckily (or luckily?), he survived, only losing the sight of one eye. Even so, after his death his influence on Karl Marx was to be very significant. But here again he was in some manner unlucky. His world-changing ambitions did materialize, but only after his death, and as a materialist, to not see the fruit of your work in your one and only lifetime is simply the end of the matter.

But Saint-Simon did have a profound impact on Marx, and this in turn did change the course of Western history. The key thing to notice here is the manner in which Saint-Simon rejected metaphysics, moral realism, theology, and every other frame of transcendent and spiritual meaning, and then set about understanding the human social world, and the human construction of economic and political power, as a natural science. This was enormously appealing to Marx.

Through Marx, as the first of the three great fathers of classical sociology, a functionally atheistic and reductively materialist social scientific outlook on the nature and meaning of human affairs gets into the air. And by our day "scientific" methodological atheism and interpretive materialism have totally reframed the humanities. Our humanities faculties now firmly contain the interpretation of human meaning to sit exclusively *within* the domain of entirely cultural, contingent, and poetic meaning constructions. But a *real* knowledge of what is actually going on in the human world, and what cultural and (since Freud) psychological meaning is *really* all about, is had by the positivist scientists of society and the individual. Thus, the long wisdom traditions of Western culture are excised from metaphysical and theological truth and all substantive moral and high meaning is reinterpreted through a functionally atheist and methodologically materialist lens. This is perhaps the most profound intellectual revolution of the Western intellectual landscape since Plato effectively isolated the purely pragmatic and linguistically constructivist outlook of the sophists from the quest for truth. Via Saint-Simon, Plato's academic legacy is undone.

It is worth pointing out that until the late nineteenth century, there were no faculties in the universities called "the sciences." When Kant published his last book in 1798, titled *The Conflict of the Faculties*, he was not writing about any "sciences versus the humanities" clash, for there were no science faculties in any Western universities at the turn of the nineteenth century. The conflict Kant was writing about was between the traditional and carefully state-regulated faculties of theology, medicine, and law, on the one hand, and philosophy (which included what we would now call science as "natural philosophy"), on the other hand.

Kant thought that of course traditional faculties should be tightly controlled by censors and government authorities, for they were important for good public order. Philosophy, on the other hand, should be free to say whatever it likes, and have no censorship controls, because philosophy is concerned with purely private intellectual freedoms. Kant wrote *The Conflict of the Faculties* because he had been censored for his theological views. Kant's argument was that when he talked on theological matters he did so as a philosophy, for the private edification of free and responsible citizens, hence he should be allowed to say anything he likes; he was not writing about theology as a theologian! It falls to Thomas Huxley—as we shall explore soon—to purge the universities of the influence of the clergy and to set the sciences up as fully autonomous faculties in the Anglophone universities of the late nineteenth century. It is the disembedding of science and logic from the higher disciplines—most centrally theology—that Saint-Simon, Marx, and Huxley set in motion. And indeed, this move makes the humanities subordinate to, and interpreted by, the social sciences when it comes to "knowledge." This is a truly radical reframing of Western knowledge and meaning, and its impact can scarcely be overstated. This reframing is centrally characteristic of nineteenth and twentieth century progressivism.

As already explored in the previous chapter, Marx thought he had no need of philosophy or religion at all. Praxis—practically *changing* the world, via the exercise of political, economic, scientific, militant, and propagandizing *power*—replaces theory, metaphysics, and religion, as far as Marx is concerned. Ironically, however, positivism itself was, from its origins, a secular religion promoting atheist metaphysical truths. For the myth of any purely positive science of human affairs that is simply fact-based, and simply objectively yet non-metaphysically true, is an act of faith that cannot be justified by "pure" Enlightenment reason, or "pure" Enlightenment science. Indeed—contra Kant—Enlightenment epistemic purity is impossible to realize. Positivism is a religious faith in the truth-revealing powers of secular sense and reason with no divine or natural warrant, but that simply *posits* truth-revealing epistemic powers to—as Nietzsche might put it—"all too human" secular sense and reason.[5]

Putting my sociology-of-knowledge hat on, it is clear that an enormously powerful influence in the modern history of ideas is intellectual *fashion*. A secular-humanist fashion took a hold of many progressive movers and shakers in the nineteenth century such that they simply *believed* in what Herbert Butterfield called the "Whig interpretation of history."[6] Here secular scientific reason defined truth and progress, and anything that broke with the religious, metaphysical, and superstitious past was a casting aside of myths and a bold and noble striving forth into progress. Despite two world wars, the atomic bomb, the Man-made extinction of species and decimation of natural ecosystems, ever accelerating under neoliberal globalization, and no sign of any virtuous cosmopolitan world order of universal reason and peace, we still believe in an Enlightenment-framed secular utopia. This remains very culturally powerful in its collective mythic attractiveness. And the central weapon in this forward march of progress was the late nineteenth- and twentieth-century "war" of science against religion.

HUXLEY AND THE SCIENCE-AND-RELIGION CONFLICT MYTH

You may be unaware of this, but Christian natural theology and modern science were typically of one piece until the late nineteenth century. For example, as a young man Charles Darwin was a huge admirer of William Paley's *Natural Theology* (1802). Paley is famous for his analogy of the

---

5. In Nietzsche's 1878 book *Human, All Too Human*, Nietzsche abandons systematic argument and moves into his now well-known aphoristic style of writing. This shows a move away from the very idea of objective truth and into the embracing of meaning making as a purely poetic enterprise. We will look more closely at European counter-Enlightenment trajectories and their relation to postmodernism in the next chapter.

6. Butterfield, *Whig Interpretation of History*.

watchmaker, where one can infer the mind of a designer by the presence of a complex and brilliant machine, such as a watch. Paley thought that the complexity and intricate coordinated functionality of plants and animals equally demonstrated that nature has a divine Creator.

In a Christian Enlightenment manner, Paley combined utilitarian moral philosophy and careful observations of the natural world to produce "natural theology" arguments that paralleled his interpretation of the Christian doctrine of creation, yet without appealing to Scripture itself. Paley employs a conceptual parallelism that seeks to show how "pure" scientific reason is harmonious with the Christian revelation. This was very popular in the Anglophone world in the early half of the nineteenth century.

The idea that science was inherently and perpetually at war with religion was actually created by liberal Protestant theologians in the late nineteenth century, who meant "Roman Catholic" and "superstitious" when they used the word "religion."[7] As already noted, in the nineteenth century German liberal Protestants were busy debunking traditional orthodox Christian doctrines with their functionally atheist scientific studies of history and Scripture. This theological enterprise produced the radical progressive atheism of Marx et al. in the 1840s. These progressives were a fringe movement in respectable educated circles in the nineteenth century. In broad culturally acceptable terms, the idea that new advances in science and the Christian faith were anything other than complementary was not at all common. When it comes to Darwin, there was nothing like a concerted Christian rejection of his natural philosophy until the 1920s among American fundamentalists.[8] But what *was* going on in England at the exact same time as Darwin published his *Origin of Species* (1859) was a carefully planned and expertly executed enterprise in professionalizing science, separating it out from philosophy, containing the influence of the clergy in the universities to a discretely religious domain, and alienating clergy and amateur women from the scientific study of nature as much as possible. The mastermind behind this venture was Thomas Huxley.[9]

---

7. See Draper, *History of the Conflict Between Science and Religion* (1876); White, *History of the Warfare of Science with Theology* (1896). No contemporary historian of science and religion sees these two influential books, and the conflict thesis they advanced, as anything other than historically false and propagandistic. Even so, the false narrative of the conflict thesis is more or less assumed in the post-Christian secular academy.

8. See Numbers, *Creationists*.

9. See Stanley, *Huxley's Church and Maxwell's Demon*; Lightman, *Rethinking History, Science, and Religion*.

What Huxley was doing was territorializing science and religion.[10] This follows naturally from Kant's purification of science from faith and reason from metaphysics. Huxley was delineating the proper territory of science as the public, secular, useful, and factual reality domain of the natural world from the proper territory of religion, which was the private, spiritual, speculative, and personal belief domain of the supernatural. Making religion firmly otherworldly, and of no direct relevance to knowledge, education, science, law, and commerce was his aim. He had remarkable success.

As already noted, Huxley coined the term "agnostic" to describe his noncommittal outlook on religion. He was convinced by evidence about things that evidence—scientific and rational evidence—could demonstrate. About all other things he had no particular view. This is English-styled strategic positivism. Huxley was able to pass this off as a real-world positivism that simply had no interest in religion, subtly making science about practical reality as if such a stance needed no metaphysical or theological warrant, and as if metaphysics and theology were obviously speculative fantasies. But he knew what he was doing. He was replacing the public high truth authority of religion with science. And he was making metaphysical materialism—which empiricism cannot justify—into the functional and supposedly non-metaphysical scientific naturalism that we now associate simply with being factual. This was a theological and metaphysical sleight of hand that worked like a charm.

The Anglo-American secular positivist trajectory that Huxley pioneered had a magnificently successful trajectory from about 1870 to about 1970. Effectively the West's high intellectual culture was de-Christianized and made secular and scientific over that century. A number of Huxley's close associates—such as the social Darwinist Herbert Spencer—dropped the agnostic theatrics and simply asserted that scientific objectivity and atheism are obvious factually and rationally necessary correlates. Bertrand Russell in the early to mid-twentieth century becomes a pin-up boy for Huxleyite scientific positivism as a non-metaphysical (i.e., simply factual) atheist philosophy, and White and Draper's perpetual "war" between science and religion is taken away from its liberal Protestant origins and simply grafted into scientific atheism and the mythos of progressive atheism. Thus does the Enlightenment mythology of pure science and pure reason get drafted into a secularizing and de-Christianizing public reform campaign. Even so,

---

10. See this very helpful book on this astonishing innovation in the modern Western lifeworld: Harrison, *Territories of Science and Religion*.

the warrants of this stance are *mere assertions* that *cannot possibly be true* in purely empiricist or purely rational self-grounding foundationalist terms. It is, essentially, a highly pragmatically successful confidence trick.

LIBERALISM AND PRAGMATISM

This move to treat only the apparent material world as real cannot be justified as an actual knowledge of reality by the only grounds deemed admissible by the Enlightenment (pure sense and pure reason). Yet positivism as a type of phenomenological empirical pragmatism—where science is *deemed* to be true because it instrumentally *works*, and non-science (i.e., religion, metaphysics, magic) are *deemed* to be false because they do not work—is where the more sophisticated thinkers of nineteenth- and twentieth-century positivism went. American pragmatists, such as William James, and sophisticated English utilitarians, such as John Stuart Mill, understood sense and reason to be practically true even if they were not metaphysically true. However, once truth is reduced to a matter of practical usefulness, the tendency to displace truth with power is an open door inviting cunning and brilliant linguistic advocates of sophistry to reenter. This is where pragmatic anti-metaphysical positivism ends up going in the 1970s, but we are not at that point in our story just yet.

A central feature of the mythos of the Enlightenment is the notion of freedom. Here, the liberated individual is no longer a slavish conformist to authorities that mediate divine and metaphysical truths that, so the story goes, no one really understands. Instead, all rational people now participate in the self-governing freedom of only adhering to what they themselves fully understand and take full individual responsibility for. The political lifeform of liberal democracy arises out of this vision. In the Age of Reason, the people themselves are the final authority of just governance. Liberal democracy—which tends toward the stance that there is no higher metaphysical or theological warrants for just rule than the will of the people[11]—

---

11. This is complicated. Famously, the Christian Enlightenment notion evident in the 1776 Declaration of the Independence of the thirteen united States of America refers both to the "Laws of Nature and of Nature's God" and goes on to state: "We hold these truths to be self-evident, that all men are created equal, that they are endowed by their Creator with certain unalienable Rights, that among these are Life, Liberty and the pursuit of Happiness. That to secure these rights, Governments are instituted among Men, deriving their just powers from the consent of the governed, That whenever any Form of Government becomes destructive of these ends, it is the Right of the People to alter

is premised on the validity of secular positivism. In practice this tends to reduce political ideas to the very mundane horizons of consumption and economics. But leaving the high-ideals-debasing trajectory of liberal democracy to one side for the present, let us look at the relationship between positivism and liberalism.

In his famous essay *On Liberty* John Stuart Mill notes that while people should not have their opinions censored in a liberal democracy, "no belief which is contrary to truth can be really useful."[12] Here the useful is the true, but equally the true is the useful. False opinions about matters of fact are destructive to the genuine human utility of a liberal democracy. And this is in part why there should be no censorship. And open truth-seeking public debate is necessary for the common good in a liberal democratic polity. Truth is very important to Mill, politically. And the truths he has in mind are positivist truths of sense and reason. The way this functionally works is that matters of objectively demonstrable scientific fact and logically valid reasoning can be understood and their truth authority can be accepted by all right-thinking people of reasonable intelligence and good will. This becomes the basis of common truth for the common good that can be universally recognized as—to quote the American Declaration of Independence—self-evident. On the other hand, there are opinions about metaphysical, theological, and religious matters, as well as artistic and moral tastes, regarding which there are no commonly accepted objective criteria, and about which people of good will may and do disagree. A liberal society allows for vigorous public debate about such contestable matters, and does not shy from offense when vigorous but non-violent disagreement cannot be avoided.

The entire arrangement is premised on the distinction between objective public truths, which it is always of genuine utility to recognize, and subjective opinions, values, and spiritual beliefs, about which people of good will and intelligence may disagree. Keeping matters of public order to matters of

---

or to abolish it, and to institute new Government, laying its foundation on such principles and organizing its powers in such form, as to them shall seem most likely to effect their Safety and Happiness." Liberal Democracy does not necessarily lead to the total secularization and pragmatizing of political power, and does not necessarily remove all transcendent and theological horizons of meaning from political power. However, where Western culture has embraced the de-Christianizing war of science against religion and the reduction of meaning to a materialist and pragmatic human frame alone, then secular positivism does in practice (even if not in theory) tend to remove high metaphysical and theological warrants from political authority.

12. Mill, *On Liberty*, 24.

objectively recognized avoidance of physical harms, and allowing a plurality and liberality in personal subjective values, beliefs, and tastes (which the polity should not trespass into) enables liberal democracy to work.

We will look into this further in the next chapter, but when a public commitment to objective factual truth and bivalent (true-or-false) rational validity evaporates, so does liberal democracy. If positivism fails, and we are committed to Enlightenment pure experience and pure reason, so does liberal democracy. This is a significant feature of gender theory's commitment to censorship and highly non-liberal state and legal public control structures. Gender theory has abandoned modern positivism, and it also abandons modern liberalism.

THE 1980S AND THE FALL OF LOGICAL POSITIVISM

Logical positivism was the last attempt to make functionally atheist science and bivalent pure logic the truth criteria defining public reality in the Western academy. I remember studying A. J. Ayer in the 1980s when his logical positivism was crumbling into self-contradictory linguistic dust.

Logical positivism, a movement started in the 1930s, was a combination of British analytic philosophy, Anglo materialist positivism, and deflationary anti-metaphysical linguistic philosophy. To very briefly unpack these three streams, analytic philosophy treats sentences as pure, logically structured sums that are either logically valid, and hence "obtain," or logically invalid, and hence "do not obtain." But analytic philosophy is also very keen to define the meanings of the words used in arguments. The central claim of defining the meaning of words in logical positivism was scientific positivism. If a word did not refer to a material and objectively verifiable thing or state of affairs it was considered *literal nonsense*, and not philosophically valid. This is the anti-metaphysical deflationary aspect of the movement. Modern Anglophone linguistic philosophy emerges well after the 1930s and is often associated with Wittgenstein. Wittgenstein's 1921 text *Tractatus Logico-Philosophicus* is often seen as a significant "Vienna Circle" influence on logical positivism, but his posthumously published *Philosophical Investigations* (1953) shows a strong swing away from logical positivism and toward a richer understanding of linguistic meaning than the conveyance of reductively rational arguments about strictly empirical information. A key notion in *Philosophical Investigations* is the "language game." Here the meaning of words is always defined contextually by the meaning of other words, as situated in specific lifeworlds and communities of practice. Thus, different "language games" can be unconnected to each other if the rich matrix of meanings in one context are not known or used in another context. The logic and meaning, then, of a religious language game can be incommensurate with the logic and meaning of a scientific language game, but this does not make one game right and the other game wrong, and it is not appropriate to judge meaning in one context by the standard of another context. Even though there were inherent tensions between logical positivism and Wittgenstein-influenced linguistic philosophy, there was considerable Anglophone cross-fertilization going on between positivist and linguistic philosophy from the 1950s, for some decades.

Logical positivism was a very popular movement in English-language philosophy between the 1930s and the 1980s. Its popularity in philosophical circles was tied to the popularity of secularizing scientific atheism as a progressive truth discourse in elite academic philosophy circles over this cultural period. It largely died in the 1980s because its central claim—that a statement is only meaningful if it can be empirically verified—could not itself be empirically verified. So dies the Enlightenment vision of pure sensory knowledge and pure logical validity in twentieth-century Anglophone philosophy. So ends the secular atheist religion of scientific truth.

Other things are also going on in the 1980s. The lifeworld of liberal democracy has been in constant motion since it first got into the air with the American and French Revolutions, then really lifted across Europe in 1848, then finally moved toward full adult suffrage in the early twentieth century. It is a recent form of government deeply tied to the Enlightenment, but as the world the Enlightenment created shifts into ever more pragmatic and ever more post-metaphysical modes of social organization, its future is hard to discern. The rise of econometric neoliberalism, crassly materialist consumerism, "post-ideological" pragmatism in politics in the 1980s, and the rise of powerful online public information-projection and control technologies of the 1980s cuts against the grain of positivist, liberal, and even secular modernity. By this time postmodernism was moving firmly into place in our academies.

AND SCIENCE?

Positivism is no longer viable. There are, shall we say, sad reasons for this that concern the loss of a widespread cultural, institutional, and commercial commitment to scientific truth. But there are also excellent reasons why a naïve materialist confidence in objective scientific truth—as an ersatz public religion—has become impossible to sustain academically.

Very interesting work in the 1950s by Thomas Kuhn (*The Structure of Scientific Revolutions*, 1957) and Michael Polanyi (*Personal Knowledge*, 1958) in the history and sociology of science encouraged a new appreciation in the Anglophone world of how historically and humanly situated scientific knowledge-construction really is. *The Social Construction of Reality* in 1966 by Peter Berger and Thomas Luckmann brought Continental trajectories in the sociology of knowledge to a broad Anglo-American audience, making us more aware of what a complex and cultural thing natural knowledge itself is. These trajectories would continue to expand leading to highly nuanced appreciations of the history of science and of the richly human nature of scientific practice. This has given rise to the flourishing new domains of science-studies thinkers (like Bruno Latour),[13] richly philosophically open thinkers about the nature and meaning of science (such as Paul Feyerabend),[14] and historical scholars working on the many contingent and cultural forces shaping scientific ideas and practices (like Stephen Gawkroger[15] and Steve Shapin).[16] It is no longer possible to assert that science is simply about the obvious facts now. The way we build, test, disseminate, fund, and learn natural facts—which indeed are artifacts of human knowledge—is well understood today.

Possibly the last gasp for Enlightenment-shaped religiously atheist positivism was the so-called New Atheist surge around the turn of the twenty-first century. This publishing phenomenon advocated a no-nonsense, scientific, purely factual, and purely rational critique of all things religious and superstitious in public discourse. New Atheism was the publishing bonanza surrounding the anti-religious advocacy of scientism by Christopher Hitchens, Richard Dawkins, Sam Harris, and Daniel Dennett. These four were in fact conservative throwbacks upholding fashionable atheist orthodoxies

---

13. Latour, *We Have Never Been Modern*.
14. Feyerabend, *Tyranny of Science*.
15. Gawkroger, *Emergence of a Scientific Culture*.
16. Shapin, *Never Pure*.

from the scientistic de-Christianizing academy of the 1960s to the 1990s. However, such orthodoxies became less influential under the neoliberal decline of state funding for pure scientific research and a widespread shift toward a more pragmatic and image-concerned politics. It is also the case that the influence of the Christian religion was no longer a significant public foil for positivist atheism to oppose. Whether a tradition-defying scientific atheism can really stand on its own feet without a significant and publicly assumed religious consciousness to progressively oppose seems unlikely. Sociologically, it looks like nineteenth- and twentieth-century scientific atheism rather needs a strong public Christianity to define itself against.

The present (as I write) "canceling" fervor directed toward Richard Dawkins—not from religious people (who have never canceled him), but from gender-inclusivity advocates—is a very interesting case-study in what is going on with the decline of old-fashioned positivist atheism.

Full disclosure, as a Christian with a keen interest in "science and religion" I must say I am a bit sad to see the old rivalry of positivist atheism against religious fundamentalism fade into the past. There were aspects about that Enlightenment-framed clash of beliefs and commitments that were quite invigorating. Be that as it may, let us proceed.

In 2021 the American Humanist Association retroactively stripped Richard Dawkins of his 1996 "Humanist of the Year" award because he was "using the guise of scientific discourse" in a manner that was "demean[ing of] marginalized groups." The marginalized groups Dawkins is charged with demeaning are "some men [who] choose to identify as women, and some women [who] choose to identify as men." Dawkins asks his readers to discuss whether, as a science-respecting person, one should risk being vilified for denying that such people "literally are what they identify as."[17] Dawkins's basic crime against humanism here is his scientific belligerence, as a respected biologist, to say that the human sex binary is an unchangeable and factual reality, no matter how you subjectively feel about your gender identity. Apparently this is now a humanist "heresy" of the first order.

In a fascinating twist, Dawkins finds himself in the public crosshairs as a prominent member of the old-world atheist scientific priest-caste in a culture undergoing a new anti-clerical revolt (against scientific positivists). Dawkins is thus publicly denounced by the American Humanist Society in the name of Diversity, Equity, and Inclusion (DEI), as an opponent of

---

17. Flood, "Richard Dawkins Loses 'Humanist of the Year' Title over Trans Comments."

liberty, humanity, and the universal human right of all individuals to define their gender identity exactly how they wish to.

We seem to have come full circle. We seem back in the revolutionary age of a revolt against all established truths, against all established and respected authorities, and there is a new determined movement to uproot everything and re-create the world. But this uprooting and re-creating is no longer being done in the name of pure knowledge and pure logic. Pure knowledge and pure logic turned out to be unobtainable dreams. Hence, science is no longer a truth discourse, but it is simply a power discourse.

Whether modern science itself can survive the loss of respect for sensory and rational truth is yet to be seen. My sense is that it will not survive as a pursuit of truth, but it will increasingly evolve into well-funded technocratic sorcery of unimaginable manipulative power. We can presently observe staggering advances in AI and an ever self-enhancing technofeudal surveillance capitalism becoming increasingly integrated with the information-controlling security state. The reach of non-elected global interest powers, such as the World Economic Forum, and of ever more effective drone warfare capabilities into the domain of global and even domestic security, rather seems to ring the full-time bell on the short experiment in liberal democracy and international cosmopolitanism. And could it even be—with our smartphones, our algorithmically choreographed lives, and our information-technology–controlled state bureaucracies—that we have never lived in a more potent and autocratic age of magic?

THE DEMISE OF POSITIVISM AND THE POSTMODERN RISE OF GENDER THEORY

The manner in which gender theory not only denies any objective meaning to the notion of gender identity but also denies any objective scientific meaning to the notion of sex is symptomatic of the failure of modern positivism. But it is one thing to question the objectivity and purity of scientific knowledge claims; it is another thing to throw out the idea of objective scientific truth altogether. To understand that move we need to understand postmodernism. Yet, we cannot go straight to postmodernism yet. We need to have a closer look at two very significant trajectories that shape the postmodern consciousness. These trajectories are linguistic deflation and logical formalism.

6

Linguistic Deflation and Analytic Formalism

IN THIS CHAPTER I will seek to explain to you how weeding all high meanings out of words, reducing our understanding of reason to formal logic, and replacing truth with practical power are all deeply Western thought enterprises. Long ago among the pre-classical and classical Greeks, the sophists were masters of these argumentative skill sets. Indeed, the very academy in Athens that Plato set up to counter sophistry with philosophy rapidly became the home of analytical skepticism after Plato died, though Middle Platonism from the second century BC and Neoplatonism from the third century AD are returns to Plato's vision of philosophy. Which is to say that sophistry is never far from philosophy in the West. This is evident from the very beginning of the birth of the Western university in the late eleventh century AD. You may be unaware of this, but it was the Roman Catholic Church that established the Western university in Paris, Bologna, Oxford, and Cambridge, with special papal privileges as dedicated learning precincts. And in this now nine-hundred-year-old university tradition there is a long theological backstory to linguistic deflation and analytical formalism.

You may be surprised to see the word "theology" here, but when it comes to the mystery of communicable meaning, until very recently language and reason were thought of as super-human realities, and human expressions of these divine gifts were understood theologically. Assumptions about the nature of language, high meanings, and reason that are theologically inflected are still assumed in the habits and prejudices of secularized Western culture. If we assume that reality itself displays a cosmic order, this is a very old theological prejudice. If we bow to the judge at a court (like we are expected to do) this practice is embedded in categories of authority that are ultimately theologically warranted. Such assumptions and habits persist today, even though our intellectual culture has been systematically dismantling theoretical structures around those remnant customs for the past couple of centuries. By now it is simply the case that our categories of knowledge and theory no longer connect with older theological habits and assumptions.

By the last decade of the twentieth century we see the decisive triumph of firmly secularized theoretical trajectories that are completely linguistically deflationary. This theoretical triumph looks with disdain on older theological trajectories that were in some manner wedded to divine and metaphysical mysteries. By the close of the twentieth century, linguistic theory opens up a new vista in Western intellectual development. This vista is given to us by the performative and entirely poetic liberation of language and logic from all essential meanings. This movement from twentieth-century deflationary and formalistic linguistic philosophy into complete poetic irrealism with Judith Butler is a key feature of gender theory.

We are going to cover a lot of ground in this chapter because I wish to push behind the recent imposition of the interpretive veil of methodological materialism on our theoretical assumptions about language and reason. I have no particular theological point to make by doing this, but the way developments in theology eventually lead to complete linguistic irrealism should be understood if we are properly to appreciate this seismic shift in our intellectual culture's approach to meaningful language, an approach that Butler both rides and promotes.

To start the ball rolling, let us go to the mid-point between the 1970s appearance of the French/American new intellectual fashion called postmodernism, and that fashion's movement from avant-garde theory into a mainstream cultural reformation movement with Butler's third-wave feminism in the 1990s. Let us start with the dying of modern British analytic and linguistic philosophy in the 1980s. This happens to be the decade when I was at university as a bright-eyed youth, cutting my teeth on serious intellectual food for the first time. I have to say, it was quite a disappointing feed.

AUSTRALIAN UNDERGRADUATE PHILOSOPHY IN THE 1980S

Back in the 1980s when I was doing my undergraduate studies in philosophy, A. J. Ayer's 1936 book *Language, Truth and Logic* was our philosophical Bible. Ayer was an exponent of the previously discussed and now defunct species of British philosophy called "logical positivism."

In fine analytic style, the exploration of life's big questions at my university had these characteristics: it transformed living sentences into dead grammatical equations; it deformed breathing and beating human yearnings for transcendence into dry straw effigies, which it then burnt as either logically incoherent or credulous and puerile; it disallowed any substantive qualitative or transcendent meaning to anything. I experienced analytical philosophy as an exercise in—as Simon Blackburn later put it—"conceptual engineering,"[1] where the only clear design aim seemed to be to show how smart you were because you believed nothing and could fault everything.[2] As one analytic colleague of mine jokingly (?) explained to me, the first law of his guild was: "if you can't say anything nasty, don't say anything at all." To be fair to my colleague, purifying science from faith and purifying logic from metaphysics is the clear Enlightenment motive driving the meaning deflations and logical reductions of analytic philosophy.

I am grateful for my undergraduate education because analytic philosophy piqued my interest in all those thinkers I was supposed to find illogical and puerile. Some years after I had completed my undergraduate studies I came to realize that Western linguistic deflation and analytic

---

1. Blackburn, *Think*, 2.

2. Despite claiming in *Think* that what he redescribes as philosophy is concerned with the big questions of the human experience, Blackburn is relentlessly deflationary as regards all the major themes of traditional philosophy. And here he speaks with unflinching ignorance and firmly outside of his actual expertise domain as an engineer of dogmatically modernist, materialist, and pragmatic "concepts." For a peerlessly ignorant and fatuously dismissive example of how analytic debunkers of Blackburn's type routinely treat serious philosophers, see Blackburn, *Plato's Republic*. In the introduction of this book Blackburn correctly notes that he himself is "neither a classicist nor a historian, even of the amateur variety . . . [indeed, he has] never felt Plato to be a particularly congenial author . . ." (vi). His ignorance and disdain do not stop him from presuming to write about the reception of the greatest text of Western philosophy over the past two and a half millennia. Essentially, this is the nub of the matter as Blackburn sees it: "[Plato's d]reaming is of little use, while coming to grips with the way of things surely is. And ours is a practical, scientific, empirical civilization, which provides an inhospitable climate to dreamers. It is surprising, then, that Plato is not more neglected . . ." (10).

formalism is a nine-hundred-year-old theological tradition. Definitional purification and logical rigor is a much older enterprise than the Enlightenment. However, having been secularized from the late nineteenth century on, the long and deep theological roots of this movement are now largely invisible to it.

Before properly getting underway, it is important to acknowledge that linguistically and analytically rigorous philosophy does not have to be deflationary and reductively formalistic. Indeed, I have found much benefit in reading carefully defined and logically clear work by some very fine thinkers in the broadly analytic and positivist trajectories.[3] Careful attention to definitions (where they can reasonably be had) and the application of valid logic (where bivalent rationality properly applies) to matters of demonstrable and significant fact (not excluding qualitative dimensions to facts) indeed are tools of the philosopher's trade. But these tools are not the art of philosophy itself.

To the academic tradition established by Plato, any serious conception of Justice, for example, has no catch-all and contained definition, because Justice opens up to categories of transcendent Goodness that are beyond the mastery of any human mind. But this does not mean we can know nothing about Justice. This does not mean that practical and unavoidably contingent working definitions of Justice, as used in constructing laws, cannot be formulated. This does not mean that valid reasoning and factual truths about real events are beyond our rational and empirical powers when it comes to making a legal judgment. Not at all. Of course careful definitions, valid logic, and demonstrable and authenticated factual veracity matter! But the reality is, these practical tools of clear and valid reasoning cannot be used to construct any qualitative truth or any transcendently referenced high truth. To assume, therefore, that qualitative and transcendently referenced high truths do not exist, because linguistic deflation and analytic formalism cannot construct them, is the central and catastrophic error of modern linguistic philosophy.

LINGUISTIC DEFLATION: HUMILITY OR HUBRIS?

As we will touch on when we look at Hamann, how one understands the nature and meaning of words is a point of serious relevance to how one

---

3. See, for example, Nagel, *Mind and Cosmos*; Frankfurt, *Reasons of Love*; Stock, *Material Girls*.

understands the ambitions and prospects of the Enlightenment project. In many regards Kant illustrates the attempt to philosophically contain and control the meaning of words in categories that are amenable to complete human mastery. Hamann thinks this an impossible enterprise, and hence the Enlightenment itself is doomed to fail. But lovers of the Enlightenment think Kant's project is a winner. Clearly, what Kant is trying to do can be evaluated either as an exercise in sensible intellectual humility or an exercise in reckless intellectual hubris.

In the classically modernist trajectory, the focusing down of human knowledge onto the world of immediate sense perception, practical utility, and rational action, and the limiting of conceptual structures to a watertight system of clear definitions and valid human logic, is seen as illustrative of humility and realism by its advocates. That is, the *via moderna* (the modern way) that pushes forward in the seventeenth century is seen as "humble" in comparison with what are thought of as traditionalist pretensions to transcendent and essential insight (the *via antiqua*). Modern thinking is seen as "enlightened" in comparison with the vague and credulous mystical utterances of old, which don't seem to connect with the real world of normal experience at all. This is the "enlightened humility" evaluation.

Hamann and Kierkegaard, by contrast, see this same enterprise as both proud and unrealistic. The Enlightenment pursues pretensions to a human epistemic mastery that are explicitly autonomous from the transcendent Source of true meaning and created reality. According to Hamann and Kierkegaard, the Enlightenment will not succeed in its aims because trying to understand sense perception and logical reasoning as if they can be cut off from their divine Source and evaluated under a purely human horizon of epistemic mastery will prove to be fatal to both sense and reason. For if the natural and contingent material world has its meanings and governing order because it is an essentially intelligible creation, made out of nothing (*ex nihilo*) by the overflowing love of God, then all things will revert to nothing (and human thought will only express nihilism) if reality and meaning are vainly imagined without God. If human knowledge and reason actually are a divine gift, then severing their theoretical connection to the divine Logos will produce a "purely" naturalist philosophy that is gibbering nonsense. This is the "Enlightenment hubris" evaluation. And since we are presently riffing on the Lutheran perspectives of Hamann and Kierkegaard we should probably signal the biblical take on the epistemic hubris stance as well. As the Christians Scriptures puts it, "they did not honor . . . God or give thanks to him, but they became futile in their thinking and their senseless minds were darkened. Claiming to be wise, they became fools . . ." (Romans 1:21–22).

As should by now be apparent, the Enlightenment indeed does fail, and this implies at least the possibility that the Hamann/Kierkegaard evaluation is correct. But without making any judgment between the "humility evaluation" and the "hubris evaluation" at this point, the manner in which the mastery of both sense (the positivist ambition) and reason (definitions and meanings) slips like sand though twentieth-century philosophy's intellectual fingers is hard to ignore.

THE TWENTIETH CENTURY AS THE PHILOSOPHICAL TWILIGHT OF THE ENLIGHTENMENT

Ever more concerted attempts to master human language while maintaining Enlightenment purity (no faith, no metaphysics) characterize what we call the linguistic and analytic philosophy of the twentieth century. These attempts illustrate what philosophers call a deflationary and pragmatic approach to language. Which is to say that "deflating" words of any meaning that cannot be purely scientific or purely logical and understanding "meaning" in terms of "use" rather than "truth" are signature features of the fading philosophical twilight of the Enlightenment. This fading can be seen both in its Anglophone linguistic, analytic, and pragmatic trajectories, and in its more mythopoetic and nihilist Continental trajectories. The end result of this process is that communicable linguistic meaning gets so tied up in definitional and logical knots that meaning itself can no longer be unraveled. To such a Gordian knot, Judith Butler—like Alexander the Great—brings a conquering sword and simply cuts linguistic meaning off from logic and facts. All language is, and only is, poetic and performative. Problem solved. Thus does twentieth-century linguistic, analytic philosophy die in 1990 with the publication of *Gender Troubles*.

But are facts and logic merely performative linguistic poetries? Are *true* facts about how things really are and *valid* logic that is not simply a human mind game really severed from linguistic meaning? To get to that question we need to look at the trajectory of linguistic deflation and factual and formalist irrealism from a higher historical vista than the collapse of analytical linguistic philosophy in recent decades. Let us step right back in history for a bigger picture.

It may surprise you to learn that modern deflationary approaches to language have their origins in the twelfth century, wherein the *via moderna* (the "just now" way) was first contrasted with the *via antiqua* (the ancient way) by Peter Abelard.[4] Deflationary linguistics and reductive logic are profoundly medieval enterprises, which just goes to show that Bruno Latour is correct to say that we have never really been modern.[5]

PETER ABELARD

Peter Abelard was born in 1079 and died in 1142. Today he is mainly known for his racy and traumatic love affair with another medieval genius, Héloïse. Abelard seduced his very gifted fifteen-year-old student, who, she claims, willingly consented to extra-marital sex with her teacher, and then became pregnant by him. It's more complicated than we need go into, but essentially Héloïse's uncle (Abelard's former employer and landlord) was incensed by the seduction and then apparent abduction of his ward by Abelard, and had a group of thugs castrate the brilliant scholar.

Abelard is one of the truly great thinkers of the Western tradition, and his influence remains with us to this day. I shall unpack some of the terms used here shortly, but listen to how Peter King, a Canadian expert on Abelard, describes this twelfth-century linguistic genius.

> Abelard's philosophy is the first example in the Western tradition of the cast of mind that is now called "nominalism." Although it is his view that universals are mere words (*nomina*) that is typically thought to justify the label, Abelard's nominalism—or, better, his irrealism—is in fact the hallmark of his metaphysics. He is an irrealist not only about universals, but also about propositions, events, times other than the present, natural kinds, relations, wholes, absolute space, hylomorphic composites, and the like. Instead, Abelard holds that the concrete individual, in all its richness and variety, is more than enough to populate the world. He preferred reductive, atomist, and material explanations when he could get

---

4. See Klima, "Medieval Problem of Universals," under the subheadings "Universals in the Via Antiqua" and "Universals in the Via Moderna."

5. Latour, *We Have Never Been Modern*.

them; he devoted a great deal of effort to pouring cold water on the metaphysical excesses of his predecessors and contemporaries.[6]

King is talking about a twelfth-century thinker, not about a twentieth-century thinker, but he might equally have been talking about A. J. Ayer or Simon Blackburn.

What Abelard shows us is that the Enlightenment aim of logical and factual reductionism, and metaphysical debunking is a recurrent ambition in Western intellectual life. The roots of this ambition run very deep, particularly when it comes to linguistic deflation and an obsession with formal rationality. Which is to say, twentieth-century linguistic and analytic philosophy does not appear from nowhere but is drawn out of deep Western intellectual wells. So, brace yourself for a quick plunge into some exotic (yet strangely familiar) medieval waters.

ABELARD'S WORLD

Abelard is writing at the end of what we now often disparagingly call "the Dark Ages." This is a roughly six-hundred-year period between the Western collapse of the Roman Imperium in the fifth century, and the economic and political revival of Western Europe in the eleventh century.

Whether this period was really dark or not depends on whom you ask. If you were to ask the Celtic missionaries who set up monasteries all over Europe in that period, it was a high age of Christian expansion into pagan Europe, even though not a few monks were martyred by the Vikings and other barbaric Europeans in that time.[7] For you may not be aware that even though the Emperor Constantine converted to Christianity in the fourth century, this hardly made Western Europe Christian. Christendom of the high medieval era is the fruit of the great age of European Christian missions. Europe was not made Christian by imperial decree or by the conquest of the sword; it was made Christian by the quiet and deep piety, and the community-building labor of evangelizing Celtic monks and nuns.

Of course, the collapse of the *Pax Romana* in the West led to endless internecine conflicts between city states. The high learning of Greco-Roman antiquity was largely lost as well. So things were indeed "dark" on those fronts. But come the twelfth century, and kingdoms are again large

---

6. King, *Cambridge Companion to Peter Abelard*, 65.
7. See Cahill, *How the Irish Saved Civilization*.

and powerful; cities are again bustling, cosmopolitan, and wealthy; and learning is recovering and reorganizing.[8] The cathedral schools, out of which the medieval universities will arise, are in full swing in Abelard's day, and he is—arguably—the foremost Western European thinker of his time.

ABELARD'S "NOMINALISM"

In the twelfth century, Western scholars had very little direct contact with the great masterworks of classical philosophy. Half of Plato's *Timaeus* and the short, logical *Organum* of Aristotle were all they had in Latin. But they had Augustine's writings, composed in the last years of the old Western Roman Empire.[9] Just after Abelard's death, Peter Lombard's conceptual compilation of Augustine's voluminous teachings, titled simply *Sentences*, was published. The *Sentences* immediately became the central intellectual curriculum document of the high Middle Ages. For with Abelard and Lombard a new thing had emerged in the West, the systematic logical and philosophical treatment of Christian sacred doctrine. We can call this "theology," but we could equally call it "philosophy" as there was no hard boundary isolating reason from faith in the Middle Ages.

Via a deep scholarly engagement with Augustine and the small scraps of pagan classical philosophy available to them, what we now call metaphysics was put forward in Abelard's day by thinkers we now describe as medieval realists. Medieval realism is the neat opposite of modern realism. To an early medieval realist, what you cannot see (transcendent, universal, essential, intellective forms) is more real than what you can see (immanent, particular, contingent, physical beings). For clarity's sake, whenever I refer to medieval realism in this discussion it will be capitalized (Realism, Realists), to distinguish it from its opposite, which is modern realism.

In Abelard's lifetime Realists working on metaphysics did as best as they could with what they had, but it was astonishingly crude when compared with the likes of Plato, Plotinus, and the Greek church fathers. Abelard tore Western early medieval Realism to shreds with logical and linguistic analysis.

---

8. For an excellent book on how young, vigorous, and adventurous medieval thinkers were, see Pieper, *Scholasticism*.

9. As Augustine was dying in AD 430, the Vandals had invaded Roman North Africa and had besieged the city of Hippo Regius (now known as Annaba in modern Algeria), where Augustine was the bishop.

A significant issue at the time was the problem of universals. Thinking like crude Platonists, the stance Abelard logically eviscerated held that all tables, for example, were mystically related to the Ideal Table, which was more or less a super concrete "thing" in heaven. So all universal terms—"cat," "house," any noun really—were tied to metaphysical higher forms that were in some sense the concrete perfections of all particular material beings that shared the same universal designation (i.e., all cats were formal participants in the Real Cat). Against this stance, Abelard held that universals are only *names* (hence, he is a *nominalist*) and not super-concrete metaphysical ideas. I will not here explore why traditional metaphysical Realism of the classical Platonist type is very much more intellectually careful and persuasive than the crude metaphysical Realism that Abelard dispatched, but you can read about that in another of my books if you are interested.[10]

Abelard establishes a view of reality that is particularist, autonomous from metaphysical speculations, and in which logic and language are human reason and meaning constructs rather than truth-revealing. This stance keeps reappearing in the West all the way through the medieval era, all the way through modernity, and into postmodernity. This is Abelard's *via moderna*, and he finds ancient ideas impossible to believe and hopelessly behind the times.

THE NOMINALIST/REALIST PIVOT

It is really Thomas Aquinas who makes a powerful comeback for the *via antiqua* with a renewed form of analogical Realism synthesized with Aristotelian natural philosophy in the thirteenth century. At this time all of Aristotle's writings that we now have were recovered in the West, and Aquinas was a very fine scholar of Western giants such as Augustine, and what Eastern Christian thinkers he had access to, such as the sixth-century Neoplatonist we now call Pseudo Dionysius. Recovering the analogical link between, on the one hand, metaphysically high and essential meanings and, on the other, the tangible concrete world revealed by the senses, and being a master of logic and Aristotle's entire corpus, Aquinas to this day remains significant for thinkers who take an interest in the West's high metaphysical traditions.[11]

---

10. Tyson, *Returning to Reality*.

11. For example, Erich Przywara's use of Aquinas's "analogy of being" to engage with Heidegger and other powerful German thinkers in the 1920s is of keen interest to this

It must also be recognized that in the history of Western thought, the Middle Ages is the high age of logic. Complex and sophisticated logical reasoning was the norm in scholastic philosophy and theology. Modernists tend to mock medievalists about their abstruse rational arguments—supposedly about how many angels could dance on a pin head, etc.—but this is really a mockery of the way metaphysics, theology, logic, and natural philosophy were all integrated in medieval intellectual life, rather than any serious evaluation of their logical prowess. As regards logic, they were very powerful and highly developed thinkers, with the public logical debate being the thrilling centerpiece of medieval intellectual life.

So a pivot from deflationary and logically reductive linguistic philosophy to metaphysical and theologically expansive philosophy, and back again, has been going on in Western thinking for the past nine hundred years. For just as Aquinas rises to defend an analogical metaphysics compatible with the *via antiqua* after its nominalist attack by Abelard, so William of Ockham rises to attack Aquinas's *via antiqua* with a vigorously logical nominalism in the fourteenth century. This is a well-established pattern.

OCKHAM'S RAZOR, SWINESHEAD'S CALCULATIVE RATIONALISM, AND BACON'S PRAGMATISM

William of Ockham was a fourteenth-century Franciscan. Ockham's razor—do not multiply entities beyond necessity—is now taken to mean that the simplest explanation is always the best explanation. But Ockham called it the principle of ontological economy, and its basic point was to discard any category of meaning and intelligible essence that is not particularized and materially instantiated. This is basic to the secularized modern scientific outlook, which is taken up as an anti-theological methodological principle in the late nineteenth-century "war" of science on religion.

The fourteenth century also saw the Oxford calculators embrace a universal syllogistic logic. They somewhat reductively treated nature as comprised of particular material objects that displayed necessary logical regularities, and they quantified physical entities through the use of mathematical models. This trend in Oxford directly influenced Nicolo Oresme and, later on, Galileo Galilei. The marvelously christened Richard Swineshead was one of the famous Merton College calculators at Oxford.

---

day among Christian philosophers. See, for example, the 2014 English translation by John Betz and David Hart of Przywara's *Analogia Entis*, along with their absorbing essay on it.

The matters are too involved to unpack in any detail here, but I think the calculators' determinist logic contributed to theological rationalism in the eighteenth century on the one hand and to a new level of mathematical abstraction in natural philosophy on the other hand. An abstract, reductive, determinist, and mechanistic sensibility thus embeds itself in both scholasticism and the early modern thought world. By early modernity even living beings are seen as machine-like entities by Descartes, and the world itself is seen as a set of determinate causal equations that we can simply solve. Once we have the right graphs, sums, and mathematically framed theorems, this equips us with a true knowledge of natural necessity. This knowledge, as Francis Bacon discerned, can be used for power over nature.[12]

Francis Bacon's name is justly connected to the birth of modern science, but a point that is difficult to grasp now is that in the seventeenth century nearly all pragmatic advocates of the new mathematico-experimental learning (which we now call science) were theologically motivated.[13] Bacon's vision guided the setting up of the Royal Society of London for Improving Natural Learning in the 1660s. Bacon held firmly to the belief that God had given Man a mandate to rule the earth, and while the means to achieving this mandate had been lost in the fall, they could be recovered by the practical mastery of nature through experiential learning. Such was the theological rationale behind Bacon's pursuit of "human utility and power"[14] through science.

Nominalism, mathematical reductionism, and pragmatic power as regards knowledge have a very long history in Western knowledge, yet they remain *theologically situated* innovations in Western culture, all the way up until the cultural success of progressive atheism in the academy in the late twentieth century.

Arguably the key development that decoupled nominalism, reductionism, and pragmatism from theology is the gradual but ultimately complete pulling away of the natural from the supernatural over a period of about eight centuries. The evolution of the meanings of the words "natural" and "supernatural" has a very long backstory,[15] which we cannot stop

---

12. See Henry, *Knowledge Is Power*.
13. See Harrison, *Fall of Man and the Foundations of Science*, 186–244.
14. Bacon, *New Atlantis and the Great Instauration*, 16.
15. For two texts I have found to be very helpful in looking at the complex and evolving relation of the natural to the supernatural in Western thinking, see Bartlett, *Natural and the Supernatural in the Middle Ages*; de Lubac, *Mystery of the Supernatural*.

to trace here, but the final outcome of that history is the collapse of any functional integration of the natural and the supernatural, followed by the displacement of the supernatural with the natural alone. Once this development is fully mature, essential meaning tied to any transcendent frame of cosmic intelligence (as the source of the human intelligibility of an ordered cosmos) can be discarded. Once you can do that, then irrealist linguistic sophistry can run riot.

We shall now briefly look at the manner in which philosophy and theology gradually become isolated into the separate domains of the natural and the supernatural. This gradual separation has a long Western backstory, which we can start, yet again, with Abelard.

A FUNCTIONAL DUALISM REGARDING THE NATURAL AND THE SUPERNATURAL

Abelard is a new kind of dualist. On the one hand, there is reason and the tangible world of particular concrete things; on the other hand, there is sacred doctrine. Abelard keeps them methodologically separated, but accepts, as an article of faith, that the natural world is undergirded by theological truths that cannot be justified by sense or reason. In this way there is a clear methodological autonomy for natural philosophy (science) and purely rational reason from religion and faith. But it was a mitigated autonomy where the methodologically autonomous natural and linguistic domain is nested within the divine truths of faith. You could get into trouble if your natural and rational arguments contradicted key orthodox doctrines, of course—and a highly able thinker like Abelard could be very slippery in how he framed anything that might not quite fit orthodoxy, so pinning him down to heresy would be no easy feat—but there was also a lot of room for disagreement within orthodoxy as well, and sometimes radically divergent interpretation of sacred doctrine could still be orthodox.

To Abelard, revealed Scripture and ecclesial authority are to be totally accepted, but reasoned arguments about those truths, and arguments in the domain of natural philosophy and ethics, are entirely fair game for logical dispute. His famous book *Sic et Non* ("Yes and No") cites 158 examples of orthodox theologians writing on different questions who come to opposite conclusions. In cunning fashion Abelard explains how—via careful attention to the differences in the exact meaning of words in the hands of different thinkers—one might reconcile these contradictions, but he does not reconcile them. Exactly what his point is, is left in the air. It is by no means impossible that he was making—as Peter King described it—an irrealist point about the flexibility and ultimate undecidability of human linguistic meaning. This in itself is not incompatible with orthodoxy, as the tradition of negative (apophatic) theology, powerfully established in Eastern Christianity well before Abelard's time, holds that what you *cannot* say about God is more valid than what you *can* say about God, even though positive (cataphatic) theology is doctrinally necessary.[16] But the significant factor here is that Abelard largely invents Western systematic theology, and this invention entails a strange methodological dualism between the natural realm, in which language and knowledge are situated, and the supernatural realm of ultimate meaning and ecclesial authority, which perhaps human reason and language can only at best gesture toward.

It is a very long story, but this dualistic tension between the human and the divine finally blows up in the nineteenth century. It blows up because the habit of situating what is humanly knowable and the sayable about the natural and temporal world within an ontological framework resplendent with unknowable and unsayable eternal realities[17] gets dropped by the Kantian phenomenological reduction.

Before the separation of nature and supernature, "naturalism" was just the sensible idea that the normal operations of nature are not miraculous, and indeed, this is what makes nature predictable and rationally comprehensible. Significantly, the intelligibility of nature was thought of as a created providence—a divine gift—in the West until very recently (the late nineteenth century). But the idea that nature itself could be ordered, and providentially ordered most of the time for the provision of our natural

---

16. The fifth-century, probably Syrian Orthodox, theologian known to us as Pseudo Dionysius the Areopagite was well known in Western theology in the twelfth century thanks to Latin translations by John Scotus Eriugena in the ninth century. In the West, one of the most able exponents of negative theology was the fifteenth-century theologian Nicholas of Cusa. Thomas Aquinas was also deeply influenced by Saint Dionysius, as he was then known.

17. See Gerson, *Ancient Epistemology*. Gerson points out that in classical Platonist and Neoplatonist thinking, epistemology (the science of human knowledge) is never self-standing or the foundation for our science of being (ontology). Rather, ontology, where being is inherently divinely sourced, is what enables our ordinary human knowledge and logic to participate to some degree in truth. All the developments we have been discussing—nominalism, reductionism, pragmatism—make this ancient way progressively harder to follow, until any meaningful knowledge of the transcendent and Being itself is assumed to be impossible.

needs, without an Orderer, without a cosmic Logos making the world a rational and ordered unity that natural philosophy could understand, takes a long time to appear. When it does—by the late nineteenth century—a scientistic atheism appears in which "naturalism" has now transformed to become anti-theological and anti-supernaturalist.

Once you can think about nature without any reference to the divine warrants of religion and faith then the manner in which Abelard's irrealism was held in check by a divine horizon of meaning above human meaning constructions, and by an earthly religious authority, is on the way to dissipating. Irrealism can break out of the discretely human domain, and became the entire domain of meaning only after the natural can be held to be fully discrete from the supernatural, rendering the supernatural functionally obsolete in the day-to-day world. This liberation of irrealism from any transcendent horizon of meaning is a profound rejection of the very deepest and most fundamental commitments of the Western intellectual university tradition. As you may know, Oxford University's biblical motto is *Dominus Illuminatio Mea*, "The Lord is my light." The Catholic Church birthed the Western university. A big cultural ship with a lot of forward momentum takes a long time to turn. This particular turn toward the purely natural takes about nine centuries to actualize, and the reason the final flourish of linguistic deflation and rationalist formalism in the twentieth century does *not* give way to a revived high ontology, as it predictably did in the past, is largely because of the secularization that entirely changes Western intellectual culture over the century from the 1870s to the 1970s, as we have already noted. This is the distinctive secularization produced by an anti-supernatural naturalism.

Something else that goes on in the late nineteenth and early twentieth centuries is the application of linguistic and performative constructivism to law and government.

BLACK-BOX PROCEDURALISM IN LAW

In the late nineteenth century, the influential British jurist Albert Venn Dicey brought precise and reductive definitions by means of linguistic deflation, and applied rigorous formal logic, admitting of no high grounds of meaning beyond syllogistic bivalence, to the meaning of laws and the notion of sovereignty. Dicey's 1885 text, *Introduction to the Study of the Law of the Constitution*, effectively locks off older categories of divine authority and transcendent reality from the meaning of law and the authority of parliament. This is a significant aspect of the great secularizing push in late–nineteenth-century England that we have already touched on when looking at Thomas Huxley and the progressive determination to replace religion with science in higher learning and public life.

Dicey's *Introduction to the Study of the Law of the Constitution* is a core legal theory document promoting the development of an entirely procedural notion of parliamentary sovereignty. Dicey notes:

> Parliament can legally legislate on any topic whatever which, in the judgment of Parliament, is a fit subject for legislation. There is no power which, under the English constitution, can come into rivalry with the legislative sovereignty of Parliament.[18]

Significantly, the reduction of the creation of legal meaning to nothing but Parliament's formally correct act of writing legislation, which is then backed up by the enforcement power of the state, connects constructed linguistic formulations with performative power, with no horizon of meaning above either language or power other than correct procedural assertion. Dicey notes:

> The principle . . . of parliamentary sovereignty means neither more nor less than this, namely, that "Parliament" has "the right to make or unmake any law whatever, and further, that no person or body is recognized by the law of England as having a right to override or set aside the legislation of Parliament."[19]
>
> A law may, for our present purpose, be defined as "any rule which will be enforced by the Courts."[20]

English law had been gradually heading toward this conception of parliamentary sovereignty since the Bill of Rights in 1689, and Dicey's understanding of parliamentary sovereignty now seems entirely obvious to most citizens of liberal secular democracies in the English law tradition, but this is, in fact, a significant development with significant ramifications.

Linking back to Dicey's stance, the barrister and legal scholar Jonathan Horton KC has written a fascinating doctoral dissertation on parliamentary

---

18. Dicey, *Introduction*, 24. As cited in Horton, "Limits of Legislation," 83.
19. Dicey, *Introduction*, xxxvi n1. As cited in Horton, "Limits of Legislation," 83.
20. Dicey, *Introduction*, 26n1. As cited in Horton, "Limits of Legislation," 83.

hyperactivity in the English law tradition.[21] Parliamentary hyperactivity is a historical phenomenon where, since the late nineteenth century, English and English-origin parliaments have produced an ever-increasing quantity of laws in each parliamentary sitting. This process is now almost impossible to keep up with, and we are becoming entangled in a dense thicket of often-contradicting blocks of rules and norms that citizens, corporations, the judiciary, and lawyers now have to negotiate.

Horton notes: "This situation has been brought about by conflating an authority which Parliament acquired in the seventeenth and eighteenth centuries with the legislation it produces. . . . [Horton finds that this] less than fully justified conferral upon legislation of authority [encourages a less than fully justified] activist and ambitious role for Parliament via legislation."[22]

In other words, because we now assume that parliament has the authority to make whatever laws it likes, provided it follows the proper democratic and legal procedures, parliament indeed *does* make up whatever laws it likes, whether we really need them or not, and whether those laws have a meaningfully just authority or not. Over time laws become both more expansive in their scope and more fine-grained in their applicable formulation, which gives the judiciary less scope of interpretation as various activist agendas are pursued by political parties through legislation. The independence of the judiciary from executive government is thus functionally shrunk by this process, which facilitates legislative activism. The authority of law is being both trivialized and politicized, and we are being hemmed in at all angles by legal frameworks that have become enormous and unruly. We find ourselves in the situation where we are at the mercy of "the 'black box' in the chain of legitimation of legislation."[23]

Horton notes how the legal scholar Luc Wintgens wonders about what this "black box" means for the authority of law. When sovereignty was vested more fully in the monarch in the English tradition, the king or queen exercised the divine prerogatives of sovereignty in a manner that was constrained, as they do not have the authority to violate the laws of God as expressed by Scripture and church, as well as expressed in the terms of natural justice though venerable custom and common sense. Parliament, however, has no limits on its legislative scope at all, because its authority in a secular liberal democracy is purely formal and procedural. Hence,

21. Horton, "Limits of Legislation."
22. Horton, "Limits of Legislation," 2.
23. Horton, "Limits of Legislation," 289.

Wintgens notes, "the magic of the black box prevents anyone questioning the outputs in any of its aspects."[24] In effect, laws become just by definition, by virtue of them being enacted by parliament. Laws are now performative and poetic human constructions, and their only justification for being "just" is procedural. Law has become a game of linguistic construction, and the constructors of legal words now see themselves as *creating* law and thus *creating* justice, rather than partially and lightly *discovering* naturally just realities that stand above human linguistic constructions. The high, essential, and transcendent horizons of meaning are being excised from law, and laws are becoming purely human, purely linguistic, and purely power-regulating legislative constructs, whose creation is now performed by the act of legislation. This is where the "purity" of the Enlightenment—the purging of meaning from faith and the purging of logic from any essential and metaphysical notion of reason—takes us.

DEFLATION, FORMALISM, AND THE END OF ENLIGHTENMENT

The long and sophisticated Western traditions of linguistic deflation and logical formalism have existed in strange tension with high and traditional meanings embedded in theology and metaphysics from the time of Peter Abelard to Immanuel Kant. That tension has largely held back linguistics and analytics from taking off into an unfettered irrealism. Kant opens a door for these trajectories to take us into a new region of irrealism, should we be bold or foolish enough to enter, by bracketing out faith and metaphysics from sense and reason. By the late nineteenth century this Enlightenment reductionism has become integral with our very form of government and law. The twentieth century is largely the story of throwing off older (Christian) embedded categories of high public meaning and authority, which largely succeeds by the 1970s. The manner in which language is looked to as an attempt to hold onto Enlightenment sense and reason via a deflationary positivist approach to meaning and a purely formal approach to reason ends up being self-defeating as *all* meanings simply dissolve into entirely humanly constructed power. We are now ripe for the rise of postmodernism. We are now ripe for the appearance of gender theory.

---

24. Horton, "Limits of Legislation," 289. Horton here cites Wintgens, *Legisprudence*, 213–14n3.

7

Postmodernism

POSTMODERNISM GENUINELY GETS SOME things right. Notably, it really does grasp that anti-metaphysical and anti-theological scientific positivism cannot give us truth. It really grasps that all human meanings are discovered through and mediated by language. These are genuine truths, and postmodernism cannot be simply debunked. In this chapter we shall draw out these truths, for we do not want to burn straw effigies of postmodernism.

However, postmodernism retains continuity with key aspects of the Enlightenment purity project. Being continuous with those very trajectories that bring modernity to an end, postmodernity is itself hardly an adequate response to the failings of Enlightenment modernity. It is more a macabre celebration of the failure of modernity, and a valorizing of vandalisms toward the real achievements of the Western intellectual tradition than any serious way forward for the West. Thus, core features of postmodernism are profoundly deceptive, self-defeating, and simply wrong. Nothing illustrates the vacuity, the aporia, and the commitment to irrational and anti-truth power games of postmodernism more clearly than does gender theory.

Postmodernism comes to accept the philosophical incoherence of modern positivism and becomes—I would say—*hyper*-Kantian in rejecting *any* real knowledge of reality. It also tends to be hyper-Kantian in retaining the Enlightenment rejection of metaphysical and theological truth, even though the traditional truth claims of high meaning and revelation were never justified by a commitment to either pure empiricism or pure rationalism. Which is to say that postmodernism has no compelling grounds in reason or fact to reject faith-received divine illumination, but *does* reject traditional truth claims out of its own quasi-religious and methodologically atheist faith commitments. That is, postmodernism is incoherently committed to the at least *functional truth* of Enlightenment anti-metaphysical and anti-theological epistemic prejudices. This reveals postmodernism as sophistry. For while postmodernists are notoriously slippery in their determination not to make any coherent or essentially meaningful truth claim, their very commitment to *not* making a truth claim reveals they do in fact hold to a truth. This truth is the self-defeating formulation that no truth claim can be true.

Postmodernism is, then, a strange embracing of the failure of modern positivism. That is, because atheist and materialist positivist accounts of truth are not philosophically viable (assuming *pure* reason and *pure* experience foundational justifications), postmodernism *believes* that we cannot have *any* truth at all. The very failure of modern positivism is taken to mean that Kant's Enlightenment stance on the unknowability of reality in itself is (ironically) true. But while Kant wanted anti-realist science to be a practical (albeit not metaphysically justified) *truth* discourse, postmodernism is more consistent than Kant in its anti-realism (now irrealism) toward science, as it treats science as an entirely human linguistic construction that is only a tool of human power and imagination. Here, science is no longer about truth but simply gives us power over other humans, and over the human linguistic construct that we call "nature."

In sum, to the postmodernist, if one cannot have modern positivist anti-metaphysical and anti-theological truth, then one cannot have truth at all, for any sort of return to speculation and faith is ruled out for Enlightenment and anti-Christian prejudicial "reasons." But here is the rub: gender theory wants to unmask the *falsehood* of fact-based notions of sex, because one cannot know the truth about reality, which is to imply that it is *really true* that you cannot know the truth about the facts of sex. This is an exercise in self-defeating intellectual futility. But we will attack gender theory's postmodern self-defeatism later in the book. For now, we need a working understanding of what Jean-François Lyotard called "the postmodern condition."

The postmodern condition really gets into the air in the 1970s, but this was a movement that some could see was on its way, right back in the eighteenth century. So we will start with four well-known counter-Enlightenment thinkers, two Christians and two atheists. We shall put Johann

Georg Hamann and Søren Kierkegaard together, and Friedrich Nietzsche and Arthur Schopenhauer together, before skipping through the implosion of twentieth-century positivism very quickly, and on to the rise of French postmodernism in the 1970s, and its uptake in America in the same decade.

HAMANN'S THEOLOGICAL CRITIQUE OF THE ENLIGHTENMENT

As we briefly touched on, Aristotle maintains that the "first philosophy" presuppositions of any truth-seeking intellectual enterprise require a *philosophical commitment* to respecting the natural truths of sense and reason.[1] If you cannot trust sense and reason to be at least partially truth-revealing, you are not undertaking philosophy in good faith as a truth-seeking enterprise.

If Aristotle is right—and I think gender theory provides excellent circumstantial evidence to suggest that he is—then there are serious problems with the Enlightenment desire to purify sense and reason from all traditional first principles. To state the ancient insight again, to Aristotle the first principles of sense and reason cannot be proven *by* sense and reason, but one must have *good faith* that real truths about nature reach us through a careful approach to sense and reason, if one is even going to get started in using sense and reason as truth-revealing knowledge gateways.

Contrary to Aristotle, the Kantian approach does not accept that reality itself can be known, and accepts no "good faith" foundation for sense and reason that cannot be demonstrated outside of the internal mental givens of the categories of sense and reason. Or, to put the same point slightly differently, *our own* sensorium and *our own* categories of reason—not meaningful nature and not cosmic reason—are now the first principles of human knowledge. Knowledge and meaning itself become *radically anthropocentric* under the Enlightenment, and the birth of modern atheism, an amoral and strictly pragmatic approach to nature, and the de-Christianization of Western intellectual culture flows directly out of that epistemic anthropocentrism. It is a few highly intelligent theologians who immediately notice these serious perils that are central to the Enlightenment project, though they are—unsurprisingly—ecclesial and academic outsiders to the spirit of their times.

---

1. See note 10 in chapter 3, above.

In Kant's own lifetime, it was one of his close friends who saw most clearly what a disaster the enlightened purification of reason and logic would be for the West. That friend was Johann Georg Hamann.

Hamann's short essay "Metacritique on the Purism of Reason"[2] was written in 1784 in response to Kant's *Critique of Pure Reason*. Hamann did not publish this devastating analysis of Kant's pivotal text in Enlightenment philosophy, out of personal regard for his friend. A number of Hamann's philosophical friends read the essay, though, and it was published in 1800, twelve years after Hamann's death.

To Hamann there were a range of impossible abstractions performed by Kant in order to try to make his system of pure reason fly.[3] Hamann does not believe Kant's approach actually works. There are at least three sorts of problems Hamann identifies with Kant's phenomenologically "pure reason": (1), phenomena and noumena can only be artificially abstracted from each other; (2), all arguments must use language, and language itself is never rationally and empirically pure; (3), the horizon of meaning that makes language work is divine, such that meaning and intelligibility ultimately disappear, or are reduced to mere tools of power, if you are determined to isolate reason from theology.

The idea that you can meaningfully treat phenomena not as an appearing *of reality*, but just as *an appearing*, is a remarkable conceptual fiction that is embraced by Kant for one reason only; it removes the need for any trust in the necessarily indemonstrable relationship between intelligible reality and the human mind. Performing the "thought experiment" of centering our understanding of reason and sensory knowledge in our own experience alone, without reference to reality itself, removes the need for speculative metaphysics. That is, it removes Aristotelian first principles. But this is literally the removal of the world in order to obtain self-grounding certainty in "pure" human reason, and "pure" human sense. It is the swapping of the rich and mysterious wonder of actual reality for the clear and certain knowledge of an abstract fantasy. Hamann will have none of it. Let

---

2. Haynes, *Hamann: Writings on Philosophy and Language*, 205–18.

3. For the most accessible English selection of Hamann's writings there is still no better text than Smith, *J. G. Hamann*. Because Hamann was an ironist, a Christian, and a deeply philosophically read linguist—teaching himself eleven languages—his original and typically German writings are very difficult for the non-specialist to follow and appreciate. But I have found Kenneth Haynes's translations of a collection of Hamann's essays, with extensive explanatory notes, very helpful. See again Haynes, *Hamann: Writings on Philosophy and Language*.

reality be beyond our determinate and certain total knowledge. Let any actual knowledge of reality be ever and always "contaminated" by trust in meanings and actualities that we cannot rationally and epistemically master. For that is the real world after all!

Then there is language. One of the most highly regarded contemporary philosophers of the past seventy years is Charles Taylor. In his 2016 book, *The Language Animal*, Taylor unpacks what he calls the HHH model of language. This is a model Taylor draws from the tradition of Hamann, Herder, and Humbolt. These are thinkers who understand that the real nature of linguistic meaning goes "far beyond that of encoding and communication information."[4] For the fact is, language is a dazzling and astonishing mystery. For while words are just sounds, and—as different languages demonstrate—there is nothing meaning-carrying about articulated sounds in themselves, intelligible meaning finds culturally created and learned words a viable medium for the meeting of human minds, and for the engagement of meaningful experiences and thoughts with an oh so rich and meaningful reality. To Hamann there is an astonishing irony in Kant using language to argue for the abstract purging of facts and logic from all high mystery and all essential meaning. But to make any meaningful linguistic communication of meaning at all is to rise far above "pure" logic and "pure" sense. Kant's very mode of expression—language—denies the seriousness and even possibility of the kind of abstracted and purified sense and logic that Kant is endeavoring to disclose to us (via the dazzling natural miracle of language).

To Hamann, human languages are entirely natural and—as Taylor puts it—we are language animals. Yet, at the same time, Language Itself—communicating intelligible meaning—is inescapably divine, and as language users we live and move and have all of our intelligible meanings within the Divine Logos (as does all of reality).[5] So Hamann thinks the very aim of removing thought and meaning from their connection to theology and metaphysics is to mistake abstract constructs for reality. More than that, he does not even think such an endeavor is in fact *possible*. To make even bad and false arguments—arguments that bracket out the transcendent and the divine—one must use divine and transcendent language.

As I will unpack a bit further after looking at Kierkegaard, the reason it is important to bring up theological critiques of the anti-faith and

---

4. Taylor, *Language Animal*, ix.
5. See Betz, *Christ the Logos of Creation*.

anti-metaphysical purity method of the Enlightenment project is that there are a range of ways one might find that the Enlightenment does not work. But however one might approach it, the Enlightenment project does *not* in fact work. Post-positivist, anti-faith, and anti-metaphysical postmodern critiques of the Enlightenment vision of modernity—and these critiques are, at core, linguistic critiques—*do* really have a point. So there are things that Judith Butler and Johann Georg Hamann agree on. There are, of course, also things they disagree on. More on that later.

KIERKEGAARD'S THEOLOGICAL CRITIQUE OF THE ENLIGHTENMENT

Here I will also focus on just three criticisms Søren Kierkegaard makes of the Enlightenment roots of what became the Marxist-influenced and atheistic positivist movement we now typically call "progressivism." Kierkegaard notes that: (1) doubt is self-defeating as a first principle; (2) real existence requires the rejection of idealist and positivist abstractions; (3) existence links us to the real, which is not, ultimately, the phenomenological spatiotemporal manifold of "pure" experience and mathematical logic. It is, rather, God.

Again, you may be wondering what Kierkegaard's three counter-Enlightenment claims have to do with postmodernism. This will be unpacked as we go, but the main reason for this line of approach is to point out that postmodernism is premised on very sensible critiques of the impossible truth claims of Enlightenment trends. Reductive positivism, idealist romantic speculation, and old-school rationalism really are philosophical duds. It is also the case that the responses postmodernism makes to the failures of secular modernity are simply mad. Significantly, there are other types of responses to the failure of the Enlightenment project that allow us a reasonable knowledge of objective natural truth and an understanding of high meaning that is not simply made up, and Hamann and Kierkegaard show us such another way.

In his book *Johannes Climacus, or De omnibus dubitandum est*[6] ("everything must be doubted") Kierkegaard has an ironic but very effective dig at a central article of Enlightenment faith: doubting everything. As the ancient skeptics knew, skepticism has the serious internal-coherence problem that if you doubt everything you must also doubt the skeptical stance

---

6. Kierkegaard, *Philosophical Fragments* and *Johannes Climacus*.

itself. As a result, ancient skeptics typically did not advocate "pure" skepticism, but rather a mitigated, pragmatic, and limited skepticism. The idea that it is virtuous to doubt all and every received truth is one that cannot be sustained on skeptical grounds. Kierkegaard wants those who embrace the enlightened and positivist enthusiasm for the virtue of doubting all theological truth claims to genuinely appreciate that this is not a stance that skepticism itself can sustain. Rather the enlightened anti-religious posture is a perverse faith stance committed to not having faith in anything (except the stance of not having faith). The entirely negative epistemic principle of doubting everything—of accepting nothing on any sort of faith, of requiring only rational and empirical indubitable demonstrations of truth—is simply the destruction of *all* knowledge and *all* belief. The Enlightenment search for pure and absolute demonstrations is a pipe dream. But if it is a pipe dream, on what basis do we assume, with Kant, that we are now "grown up" and no longer need faith?

Kierkegaard invented the now well-known term "existential." Twentieth-century atheists—Martin Heidegger and Jean-Paul Sartre in particular—effectively plagiarized and repurposed Kierkegaard's work to make the exact opposite arguments to Kierkegaard. But let us not concern ourselves here with atheistic and twentieth-century existentialism, but look rather at what Kierkegaard himself was saying.

When it comes to what is truly important in our actual lives, Kierkegaard maintains that what really matters is the manner in which we live with integrity (or not) toward that which we believe to be of highest meaning and importance. In the twentieth century Martin Buber—working directly within Kierkegaard's trajectory, but as a Jew not a Lutheran—points out the manner in which our high-belief commitments are demonstrated in how we actually live as spiritual, relational, and social beings.[7] That is, existentially, *no one* really lives as if there is no truth or meaning in the world and all meanings and values are simply made up. Nihilistic constructivism is *an existential lie*.

Kierkegaard is interested in real truthfulness, not in abstract mind games *about* "truth." Existential truth concerns our own most basic choices and actions in our concrete and particular, actual existence. This is what Kierkegaard means by the term "existential." Abstract and ideal mind games (and Kierkegaard has Hegel in his sights) have diddly-squat to do

---

7. Buber, *I and Thou*.

with existential truth, no matter how brilliant and seductive they might be as intellectual systems.

Closer to the ordinary Dane of the 1840s, Kierkegaard insist that faith in God is not a matter of abstract belief in the objective truth of certain doctrines and the conventional performance of respectable religious and moral expectations. Existential faith is faith that encounters God as ultimate and divine Truth, as—within the Christian tradition—a totally transformative miraculous transition from a life that is conventionally normal but dead in sin to participation in the resurrected life of Christ himself. Significantly, the idea that science or historical scholarship has anything directly to do with the transformative encounter of the sinner with the saving, life-giving work of God, here and now, is a frightening existential category error. Kierkegaard has nothing but scorn for the liberal Protestant trajectory of defining truth via the conveniently "objective" categories of historical credibility, of rational validity, and of scientific demonstration. This is nothing but replacing faith with sin, and the resultant "Christianity" has no existential truth in it. In his masterpiece on faith and sin as epistemic categories[8] Kierkegaard notes that "subjective truth" (and here he means existential truth that works itself out in a genuine Christian life) does not rest on the so-called "objective truths" or modern functionally atheist historicism and scientism, but nonetheless, following hard after "subjective truth" is the only way to "objective truth" in the end. Which is to say that only the truth-seeking existential "how" leads to a genuine knowledge of the objectively true "what." Trying to get to existential truth by getting your "what" right first is a futile and in fact sinful (i.e., epistemically proud) dead end that will never work. Or, as one fine Kierkegaard scholar put it, for Kierkegaard, "the truth is the way," meaning a truthful way of good faith in God leads to Truth itself.[9] But this high Truth is God grasping us, it is not us grasping God. And this is the condition for any ultimate knowledge of Truth, as it is—perhaps along Aristotle's lines—a divine gift, not a human right. The proud cannot know the truth in their sin.

Now that may be more theological than you are comfortable with, but again, the central point of this introduction to postmodernism is that while the failures of the Enlightenment purity project are unavoidable—and postmodernists are correct to point them out—there are different ways of interpreting that failure. The way Hamann and Kierkegaard interpret

---

8. Kierkegaard, *Concluding Unscientific Postscript*.
9. Simpson, *Truth Is the Way*.

that failure is premised on the conviction that the Enlightenment desire to abandon religious faith and metaphysical speculation was the wrong turn that inevitably leads to the failure of the Enlightenment. While they are both radical countercultural denouncers of the Enlightenment, they are intellectually motivated by their continuity with orthodox Christian faith and high metaphysical mysteries. This, however, is not how postmodernists interpret the failure of the Enlightenment. Our postmodernists interpret the failure of the Enlightenment as the collapse of the entire project of Western philosophy and Christian theology since Plato, and a return to the poetic anarchic liberalism of the sophists.

Apart from the trends we have already looked at with the progressive atheism of Ludwig Feuerbach and Karl Marx, on the one hand, and atheist French and Anglo-American positivism, on the other hand, significant post-Christian counter-Enlightenment developments are going on in the Continent in the second half of the nineteenth century. Let us now turn very briefly to Schopenhauer and Nietzsche.

SCHOPENHAUER AND THE WORLD AS WILL AND REPRESENTATION

Arthur Schopenhauer goes beyond Kant in holding that the phenomenological world of representation actually *is* the world, which makes Schopenhauer strangely Hegelian (in a Vedantic Hindu manner) in asserting that Will (Spirit in Hegel) is at once the objective but irrational and amoral reality of how things really are, as well as an evolving subjective reality expressed creatively through human awareness and action. That is, will and representation are not in any discrete sense merely internal mental phenomena; they are a unity constitutive of the phenomenal world itself. This is a spiritual atheism where struggle, irrational will, and representative knowledge are not expressions of subjective or divine Will/Spirit *over and above* creation, but express *Will and reality in unity*.

To Schopenhauer's Vedantic outlook, creation and destruction are ultimately one, suffering and pleasure are ultimately one, good and evil are ultimately one, reality is ultimately will and representation. However, destruction, suffering, evil, and will are primary and eternal, whereas creation, pleasure, good, and meaningful representation are fleeting and imaginative constructs that are derivative of primal reality. The influence of Eastern thought is strong on his work, and this signals *both* a profound rejection of the rationalist and positivist trajectories of the Enlightenment *and* the birth of a new and dark spiritual energy in Western philosophy. This new spiritual energy is just itching to break free of traditional Christian defined categories of good and evil, truth and falsehood, God and the devil. This is the celebration of the dark, irrational, and ultimately meaningless poetry of entirely willful existence and entirely representative though non-essentially referenced poetic "meaning."

We will not dig deeper into Schopenhauer here, but it is worth noting that from early in the nineteenth century there have been powerful alternatives to the light-filled and rationally harmonious vision of Kant's Age of Reason. The secularized Christian cultural world of faith-purged reason, metaphysics-purged science, and universal cosmopolitan peace and prosperity that Kant envisioned does not necessarily follow from getting rid of faith and transcendent essential meaning. Indeed, the celebration of irrational will and anarchic suffering can arise out of the Enlightenment project's determination to free us from Christian faith and traditional metaphysics. This anarchic celebration of *sheer* will and *sheer* poetic and performative representation is by no means absent from today's queer postmodernism.

It seems that some contemporary positivists, such as Richard Dawkins,[10] are now discovering that liberating the West from the so-called "God delusion" of the Christian faith leaves the West with a gaping theological and metaphysical vacuum that must be filled by something. For many people, faith in science is not adequate to the theological and metaphysical task now at hand. Indeed, whether the very idea of scientific truth can survive the collapse of the Christian cultural commitments to the theologically warranted categories of natural truths, which gave rise to modern science, is in serious doubt. Obvious scientific facts, and good quality peer-reviewed and openly scrutinized evidence, are now in serious trouble should the will-and-representation agendas of gender-identity

---

10. Dawkins's admission of being a "cultural Christian" in his public debate with Ayaan Ali in 2024 is fascinating. Ali is a very theologically and metaphysically intelligent person, who, though once an atheist, became aware of the inability of culture to sustain its high vision of meaning and freedom without high theological warrants. Dawkins, brilliant scientist though he is, simply cannot follow her reasoning, as he has almost no theological or metaphysical intelligence. But he does grasp that the values and common beliefs of a Western way of life are embedded in the cultural formation of the West in the Christian religion. UnHerd, "Richard Dawkins vs Ayaan Hirsi Ali."

advocates deem the "so-called facts of sex"[11] to be wrong and immoral. But back to the nineteenth century.

NIETZSCHE: THE DEATH OF GOD AND THE DEATH OF MAN

Friedrich Nietzsche makes significant discoveries about the ramifications of counter-Enlightenment atheism. As a teenager he read David Strauss and Ludwig Feuerbach, concluding that the Christian faith was indeed a manufactured myth and a projection of ourselves onto the cosmos (we make God in our own image). He then discovered Schopenhauer's root-and-branch critique of "the horrors and absurdities of religion,"[12] which is also sensitive to why religion is so strongly adhered to as—in Schopenhauer's view—a shield from truth. Accepting the central arguments of these three thinkers, Nietzsche clearly grasps that if God is dead, then Man is dead, and, indeed, all categories of essential meaning, right and wrong, truth and falsehood, are dead too. Notably, when there is no God in whose image we are made, then there is no referent that can define human nature in any essential and intrinsically meaningful terms. Significantly also, after the death of God, the distinction between mad and sane is wiped away. Zarathustra, Nietzsche, and Foucault are a unity here. The wide-eyed prophetic madman of Zarathustra sees that the truth horizon to meaning itself has been wiped away with the discarding of God. The mad prophet's vision is in stark contrast to both conventional Christians, who merely turn the handle on a dead belief, as well as culturally Christian atheists, who pretend the only thing that has changed after God dies is that one no longer needs to go to church on a Sunday. While they are culturally "sane," these are the immoral, the small, and the deluded poor excuses for real men and women, whom Nietzsche despises. Only the mad and the deviant can be truly great.

God anchored truth to a frame of reality above the arbitrary contingencies and competing perspectives of human knowledge in Western culture, even as that frame is ever beyond human mastery. But once cut free from that anchor to higher meaning, everything is at sea, all fixed points disappear, everything changes. Now science, morals, shared meanings, political conventions are all functions of meaningless flux, they are all relative

---

11. Butler, *Who's Afraid*, 190.

12. For a very helpful selected collection of Schopenhauer's thoughts on religion, see Schopenhauer, *Horrors and Absurdities of Religion*.

and contingent perspectives, power is without authority, glory is an illusion, the world itself is an incoherent conglomerate of entirely imagined and made-up mythic narratives. After the death of God *only* myth is left. Is this where the Age of Reason takes us?

In *Twilight of the Idols* (1889) Nietzsche explains that he does philosophy with a hammer. That is, any system of knowledge and ideas, any moral philosophy, any religious belief system, any construction of artistic or cultural meaning, he taps with his hammer, listening for that inner ringing sound that shows it up as an idol. An idol to Nietzsche is a human idea that serves human purposes, where the people who build and worship such idols delude themselves that they have not simply made it up. Crucially, made up abstractions and projections that are then delusionally believed—as if they are truth discoveries—Nietzsche finds to be dishonest and small hearted. Such idols are cultural artifacts that are used to try to control and ultimately escape the seething and irrational creative energies of Life.

In *The Birth of Tragedy* (1872) Nietzsche claims that Life is a raw force of cruel, joyous, violent, and ecstatic sexual energy, untrammeled by safe and routinized customs and conventions. Nietzsche postulates such a raw Dionysian energy in the barbaric pre-Homeric Greeks, which is then dialectically integrated with Apollonian reason and artistry, without being diluted, in the early classical tragedy plays. The spectator watches the absurd impossibilities of the doomed clash of nature and culture, but this is reality; this is the pinnacle expression of human life. This Nietzsche saw as the high point of Greek life, and things go seriously downhill from here. He sees a moralizing and civilizational dampening of the energy of Life, in the cause of safety and control, in the rise of philosophy (particularly Plato), then religion (particularly Judaism and Christianity). This is an immoral and poetically deadening fall from that life-affirming, power embracing, physical and psychic energy of Life. Greatness is poetically made, in harmony with absurd and violent reality, by those who are both free and determined poetic channels of Life. But perhaps I wax too poetic.

Coming back to the dull grey on grey of a more analytic mythology, Nietzsche establishes what philosophers have since called perspectivism and an appreciation for poetic myth-making as the most primary reality of human meaning. Assuming there are no high anchor points to truth and meaning, as a horizon that overshadows and partially gives itself to human knowledge and meaning-constructions, Nietzsche shows us that truth and meaning are fictive, imaginative *projections* onto a *meaningless* and ultimately *pointless* physical reality.

Can you see the roots of postmodernism in the nineteenth century's counter-Enlightenment atheism now? If you combine that sophistic anti-Christian Continental trajectory with the philosophical failure of twentieth-century positivism, and with the collapse of cultural Christianity in the 1960s, then you can see that our high-meaning culture is in a state of serious crisis, and the dogs of destruction are about to be released. That release we now call postmodernism, and it gets into the air in the France of the 1970s. But postmodernism has deep roots in ideas and intellectual fashions that well pre-date the 1970s. Postmodernism does not come out of nowhere, without father or mother or genealogy. Postmodernity is the direct progeny of Enlightenment modernity. Yet, we can better appreciate its twentieth-century expression if, instead of going straight to post-1968 France, we turn first to the interwar years in Germany and France. So we start with Heidegger and Sartre.

HEIDEGGER AND SARTRE: POST-WAR ATHEIST EXISTENTIALISM

Martin Heidegger was raised a German Catholic who, as a young man, entered training to become a Catholic priest. He had a solid background in Aristotle. At some point as a relatively young man, he lost his faith and abandoned the priesthood. Throughout his life he had a string of tangled sexual relationships with various friends and students. He appropriated various aspects of Kierkegaard's existentialism and Nietzsche's poeticism, and reformulated the category of "being" to be entirely temporal (not eternal) and atheist (replacing God with Void). When I read him, Heidegger seems to utter indubitable pronouncements like a German mystic who has his own personal conduit with the Divine (in this case, Heidegger's own mind). He reads to me like an anti-onto-theological theologian, and a post-metaphysical metaphysician.

Notoriously, Heidegger was a supporter of the Nazi regime, even though that regime disappointed him because it did not put him in charge of the philosophical formulation of the Nazis' aims and rationale. Heidegger never admitted to fault as regards his own involvement in Nazi Germany, though (after the war) he did criticize that regime for not recognizing his genius. Heidegger was also a very influential figure in what became known as the philosophy of technology. He is a significant and complex thinker. But there are only two aspects of his thought that I wish to draw attention to here in opening up contemporary postmodern thought. These are his understanding of time, and his understanding of death.

Time has no outside to Heidegger. The unmoving riverbed of ever-flowing time is eternity in traditional philosophy and theology, but—to use this analogy—time is a bottomless ocean to Heidegger that does not flow over any fixed pre- or super-temporal reality. We, at least, are in time, and there is no "beyond time" to which our spirit belongs, so the flow of time *is* our life, with the only horizon to that flow being its inevitable cessation when we die. When we die we are simply gone, for we only have our being within time. But we do have a directional temporal horizon, such that after we are thrown into temporal being, we are ever moving toward the nonbeing of death.

What, you may wonder, has this got to do with postmodernism?

Human life is here entirely defined by historical contingency and metaphysical nihilism[13] (i.e., higher meaning defined by Nothing). This becomes the edgy atheist existentialism of the post-war period. Jean-Paul Sartre is doing a similar thing, albeit in a French register. But Sartre is a less (anti-)metaphysical and a less (anti-)theological thinker than Heidegger, and simply not German, so the Frenchman is perhaps more voluntarist than Heidegger, and is interested in venturing his own meaning. Sartre insists that each individual must take full responsibility for creating their own meaning. Accepting that the universe has no meaning, and that it is up to each individual to create their own meaning—as this is what it means to simply "find oneself" as an existing being—poetic nihilism becomes the avant garde and sexy new post-war Continental philosophy. Of course Heidegger and Sartre reject all things Christian, particularly as concerning sexual relations. By the time the sexual revolution and anti-Christian progressivism of the 1960s youth movements arise, Heidegger and Sartre are preachers of a new liberation for high-horizon-free meaning-making with ready and young audiences.

---

13. Heidegger refuses to acknowledge that he himself is a metaphysical thinker, but that is a complicated story we shall not explore here.

POSTMODERNISM

THE POSTMODERNISTS: LYOTARD, DERRIDA, AND RORTY

There is quite a progressive mythology around 1968 in the Western university scene. This is the first generation of Baby Boomers coming of age at the height of the post-war boom. The youths of 1968 had only ever known peace (unless they were conscripted to Vietnam), prosperity, and new horizons of opportunity. It was also the height of the Cold War and the era of sex, drugs, and rock and roll. Radicals in university and hippies dropping out of university were all pushing for change. Affluent and fashionably countercultural young hedonists looking to have a good time, and make a better world, flexed their strength against the authority of their parents' generation and more or less pushed them over. The 1960s and 1970s are when Michel Foucault is an older (but not too old) radical figure speaking for the young and restless in the optimistic cause of overturning the old and bringing in the new.

Let us now move from intellectual backstories and historical contexts to ideas.

In 1979 Jean-François Lyotard explained "the postmodern condition" as "a war on totality" and its posture is "incredulity towards metanarratives."[14] In other words, all knowledge is stories, but there is no one "big" story that judges the truth and validity of "smaller" stories. For all stories are small stories, and they are always situated within contingent culturally and politically constructed perspectives. That is, postmodernism rejects the validity of any "totalizing" attempt to get at objective and universal truth. Lyotard is very clear here, modern science—which has dissolved so many previous theological and spiritual metanarratives—cannot itself be treated as a metanarrative. At this point positivism was on its last philosophical legs, so Lyotard's timing was apposite. From here on it becomes a trendy and sophisticated stance (which is not actually silly) that science is also always perspectival, and "it" (though who can say what "science" is?) is best understood as a multiplex of shifting and contingent culturally and politically situated knowledge-constructions. And, of course, knowledge is a linguistic construct. This brings us to Derrida.

Depending on who you listen to, Jacques Derrida is a brilliant scholar of linguistic meaning or a complete intellectual fraud. To a postmodernist there is, at least arguably, no totalizing way of saying who gets Derrida right

---

14. Lyotard, *Postmodern Condition*, 82, xxiv.

and who gets him wrong. I'm not a postmodernist but I think it is probably fair to say that he indeed is brilliant, but he uses his brilliance to make all linguistic communication fraudulent (or, playful). Here, every form of communication is what he calls a "text." All texts are comprised of signs. Signs can be de-coded into linguistic meanings, but as linguistic systems of signs are self-referential (i.e., one linguistic sign only has a meaning in relation to other linguistic signs), communication—understood in an old-fashioned sense of a direct transfer of true meanings about reality from one person to another—does not actually happen. Human language does not get to reality, for reality itself is linguistically meaningless. And when it comes to what meaning I think I am constructing, I have no real power to ensure that the self-referential linguistic constructions I am making are interpreted in the way I intend them to be understood. There is always a playful difference between the "writer" and the "reader" of any linguistic "text" such that the meaning constructions we *think* we are making might only have the (self-referential and reality-unconnected) meaning we intend it to have in our own head. In other words, if you are interested in having words used to show that any communication of real meaning is impossible, and you want to do this via a playful but cunningly subversive deconstruction of linguistic meaning as such, then Derrida is your man. By this time you should be able to see that Derrida is in many ways continuous with the complete mythic poeticism of all meaning pursued by Nietzsche because of the death of God, which has its origins in the Enlightenment project of purifying reason and perception from faith and metaphysics. The collapse of communicative intelligible meanings about reality does not just pop up unannounced with Derrida. Derrida is simply the logical conclusion of a now long arc of conceptual development, an arc that modern positivists are indeed a part of. Whether positivists like it or not, they are superseded by a shift to the *total construction* of knowledge, and the *disappearance of truth*, even as a possibility, within linguistic communication. Sophistry has arrived in the academy, and she is now very hard to dislodge. And this brings us to knowledge as a power construct.

The American postmodern pragmatist Richard Rorty maintains that "truth" is simply not a useful word any more. Accepting that knowledge relates only to our language, the point of saying things is not that one's utterances are true or false, but that they are an effective means to achieving the practical outcomes that one wants. Now Rorty was a powerful and morally serious thinker, who could run rings around most of his opponents, so

I do not wish to paint him in any fatuous or demeaning light. But the fact is, if linguistic communication is not about truth, and if politics is not about high meanings that—though beyond our mastery—are about qualitative and moral reality, then *words are just tools of power*. This is sophistry, and it is a denial both of philosophy in the Western academic tradition and of the truth value of modern science (which, before nineteenth-century positivism, presupposed divine warrants enabling our true understanding of the order and meaning of nature). To Rorty, science and, say, political discourse have great *practical* value, but the descriptions of the world that are our scientific theories, and our moral and political beliefs, and our everyday words, are not the world, and the world has no interest in them. Our *descriptions* can be (linguistically) true or false, and we can make valuations about things, actions, and affairs that we call "good" or "bad," but we should not confuse reality itself—which has no meaning and can be neither true nor false, it just is—with our words. And when it comes to words, *effect* is the thing that matters, and this effect is on other language users, primarily, and is a means to collective practical engagements with the meaningless reality that we might call science, technology, political communication, and so forth. But "truth" is not a useful word or idea.

Arguably Rorty's most important work is his 1989 text, *Contingency, Irony, and Solidarity*. We will come back to this later, but the postmodern movement by the late 1980s is increasingly mainstream in the academies, even in the Anglo-American academies that had been positivist and analytic for most of the twentieth century. At the same time, the pragmatic neoliberalism of Reagan and Thatcher is transforming the post-war "first world" (as it was then called) from Keynesian political economics of strong social welfare states and heavily regulated banking and finance sectors into Milton Friedman's small state and global liberal vision, combined with fast and furious deregulation of banking and finance. We will come back to this, but here I just wish to signal that "liberalism in a post-ideological age"[15] was really getting into the air politically at this time, which, among other things, dissolves strong ideological differences between twentieth-century left and right political ideologies. Pragmatism was in the air. Words are tools of power.

---

15. Greiner, "Australian Liberalism in a Post-Ideological Age."

THE QUEER POSTMODERNISTS: FOUCAULT AND BUTLER

We have now arrived near the conclusion of the genealogical side of this book. We are now able to see where postmodern queer gender theory came from. Gender theory came into being by a natural progression of ideas and stances that arise from following through on Immanuel Kant's "enlightened" attempt to purify sense and reason from faith and metaphysics. If I have walked you successfully along this path of conceptual development, you should now be able to see how intellectually persuasive the irrational and anti-factual stance that is queer postmodern gender theory actually is.

Gender theory is persuasive, that is, given what many of our best and brightest (or at least, most fashionably successful) thinkers have been trying to do since Immanuel Kant's *Critique of Pure Reason* was set loose on the world. And significantly, after the former intellectual aristocrat called "logical bivalence" has been banished and made academically homeless, our high culture cannot even make the obvious observations that gender theory is both false and mad. But allow me one brief observation here, presupposing the shameful analytical category of logical bivalence. If logical bivalence is not actually bunk, then *either* the Enlightenment project and Butler are right *or* Hamann and Kierkegaard are right. If this second position is correct, then Kant and gender theory are wrong.

I am getting ahead of the argument wherein I shall defend the claim that indeed there is no need to throw out the normal categories of bivalent logic and reasonable scientific and commonsense truth claims, hence we can still say that gender theory is wrong. But at present we are in the descriptive and preparatory part of that argument.

Now that we have arrived at the origins of the contemporary queer movement in the 1980s, and the origins of third-wave feminism in the 1990s, there is not actually that much to do. Given the purging of sense and reason from faith and metaphysics, followed by the death of God, the failure of positivism, the poetic and reality-non-intersecting nature of post-theological and post-metaphysical language, the instrumentalization of words, and the reduction of science and politics to power, Foucault and Butler will now appear as they really are: entirely mainstream and conventional scholars. Our wildly postmodern and queer irrealists, who deny that human sense and reason have any sort of truth-revealing powers, are ordinary members of the sophistic knowledge class that has taken over our institutions of higher learning.[16] We can now outline the basic contours of Foucault and Butler that will produce gender theory quite quickly.

We start, then, with Michel Foucault and the sociology and politics of deviance.

MICHEL FOUCAULT

Foucault's three volume[17] *History of Sexuality* (1976, 1984, 1984) is something of a Bible for contemporary queer theory. There are two central features of this trilogy. The first is the idea that in a different time and place (the homoerotic, pederastic, and *patria potestas* world of classical times) sexual desire was understood very differently to the way we now typically understand it. The second feature is the argument that bio-governance and a fixation with sexual identities in recent times is a new and novel way of controlling bodies and private sexual-behavior norms. These two narratives strongly "queer" the "natural" and "good" evaluation of the dominant sex and gender norms of the present. Recall, "queering" is a making strange of any taken-for-granted notion of right and wrong, or natural and deviant, in contemporary sex and gender norms. That Foucault himself very much idealized (and practiced)[18] the vision of sexual desire native to the pre-Christian homoerotic, pederastic, and privileged private power of

---

16. Josef Pieper warned us about this trend in 1950. See Pieper, *What Does "Academic" Mean?*

17. Three volumes were published in his lifetime, but a fourth volume was posthumously published from draft notes in 2018.

18. Johnson, "Michel Foucault: The Prophet of Pederasty" (n.p.): "Today, Foucault scholars and editors prefer to pass over his advocacy of pederasty in silence. It is striking that the volume of his *Essential Works* entitled *Ethics* includes many interviews, but not one he gave in 1978. There he argued that it was 'quite unacceptable' and an 'abuse' to assume 'that a child is incapable of explaining what happened and was incapable of giving his consent' to sex with an adult. It is a matter of public record, however, that Foucault signed a petition to the Assemblée Nationale in 1977 calling for the decriminalization of all 'consensual' sexual relations between adults and children. . . . Foucault was impressed by the fact that the Greeks 'never admitted love between two *adult men*. . . . [For them] love between two men is only valid in the form of classic pederasty.' He even told his biographer James Miller: 'Besides, to die for the love of boys: What could be more beautiful?' For Foucault, pederasty was the only truly romantic form of love." In 2021 former personal friend of Foucault Guy Sorman made credible public comments on French public TV describing Foucault's sexual encounters with Arab boys in Tunisia. See Sorman, "Was Michel Foucault a Pedophile?" (YouTube interview). See Guesmi, "Reckoning with Foucault's Alleged Sexual Abuse of Boys in Tunisia."

the male citizen is, unsurprisingly, the "perspective" tacitly underpinning the narrative of liberation and oppression that Foucault weaves. After Nietzsche, everything is perspectival, so there are no real moral truths about human sexuality; there are simply different narratives of social and culturally situated meaning that are creatively and performatively configured in all sorts of . . . interesting geometries. Out of this perspective, ironically, a new morality appears. This is the morality of affirming sex and gender deviance, and its counterpart, the shaming of sex and gender normativity as inherently oppressive.

You may have noticed that "pride" is now a central rainbow ideology trope. What "pride" now means is that individually determined deviance is good and exactly *not* shameful, and gender and sex conformism—when there is an expectation of public norm conformity—is bad and bigoted. Now this is not really a sociology of deviance stance, because sociology performs a positivist neutrality in its epistemic and methodological narratives, and is only really interested in locating how norms and their non-compliance (deviance) socially function. But here Foucault is tricky (who would have guessed?). "Power" is inextricable from any human context, so sociological knowledge itself is politically situated, so why not at least tacitly embrace the valuative claim that deviance is liberal and good while sexuality norms, as public and private governance structures, are authoritarian and bad?

Under the at least notional banner of social scientific "objectivity," and under the post-Freudian banner of a "purely" naturalistic understanding of all narratives of sexual desire, Foucault's own sexuality preferences and political interests are advanced through his work. And what he advances is that sexuality deviance is good and liberal, hence enlightened societies should valorize the deviant and shame the traditional conformists. In this way, the underlying political reform agenda—later identified as the queer reform agenda—in Foucault's *History of Sexuality* is that traditional male/female and reproductive-family–situated sex and gender norms in both public and private contexts—as upheld by contemporary bio-governance interests—must be cast aside in the name of freedom. In their place, gay liberation and Foucault's promotion of removing age of consent laws in France sets the direction of queer activism to come. Anti-discrimination legislation for homosexuals was introduced in many Western jurisdictions in the 1980s such that deviance from heterosexual norms was no longer criminalized and stigmatized in the workplace. But this was only the beginning. The contemporary queer movement is not a minority rights movement—as the GLB movement of the 1980s largely was—it is an over-throwing-of-sexuality-normativity-itself movement. More on that later.

JUDITH BUTLER

Judith Butler's *Gender Trouble: Feminism and the Subversion of Identity* hits the stands in 1990. It is important to note at the outset the strange tension that exists between Butler's "subversion of identity" and the "gender identity" legal rights and transgender political activism that has arisen out of her work. For in reality, Butler has no interest in any sort of essentialist understanding of identity at all. In contrast, the therapeutic model presupposed in "gender-affirming care" accepts that a trans child has a dissonance between the gender of their mind—which defines their *"true* identity"—and the sex of their body. Thus they have an authentic gender identity, defined by being born in the wrongly sexed body, hence the only reasonable treatment for gender dysphoria for trans children is to hormonally and medically transition their bodies so that their bodies are made to align with their inner and true gender identity.[19] But this is *not* how Butler understands the "trouble" that gender causes. For her, gender is performative, as is sex, as is identity, as are all meanings. To Butler, no one has an essential "true" self at all, let alone an identity where a transwoman is *really* female. There could be no more or less of an "identity" for a naturally sexed woman than there could be a female identity of a transwoman to Butler's formulation of identity-subverting feminism.

Intriguingly, a significant source of Butler's subversion of identity is John Austin's exploration of the performative utterance. This is consistent with the English deflationary and pragmatic approach to the meaning of language in twentieth-century English law.

As previously mentioned, A. V. Dicey's "black box" conception of the creation of English law sees law as a linguistic *making* of regulatory frameworks, legitimated by parliamentary procedures alone. This is in direct contrast to the more traditional legislative role where parliament and other ruling bodies *recognizes* the high horizons of moral meanings and deep customary categories of natural justice. The older model assumes the reality of transcendent metaphysical and theological categories of Justice and the Common Good, which good laws—written or conventionally assumed—partially express. Here, words participated in qualitative and transcendent

19. See Barnes, *Time to Think*.

realities, so human authorities were not simply at liberty to construct the meaning of justice and goodness however they determined. In contrast, the new approach simply makes law up as an entirely human linguistic construct, and there are *no innate or transcendent limits* on what laws should or can regulate. In the older model words not only described matters of factual reality but could partially signal real qualitative states and high transcendent meanings that overshadowed humanity. In the new model words were systems of self-referential definitions following grammatical rules that *generate* properly governed order. Dicey's reforms are part of the secularizing progressive push that starts up in earnest in the latter half of the nineteenth century among English elites. In English philosophy, a deflationary and pragmatic linguistic trend very much continuous with Dicey's conception of the procedural relations of parliament to public opinion and law flowered in the early twentieth century, strongly influencing the linguistic and analytic British philosopher J. L. Austin.

Austin is more complex and nuanced than Butler about whether performative utterances are a specific type of speech act, or whether all speech and meaningful acts are in the final analysis performative tools of linguistic projection unrelated to anything one might call truth about the real world.[20] In this regard Butler is a more consistent deflationary linguistic rhetorician than is Austin. But it is clear that to Butler words only refer to linguistic constructions, and all meanings are linguistic constructions, and the meaning of all human expressions are performative.

By making all human meaning creative yet entirely linguistically cocooned performances, she *de-naturalizes* both sex and gender, rendering them both *creative acts* rather than natural facts. This really is identity-subverting. Not only that, it severs language from truth and subverts facts and logic, right and wrong, and meaning and communicable intelligibility itself. It is hard-core absurdism with our Judith! But this explains the strange phenomena of males claiming to be *real* women, and also claiming that actual real women (XX chromosome sex-gene humans) do not exist, because "actual real women" are no more "real" woman than a male performing a female gender identity. For *it is only the performance of a claim that makes it meaningful*, hence there is no natural reality that any linguistic claim actually represents. So not only are all identities performative poetry that are simply uttered and required to be accepted, and hence performative of "real" gender identity, but no real natural objective meaning to the

---

20. See Austin, *How to Do Things with Words*.

word "woman" can be accepted as meaningful. Hence, made up and simply performed gender is real (and one must play along with the performance) and objective sex does not exist (and all sex-based rights must be outlawed). Welcome to gender theory!

With *Gender Trouble* Butler sets out to transform feminism; to de-naturalize it, to make the category of "female" non-exclusionary, to dispense with any sex-linked notion of gender, and to embrace the queer opposition to all and every commonly assumed category of sex-realism and gender normativity. This is called third-wave feminism because, unlike second-wave and radical feminisms, it removes the female sexed body from being the defining distinctive of what a woman is. If feminism is not defined by the needs and struggles of sex-defined females, then what is it? This is the question gender-critical feminism asks of third-wave feminism, without receiving a persuasive answer.[21]

POSTMODERNISM AND THE ENLIGHTENMENT PROJECT

Postmodernism is the logical outworking of the Enlightenment project. And the disturbing reality is that purging reason and science of faith and metaphysics has proven to be a failed project, one that results in the disappearance of valid reasoning and scientific truth. How do we evaluate this failure? Is this failure, after all, the "truth" of the matter? That is, is the absurdist rejection of any genuine relationship between intelligible meaning and reality actually how things are, and hence logic and science are just convenient and power-enabling fictions? Or is it the Enlightenment purity project itself that is misconceived?

If our sophistic and performative academics are right, then gender theory cannot be wrong—though gender theory cannot be right either, as nothing is right or wrong, and all human meaning is just performatively made up. But if the Enlightenment purity project is itself wrong, then its failure points us to other approaches that may yet allow us to have reality-connected natural and logically bivalent meanings. If that is the case, then it may yet be possible to show that gender theory is wrong.

But there are reasons other than simply intellectual ones why gender theory has been able to lodge in the structures of law, the state, and corporate and institutional power. We should look at those reasons too.

21. See Lawford-Smith, *Gender-Critical Feminism*.

8

Gender Theory Makes Sense to Our Knowledge Elites and to Our Lifeworld

MANY PEOPLE WHO FIND gender theory persuasive (even if they do not really believe it is true) and morally important are highly educated and intelligent professionals who are leaders in our society and integral members of our knowledge and ruling classes. Thinking of such people as ignorant and deluded, as if they are willfully defying obvious truth and respected authorities, is not going to achieve anything, because they *are* our knowledge and power authorities. Indeed, it is possible that they are only able to believe gender theory *because* they are highly educated and very intelligent people in positions of status and authority.

As counterintuitive as it may seem to modernists seeking to uphold science and reason, it is the Age of Reason itself that has brought gender theory into being. People who are deeply formed by their Enlightenment-framed education are often able to follow the tortuous linguistic movements of gender-theory reasoning, and cannot fault it. Less educated people cannot readily follow it, but—should circumstances arise where they are put in conflict with Diversity, Equity, and Inclusion (DEI) ideology—they find it to be both false and mad. Then again, people who are both reasonably educated and comfortable with our contemporary lifeworld will usually just go along with institutionally and legally mandated DEI expectations, even if they think it is a bizarre fad, because it is too much trouble to fight. At the level of fashionable virtue signaling, DEI also looks like it is compatible with a "you be you" sexual liberalism. It is only when gender-identity demands directly confront one's sense of appropriate norms, common sense, scientific knowledge, and safety that normal people push back. But any sort of pushback is now in serious tension with legal authority and mandated workplace regulations in many contexts. Such contexts will increasingly occur as DEI's anti sex-realist reformation of gender norms has increasing impact on ordinary people's lives. The clash between respected authority and systematically marginalized sex-realist pushback is well illustrated in the Australian legal case known as Tickle v. Giggle.

SAL GROVER AND JUSTICE ROBERT BROMWICH

Sal Grover is an Australian. In the early years of this century, and as an attractive young woman, she was a hopeful screenwriter in Hollywood. During her time there she had some terrible encounters with powerful men seeking to sexually exploit her youth and opportunity vulnerabilities. The #MeToo movement inspired Sal Grover to set up a women's-only app, which Grover called "Giggle for Girls." She found that biological males routinely and in no small number sought to access her app from its trial period on. Evidently, some males simply refuse to tolerate female-only spaces. So Grover put filtering mechanisms in place and refused to let males onto the app.

Grover is an intelligent and entrepreneurial woman, comfortably at ease in our liberal, secular, and Enlightenment-framed lifeworld, but her experiences of needing female-only safe spaces made it impossible for her to just fit in with the legal and institutional ascendance of DEI. When the transwoman Roxanne Tickle claimed to be gender-identity discriminated against because Grover refused to give that individual access to the app, Grover found herself in the Federal Court of Australia. As I write (early 2025) Grover has been successfully prosecuted in the Federal Court for indirect gender-identity discrimination. Grover lost her case to Tickle, but the matter is now under appeal both by Grover and—not satisfied with the amount of compensation Grover was required to pay—Tickle.

This case bears some examination as it illustrates just how much our knowledge and power elites have bought into gender theory.

As regards its first appearance in the Australian Federal Court, Justice Bromwich found that anyone who considers "sex to mean the sex of a person at birth, and that this is unchangeable" performs a decisive legal "fail." Justice

Bromwich ruled that unchangeable biological sex-realism "conflicts with a long history of cases decided by courts going back over 30 years. Those cases establish that, *on its ordinary meaning*, sex is changeable."[1]

Accepting that legal definitions are not defined by anything other than legal definitions, and that such definitions have absolute authority when it comes to making legal judgments, this judge has no real choice in making his observation that regardless of millennia-long assumptions and any commonsense or traditional scientific understanding of natural reality, over the past thirty years, the birth sex of a person has now *become* changeable. For, as a matter of Australian law, one's "assigned sex" indeed now can be changed by legally changing one's birth certificate in order to make the certificate align with one's gender identity. The linguistic constructivism and natural-reality disdain assumed by Justice Bromwich's ruling is striking and disturbing. Yet, after the 2013 amendment to the Australian Sex Discrimination Act (1984), there is now no biological definition of sex available in Australian law. Thus, as night follows day, because gender identity alone defines legal "sex assignment," and "sex assignment" is now defined in law as an entirely subjective and performative category, if a person identifies as female and performs broadly culturally accepted behaviors and appearances that can be argued to be compatible with how "female" is broadly performed, then in Australian law, a born male indeed can *become* female.

In the summary of his ruling Justice Bromwich seems to go further than legal linguistic purity, as he seems to be asserting that because progressive, intelligent, and informed people—such as himself—may really believe that sex is now changeable, it follows that objective biological conceptions of the natural sex binary are now dated and, for all intents and purposes, false. Hence, "on its ordinary meaning, sex is changeable." Without any apparent storm or stress, Justice Bromwich expresses a legally formalist, entirely performative, and culturally constructed conception of what sex "really" is. This notion of "reality" here is strikingly irrealist. And it seems that irrealism is now treated as unproblematic and mainstream by our legal and knowledge class.

IRREALISM

I have used the term "irrealism" a few times in this book thus far but without spelling out its philosophical meaning.

---

1. Bromwich, "Federal Court of Australia. Tickle v Giggle," 3; emphasis added.

In the philosophy of science, the term "anti-realist" was invented to distinguish modern "realism"—meaning any positivist attempt to give us an objectively true and scientifically demonstrable knowledge of material reality—from its phenomenological alternative. An "anti-realist" philosophy of science accepts skeptical empiricist solipsism such that we only know our own individual human sensorium and any claim to know reality itself is empirically indemonstrable speculation. Following the lead of Hume and Kant, most anti-realists maintain that science and logic are pragmatically "real enough," even if they are not a true knowledge of reality itself. Thus "anti-realism" and "realism" in the modern philosophy of science are definitionally tied to each other, and often don't look that different to each other in practice. They are dialectically dependent terms. Even so, modern realists claim to know reality as it really is via scientific and logical means, whereas anti-realists claim to only know the world of phenomena. Irrealism, on the other hand, is a rejection of the realist/anti-realist dyad.

Even though we have already seen a Canadian scholar of medieval thought use the term "irrealism" to describe Peter Abelard's twelfth-century nominalism, in the recent philosophy of knowledge it is the very modern twentieth-century thinker Nelson Goodman who most clearly articulated the notion of irrealism, back in the 1970s.[2] To Goodman, the idea that there are different types of descriptions of reality—be it positivist or phenomenological—is wrongheaded. It is more appropriate to say that there are different worlds opened up to our minds by different creative processes of linguistic "description." A positivist approach is one way of describing—or better, creating—a meaningful world, a phenomenologist's approach is another world creation. One world is not right and the other world wrong in relation to actual reality. There is no relation to actual reality outside of our always contextually situated and linguistically constructed worlds, so the situation we find ourselves in is that there are many worlds that often overlap in some places, and that are incommensurate in other places. This is irrealism.

Our educated elites in our knowledge class have gradually, perhaps imperceptibly, come to accept an irrealist outlook on reality and meaning. As we have explored, there are complex and persuasive reasons why irrealism has won in our intellectual high culture, even if those reasons may actually be wrong, and even if there might still actually be a real world out there that our commonsense words and scientific knowledge partially

2. See Goodman, *Ways of Worldmaking*.

understands and communicates. But the success of gender theory is not simply a function of powerful trajectories in academic circles. This success is also a function of what sociologists call our lifeworld. This is the domain of the "ordinary meaning" of "sex" that Justice Bromwich, perhaps, is referring to. To be more specific, it is our liberal consumer lifeworld that *practically reinforces* that intellectual vision of irrealist pluralism and that has recently outlawed sex-realism as obsolete. It is the way in which we now get to market, to technologically build, to creatively construct, and to socially perform our own "identities" however we see fit that makes the idea of fixed natural meanings obsolete.

THE CONSUMER LIFEWORLD AND GENDER THEORY

The social reality in which we live,[3] which European thinkers from the time of Edmund Husserl (1852–1938) have called our *Lebenswelt* (lifeworld), is not a set of abstract ideas; it is the socially assumed and reflexive world of common experiences and common expectations. These lifeworlds have developed over many generations in different societies, and they are continuously, but usually gradually, changing in their details. The rate of change in our broadly Western lifeworld since the Industrial Revolution has been unusually fast due in part to the unprecedented speed and impact of developments in science and technology. Manufacturing, warfare, information technology, finances, and mass-society management and manipulation technologies have reconfigured the social and cultural worlds in which we live in rapid and deep-reaching ways.[4] We can now often see dramatic lifeworld changes within a matter of decades. For example, the normal social environment of teenagers when I was one in the early 1980s did not have mobile phones or the internet, and this makes the social lifeworld for young people in which I grew up very different to the social lifeworld of my teenage daughter today.

The most basic reason why gender theory seems reasonable and moral to many people today has nothing directly to do with theory, but it relates to the very individualistic, constructivist, and ever fluid practices of self-construction that define the lifeworld that we now live within. This is the lifeworld of liberal, technological, and secular consumerism.

3. See Berger and Luckmann, *Social Construction of Reality*.
4. See Virilio, *Great Accelerator*. The rate of human technological impact on the natural world has also radically accelerated since 1945. See McNeill and Engelke, *Great Acceleration*.

Within this lifeworld we take it as given that people can be whoever they want to be, and do whatever they want to do. This is not because we in fact *can* be whoever we want to be or do whatever we want to do, but the cultural power of marketing, advertising, and individually tailored algorithmic consumer targeting, coupled with increasingly atomized individualism and the fragmentation of familial relationships, now reaches into every aspect of our waking lives. This consumer lifeworld is most centrally defined by the way in which it appeals to and feeds each individual's monetizable desires and fantasies (and fears and anxieties).

If you can pay for it, you can have it. In our post-Christian and morally relativist lifeworld, there is no right or wrong about what you as a consumer want. If you want to be or project yourself as a certain sort of person, there are willing providers of products and experiences that you can pay for, and you can *become* that person. That actually being anyone at all is now understood to be a constructed and performative theatre rather than any identity comprised of a real set of essential meanings, sacred responsibilities, natural realities, or ultimate obligations, is beside the point. And, of course, we now have astonishing appearance-enhancing and re-making technologies. The health and wellbeing industry is enormous and highly lucrative, as people are often self-conscious about their appearance and unhappy with their bodies. Now that we live in a flatly materialist and hyper-sexualized culture, body image is more important to us than ever before. So there is always a pill, a product, a program, a surgery you can buy that will help you re-make your appearance so that you can feel good about yourself. We have largely been socially conditioned to assume that we are self-creators when it comes to our bodies, our sexuality, and our physical appearances. We are heavily collectively formed to presuppose that "self-actualization" in whatever manner we choose, as an expression of ownership and control of our bodies, is our birthright.

It is consistently apparent that most gender-critical feminists and other liberal critics of the DEI movement make a point of saying that transmen and transwomen can express whatever identity through their bodies they like. Far be it for any modern liberal person to say that simply because they are male, they should not undergo trans-gender hormonal and surgical interventions. But the DEI movement is not liberal in return. For trans-rights activists actually wish to displace *real* women via their linguistic identity games, and they wish to pretend that there is no *real* difference between a male performing a female gender identity, and a *real* woman.

And indeed, the notion of a totally liberal identity world is not achievable, and this is not even how classical liberalism works. To Locke and Mill, objective facts govern the public domain, and here everyone respects demonstrable truth, and everyone accepts the principle of "do no harm," but in private domains and in the domain of morals and religious beliefs, you can expect that no one can force you to comply with their beliefs and values. Classical liberalism would hold that you can perform whatever gender identity you like and have whatever sexual morality you like, in the private domain, and in the domain of freely given consent. But in the public domain it is the facts of sex that determine who in objective reality is a man, and who in objective reality is a woman. So in fact, classical liberalism would not support any state-backed mandate for transwomen to enter female-only spaces, or for others to be required to address them with feminine pronouns.

What this shows is that even with people who have a deep and critical theoretical understanding of gender theory, the irrealist lifeworld assumption of something like an individual right to construct one's own identities however one chooses, and to self-actualize the performance of one's own identity however one desires, is still assumed. But actually, if you are not prepared to allow that people who are males can unproblematically expect everyone to treat them as if they are really females, then you are not upholding self-constructing irrealism as some sort of a right as regards one's gender identity.

Any serious critique of the contemporary notion of gender identity can only be modern and liberal if it is not postmodern and irrealist about the public facts of a person's sex. Modern liberalism presupposes that we can publicly agree about facts, even if we personally have different moral, religious, and private understandings of the meaning of public facts. In contrast, postmodern irrealism does *not* allow that you are entitled to believe whatever you like about your and other people's personal gender identity. You are not allowed to have, for example, the gender identity of believing that you are a real woman because your sex is objectively female. This is because postmodern irrealism is neither modern nor liberal. The liberal sex-realist—in order to be a modern liberal and a sex-realist—must maintain that there is something seriously wrong with people who expect other people to treat their obvious identity fiction as objectively true. The liberal sex-realist must require that people should not be compelled to performatively go along with opposite-sex pronouns and opposite-sex stereotyped gender-identity performances, as if those words and appearances are real. To the modern sex-realist, no one should expect a personal fantasy to be treated like a public reality. Postmodern irrealism is not liberal; it is patronizing, dishonest, and truth-compromising.

Lifeworlds, as we experience them in our lived reality, are not firstly theoretical structures; they are structures of *practice*. However, no practice is finally discrete from theory (or the other way around) because as language users we are meaning-defined beings. The connections between ideas and practices in any given lifeworld are intimate. So let us briefly explore that manner in which the modern consumer lifeworld remains deeply theoretically situated.

Now, I would much rather we had classical liberalism than the current compelled speech and state-mandated public compliance with sex-denying fantasies, but the fact is, there are reasons why contemporary neoliberalism is not classical liberalism. And those reasons are also tied up with the Enlightenment purity project that has produced gender theory.

A "PURIFIED" LIBERALISM DEFINES THE LIFEWORLD IN WHICH GENDER THEORY APPEARS

Back in the seventeenth century, John Locke inverted the meaning of some important terms. Observable and quantifiable physical attributes—size, shape, number, and so forth—became the "qualities" of real objects in the world, even though what he is actually talking about are measurable and quantifiable sensibilia. So qualities are thus quantified. This is important for the new mathematico-experimental learning we now call modern science, which is all about gaining power over nature through quantified and mechanistically determinate knowledge, in the service of human utility. When it comes to *qualitative* qualities—goodness, justice, beauty, and so forth—these are no longer thought of by Locke as the real attributes of beings; these are now human subjective and interpretive opinions. So "qualities" under Locke become objective features of reality (and he is actually referring to the merely quantitative facticity of physical objects), and the traditional understanding of qualitative qualities (which we may only ever partially correctly know) become subjective opinions that do not in fact exist in a now purely quantitative conception of objective reality.

Making "quality" refer to qualitatively meaningless objects of sensible experience and subjectivizing and privatizing qualitative meaning as opinion or belief are the key conceptual preconditions for modern liberalism.

For the liberal social arrangement is that people can agree about scientifically demonstrable matters of objective fact even if they cannot agree about what reality qualitatively means. We stick with a quantitative and demonstrable notion of the objective world—including categories of physical harm that everyone can agree on—and we allow people to believe whatever they like about the meaning and value of reality, for such beliefs are subjective opinions, not factual truths.

I am simplifying things here. Locke recognizes that a range of commonly held, qualitative, and public *beliefs and values* are required to make any society workable in practice. So while the Bill of Rights of 1688 gives a range of Englishmen religious liberty to not have to be Anglican, this liberty does not apply to Catholics. Disagreeing about religion as a matter of private and subjective belief/opinion only goes so far. Even so, modern liberalism presupposes a neat conceptual separation between, on the one hand, objective facts and objective categories of physical harms which are defining of good order in the public domain, and, on the other hand, subjective beliefs, opinions, and values, regarding which the public domain has no right to direct or interfere, for they define the sacred freedoms of the individual and private domain.

While private and natural domains were largely outside of civil law and public state control in the West prior to Locke, those domains have never been discretely "free," for religious, customary, and natural and metaphysical moral claims have usually governed people's lives in every aspect of their lives, whether there is a civic and state-controlled reach into people's private lives or not. Which is to say that while the qualitative has not been under legislative and state-controlled authority, this does not mean the qualitative has been a discretely subjective and individual domain without governance, as there were other governing authorities than the state and civil law that were significant in the "private" domain in Locke's day.

I am trying to outline to you the manner in which the modern liberal conception of a completely sacrosanct, self-governed sphere of private freedoms that is the domain of opinions, beliefs, and of all qualitative, metaphysical, and moral commitments, is a new idea. Equally, the notion of a discretely public-objective, state-governed sphere of order and control that is firmly demarcated from a discretely private-subjective, individually governed sphere of freedom is a distinctive feature of modern liberalism. But it's more complex than any actual tight demarcation really allows.

There are two complications. Firstly, there is no domain of human value, belief, or meaning that is purely individually constructed and self-governed. No one has a meaningful and valuable life by simply making up whatever values and meanings they choose for themselves. Language, meaning, beliefs, and values pre-exist the individual, and the individual is embedded in such extra-individual gifts of meaning and quality whenever he or she chooses to believe and value anything. Secondly, modern liberalism only worked because there were other functional governing structures in the domain of value and meaning, structures other than the individual and the state, which enabled liberalism to work. This second complicating feature requires further unpacking.

When Locke was inventing modern liberalism the world he lived in relied on deeply religious tacit meanings and deeply embedded customary manners, relationships, and authority networks. These are what sociologist call middle-order human institutions: extended family, local community, parish, and so forth. In our context, the bottom level of social organization is the individual life, and the top order is the state. Middle orders are human and organic; high orders are impersonal and bureaucratic. Middle-order social institutions used to deeply govern people's private lives and situate their personal life in a context of intrinsic and transcendent meaning and purpose. But what we have seen over the past four centuries is that—among other things—the ideology of "please yourself" liberalism has eroded middle-order social institutions such that, by the late twentieth century, it was only really the state and the individual that were left. In this context the personal "freedom" of the atomic individual ends up being governed by marketing forces that surreptitiously tap into people's sense of entitlement to choose whatever they want, if they have the money to buy it. So we end up with banal hedonic and material desire and fear governing our personal sense of value, meaning, and belief choices, and increasingly invasive and regulating state power governing our public actions.

Sociologists like Émile Durkheim have studied the difference between customary religious societies (such as traditional Australian Aboriginals) and modern secular societies (such as France in the early twentieth century) and made some interesting comparisons.[5] Durkheim found that modern secular and liberal societies are set up to give people maximum individual freedom, whereas traditional religious societies are set up to give people maximum collective meaning. But when individual

---

5. Durkheim, *Elementary Forms of Religious Life*.

meaning-creation becomes atomized and personally constructed, the broader culture of meaning in which individuals are situated tends strongly toward nihilism and anomie. Anomie is the breakdown of customary norms and moral conventions as individuals define their own goods in atomistic and self-centered ways. Ironically, a society that is set up for individual freedom kills society if it works too well at delivering the personal-freedom objective. And ironically, the breakdown of organic (i.e., family) and middle-order (parish, local sporting club, etc.) social institutions and authorities results in the state gaining ever deepening controlling power over individuals in order to keep social order functional.

When it comes to secularized liberalism after the great de-Christianizing century (1870–1970) transcendent horizons are increasingly flattened out of norms and public meanings, giving us what Charles Taylor calls a "secular age" where meaning is only situated within an immanent and ultimately entirely poetic frame.[6] Hedonism takes on something of a religious significance, but leads to sordid despair when over-extended, and material comfort, status, safety, and wealth-accumulation become the only meaning of life games in town, with relationships increasingly built around autonomy, career, and the pursuit of "self-actualization." Sociologists point out that what we are now seeing is the eroding of kinship structures and the loss of middle-order social institutions, and individuals are "atomized" so that they are easy for impersonal mass-media integrated commercial and governmental powers to control.[7] Throw in the algorithmic formation of our young people who have grown up with 24/7 internet connectivity via their smartphones, and you have our profoundly nihilistic and anomic life-world. No wonder there is a mental health crisis for our youth.[8]

The long and short of all this is that the neoliberal lifeworld in which we now live trades under false pretenses on classical liberal ideas that are integral with early modern categories of scientific objectivity and personal freedom. The fact is, those early classical liberal formulations were not half so serious as we are about personal freedom from middle-order meaning authorities and from kinship structures of mutual responsibility. For middle-order institutions and authoritative meaning-frameworks were still very strong in Locke's time. It is true that Hobbesian state tyranny, and the state as sole appropriator of violent power, has always been a stream

---

6. Taylor, *Secular Age*.
7. Bauman, *Liquid Modernity*.
8. Haidt, *Anxious Generation*.

within liberalism. In our day we have the ever-expanding power of the state (in league with the corporation) which together with consumerism and secularism have pretty well put middle-order authorities and institutions to the guillotine. Strangely, even though we are more manipulated at an individual level and more and more invasively regulated at a state level than at any other time in human history, we still have serious lifeworld buy-in to the notion that consumer freedom is giving us the life we want. We do not see how controlled our personal choices and freedoms are by brilliant manipulative strategists playing on our atomized and imminently framed desires and fears. Equally, the erosion of high meaning has left us in an increasingly irrealist and pragmatic culture. Gender theory is very much a part of the lifeworld we live in, and—as far as the norms and assumptions of our lifeworld go—we have no real way of showing why it is mad and not at all liberating if you happen to be a woman wanting sex-based rights.

GENDER THEORY WORKS, BUT IS IT STILL WRONG?

At this point in the book it should now be clear to you, dear reader, why gender theory works. It is deeply integral with the progressive trajectories of Western intellectual culture from the Enlightenment to postmodernity, it is integral with the formalistic and irrealist trends in the meaning of words as it impacts both law and our governing, judging, and educating institutions, and it is integral with our neoliberal and post-Christian consumer lifeworld. What chance, then, do the protection and restoration of sex-based rights for women have? What chance does the protection of minors from an aggressively evangelizing sterilization and genital-mutilation cult, protected and promoted by the state and the academy, have? For gender theory has the law, the state, the academy, the healthcare professions, and public institutions firmly in its controlling grip, and there seems to be no meaningful pushback from religious or scientific institutions.

Something can "work" and still be wrong. This is not a tricky observation. In any context where we experience a denial of natural justice or the propagation of a damaging lie due to the pragmatic power of the unscrupulous simply overriding what is good and true, we will all refuse to conflate pragmatic effectiveness with moral validity and factual truth. This is the actual moral and intellectual reality of the human experience. This is why the perpetration of what is immoral and false requires theoretical justification and concerted strategic promotion to "work."

At present, gender theory has—by means of enchanting sophistry and strategic brilliance—enormous legal and strategic cultural force behind it in its ambition to destroy heteronormativity and all sex-realist categories and norms. The present ascendent might of gender theory does not, however, make it right. Indeed, its ascendance highlights that something has gone drastically wrong with the Enlightenment project. For while that project set out to shine the truth of science and reason onto the world in the cause of liberation from ignorance and the promotion of rational humanity over irrational prejudice, it ends up justifying its opposite. While gender theory has—as this book has outlined—an impeccable Enlightenment-grounded genealogy, it denies scientific truth and promotes irrational fantasy over natural reality.

If gender theory is wrong, this cannot be shown if one assumes that the Enlightenment purity project is obviously good, right, and correct. And the Enlightenment genealogy of gender theory is impeccable. A perspective outside of the powerful currents of post-Kantian thinking is necessary to show where gender theory fails. That is why it has been so important to show how solidly mainstream gender theory actually is in relation to post-Kantian developments in Western philosophy, power, and culture. But as gender theory really does fail—it opposes scientific truth and it opposes all cultural and socially normative expressions of the natural realities of male and female sexual difference—we now have excellent reason to be suspicious of the Kantian Enlightenment purity project. For the fact is, gender theory shows us just how seriously the Enlightenment project has gone off its rails.

Gender theory is symptomatic of a *failed* Enlightenment. Pursuing a *redeemed* Enlightenment will lead us out of the intellectual and moral quagmire that is gender theory.

We move on then to the challenge of not only showing that gender theory is wrong, but identifying how its failures are tied to a failed Enlightenment purity project, and offering some indication of how we can now pursue a redeemed Enlightenment project. For we now urgently need to recover science as truth-revealing and reason as concerned not with deflationary and formal linguistic logic, but as connected to real qualitative truths of value and meaning that stand *above* the partial and poetic construction of human language. Sophists like Judith Butler force us back to first principles, and the recovery of meaningful first principles is going to be the only way out of the impossible conundrums of the officially backed fanatical irrealism of gender theory.

Why Gender Theory Is Wrong

THE NUB OF THE case against gender theory I am putting forward in this book is as follows.

The central *aims* of the Enlightenment project are to use science to liberate us from ignorance, and reason to liberate us from irrational and inhumane prejudice. These are wonderful aims that I think all modern Western people of good will should support. I certainly support these aims.

The *method* of the Kantian trajectory of the Enlightenment project is to bracket faith out from science and to bracket metaphysics out from reason. This method has proven to be a disaster that wrecks the Enlightenment project, such that the gender theory progeny of Kant's bracketings ends up promoting irrealist anti-science and irrational and deviance-affirming fantasy. Gender theory sets itself firmly against any sort of commonsense social gender norms grounded in natural reason, and against the broad dimorphisms of the natural reproductive sex binary. Is this where the Age of Reason takes us?

Bracketing faith and metaphysics out of science and reason produces gender theory. Hence, the underlying cause of the present success of gender theory is the mistaken methodology of the Enlightenment. Hence, revisiting and rebooting Enlightenment thinking, without its methodological mistakes, is what a genuine solution to the problem of gender theory really requires.

But was the Enlightenment methodology really a mistake?

I am going to unashamedly trust in the realism of commonsense bivalent logic and answer this question. *Either* this methodological bracketing of faith and metaphysics out of science and reason was a mistake *or* there really is no meaning to reality and the Enlightenment project in its entirety was delusional. Fortunately, this sort of syllogistic either/or is straightforward to solve. "There is no meaning to reality" is a negative assertion about *the meaning of reality*, which is self-defeating, hence, methodologically bracketing faith and metaphysics out from science and reason must have been a mistake. This is syllogistically valid, but is it also substantively true? There are reasonable experiential grounds underpinning commonsense sex-realist normative *beliefs* to hold that this syllogism is also substantively true.

Gender theory denies commonsense and normative conceptions of the natural realities of the human reproductive sexual binary, and hence denies the distinctive vulnerabilities of women and children to fetishizing and sexually predatory males under an imposed DEI gender-norm anarchy. Gender theory, in explicitly opposing heteronormativity, denies the need for natural-sex-linked gender norms at all. But should gender theory succeed in overturning sex-realism and eroding commonly accepted gender norms premised on the natural male/female sex binary, this cannot fail to negatively impact on the public safety of women and children and the social viability of the heterosexual reproductive family. Both of those outcomes would be destructive of the natural conditions of human reproduction and socialization. This would be unnatural, anti-humanist, and hence inherently bad.

An applied gender theory cultural revolution could only be "good" if one believes that sex-based gender norms are inherently oppressive, and if one desires to radically shrink the human population and undermine the reproductive family, presumably to be largely replaced by technology and state-run or privately run institutions. But there are two problems with this. Firstly, while it may be "good" for sex-and-gender-deviant minorities if all commonly accepted sex-based gender norms were destroyed, this would not be experienced as qualitatively or practically good for the large majority of people, and particularly for vulnerable women and children, who rely on natural-sex-based norms for their sense of sexual safety and human dignity. In a liberal democratic context, the non-conformist minority should not impose its norms on the majority. Secondly, both of these queer "moral" aims are in inherent opposition to any sort of moral realist stance where substantive goods cannot be reduced to interest preferences. The theoretical rejection of moral realism only arises because the bracketing of faith and metaphysics from science and reason is assumed to be valid, but in practice, moral realism is still assumed in our life-in-common actual experience of reality. In day-to-day interpersonal reality, qualitative and inherent moral truths remain valid no matter what non-essentialist morality-is-merely-a-power-and-interest-preference stance is pasted over the top of immoral self-interest.

In the next three chapters, we shall unpack various aspects of the above line of reasoning.

9

Gender Theory Is Wrong: Practical Arguments

THE HEART OF THE case against gender theory that I wish to put forward is that this ideological sex-irrealism is symptomatic of the methodologically induced failure of the Enlightenment project. The aims of that project—to advance human flourishing by means of better scientific knowledge and a high vision of humanizing reason—are aims I support. However, key methodological moves subverted those aims from within. It is the recovering of the good and valid aspects of the Enlightenment project, without its faulty methodology, that will most effectively counter gender theory (and save science and reason) and that will halt the reforming sex-irrealism that gender theory is now strategically and ideologically imposing on us all. But there are less "big picture" arguments that can be made as to why gender theory is wrong, which we shall now proceed to.

POSTMODERN IRREALISM CANNOT COHERENTLY DISALLOW SEX-REALISM

There are a number of ways in which gender theory hoists itself with its own petard.[1] One of the most obvious is that if all gender-identities are sex-

---

1. This is a Shakespearean turn of phrase—when Hamlet disposes by trickery his two school fellows who were the servants of the king on an errand to dispose of Hamlet—meaning to get blown up with one's own bomb.

irrealist performative constructs, and determined only by each individual's subjective sense, then why can one not have a sex-realist gender identity? That is, by gender theory's own logic, it is not consistently constructivist, but smuggles in unjustifiable absolutist and seemingly moral realist objections to sex-realism.

In gender theory, sex and gender must be co-constructed linguistic and performative cultural artifacts. Here, the meaning of our words is not real as reality has no meaning, only our words have meanings. Here meaning is an entirely linguistic construct; meaning is not a function of objective qualitative and formal essences in reality, but it is simply a useful artifice of social power relations and a means whereby we can undertake collectively useful enterprises. Morality itself—according to gender theory—is not a function of natural or divine moral truths, but it is entirely socially, politically, and legally constructed. And yet, it seems, sex-realism and any sex-linked public gender norm must be outlawed. Why? If all human speech acts are equally poetic and performative meaning-creations, then why is the meaning-creation of sex-realism wrong? And make no mistake, virtue and vice categories are *integral* with DEI political activism. Because of the virtues of DEI, sex-realism must be redescribed as *both* cis gender identity (which is not sex-realist at all) *and* as inherently immoral, as it excludes transmen and transwomen from the categories or real women and real men.

There are two problems here. Firstly, if exclusion itself is the core moral issue here, then gender theory should not *exclude* sex-realists. Secondly, how can exclusion be a *moral* problem if this is a morally *irrealist* stance? Which is to say, that to gender theory there are *no moral truths*, so the discourse of Diversity, Inclusion, and Equity is not *actually* a *moral* discourse; it is simply *a tool of power*. And it only uses moral categories because people who are *not* irrealists about moral truth can be made to feel moral guilt if moral language is deployed to advance the DEI reform agenda.

So here is the problem. I refuse to accept that I have a gender identity of a cis man. The imposed categorization of myself as a "cis man" denies my own understanding of who I am, and I do not identify as a person whose "assigned sex" just happens to align with my gender identity of being a "man." Gender identity is meant to be defined by each individual alone. Yet, it seems that I am not permitted to define my gender identity as a sex-realist man, as a man who is a man because I am biologically male. As far as I am concerned, whatever my sexual orientation may or may not be, whatever social gender-expectation non-conformism I may or may not exemplify, whatever fetishes or fantasy I may or may not entertain, *I am in fact a man because I am a biological male.* This is what a sex-realist man believes about his own "gender identity." On what grounds could gender theory deny me the right to believe in my own natural sex-defined gender identity? Am I not being illegally misgendered if anyone asserts that my real gender identity is that of a cis man? And even though the large majority of human males are sex-realist men in their own conception of their own gender, that majority is required by gender theory to renounce their sex-defined gender identity and accept that they are really cis men, whose actual biological sex is only an assignment, and has *nothing intrinsic* to do with their gender identity. The fact is, most men don't believe that they have an assigned male sex; they believe that they really are male, because of their sexual biology, and this makes them a man. But gender theory cannot allow people to believe they have a sex-realist gender identity, because—impossibly—sex-realism must be false! I say impossibly here because gender theory's irrealism makes it impossible to claim *any* gender identity is, in reality, false.

Gender theory is incoherent, is anti-liberal, and disingenuously and manipulatively uses moral realist language to advance its moral irrealist ideological objectives in practice. On what grounds could it be reasonable, moral, and even inclusive to accept that all people who gender identify as sex-realist men and woman are wrong about their own sense of their own gender identity?

And if you are a sex-realist because you believe God created humans in his image as males and females, gender theory entirely opposes your religious freedom to believe that there really actually are essential and qualitative meanings in creation. So much for liberalism and toleration! DEI—which is the genitive form of the Latin word "God"—does not permit the religious person to believe that there really is a created meaning to their own embodied sex. *Religious freedom is revoked* and a traditional orthodox Christian is no longer permitted to believe in their own religiously defined sex-realist gender identity. But again, an irrealist cannot coherently say that a religious sex-realist is *wrong* about their sense of gender identity. To a "real" irrealist, the religious sex-realist gender identity is *just as valid* as any other subjective and constructed gender identity. Once again, gender theory seems less irrealist than it claims, and only gives gender-identity recognition to the set of gender identities it deems to be "correct" possibilities, because irrealism is the *real* truth about reality (which is not proper irrealism at all).

Gender theory shoots its own theory in the head when it comes to how not irrealist and how not inclusive it is in practice. Gender theory is simply a convenient linguistic construct—a marketing tool—that does not make sense and that has no moral authority. Gender theory is, in actual usage, a tool of power used to discipline people who do not agree with it—the large majority of people as it so happens. Tyrannical, fanatical, and fantastical ideology by any other name would smell the same (apologies to Shakespeare). Gender theory is wrong.

CONVENTIONAL GENDER NORMS ARE INTEGRAL WITH NATURAL SEXUAL REPRODUCTIVE NECESSITIES

The famous second-wave feminist assertion that—as Simone de Beauvoir put it—"one is not born, but rather becomes, a woman"[2]—is usually thought to imply that culturally acceptable gender roles are entirely socially conditioned. Now this is not simply what de Beauvoir is saying, but the myth of the total constructivism of gender roles, and later, of gender identity, does originate with de Beauvoir's choice meme. This, in effect, mythic queering of the naturalness of socially acceptable gender roles plays itself out in a number of directions in feminism, both in its second- and third-wave expressions.

In second-wave feminism the overcoming of inequalities in gender roles between the sexes that are determined by sexual difference, particularly as concerns the dependence of women on men in the role of mothers, and the "limitations" women experience relative to men in casual sexual relationships, because they might get pregnant, were fought against. The score must be equalized; women's sexual bodies must not make them dependent on men or less free than men in their sexual activities. In many regards second-wave feminism is a war on the distinctives of the female sexed body in relation to the male sexed body, regarding how that plays out in power and autonomy relationships and roles.

In third-wave feminism equalizing the score between males and females—the E in DEI—is pursued by seeking to destroy social categories of sex-based gender norms entirely, by subjectivizing both gender and sex. Now, not only is one not born a woman, one is not born female either. Sex is de-naturalized, the social construction of sex-linked gender is thus

---

2. Beauvoir, *Second Sex*, 295.

de-socialized, and gender and sex are both treated as individual-identity constructions. De-naturalized sex and gender anarchy are considered real freedom. Here, anyone "imposing" one sex or another on you, or one gender or another on you, is oppressive. Thus is natural sex denied entirely and gender transformed from being social conventions that accrue around sex into a personal poetic and performative identity-creation. This is supposed to liberate everyone from oppressive social gender norms, and from oppressive assertions of what one's sex means socially.

I wish to argue here that sex-linked gender norms are both socially conditioned and natural. Such a stance is incompatible with the attempt to eliminate the natural differences between the sexes as much as possible, as promoted in much second-wave feminism, and incompatible with the attempt to de-naturalize sex itself and subjectivize gender and destroy sex-linked gender norms in third-wave feminism. But, contrary to both these feminist trajectories, maintaining that sex-linked gender norms are both socially conditioned and natural has the advantage of being true.

To start with, because something is entirely socially conditioned—such as, for example, language use—does not mean it is un-natural and is an entirely cultural phenomenon. In the analogy of language, the different words and grammar that a native speaker of a specific language learns in a specific time and place, within a specific set of relationships and conditions, is indeed entirely culturally and socially conditioned. But the capacity to be a language user is a natural human capacity, and it is a natural capacity that requires a relational and cultural context to be actualized. In this sense, the cultural conditioning context of learning a specific language is the natural context for the development of a natural capacity. Gender roles, it seems, are the same. One learns how to be a man or a woman, and the specific learning of gender roles is entirely relationally and culturally situated, but the capacity to be masculine or feminine is a function of the natural potentialities of being a sexually reproductive human. If we were not differentiated sexual beings—males and females—to start with, then there would be no gender roles. In this sense, gender roles—which are inherently different in infants, and then boys and girls, compared to men and women, because infants, boys, and girls are not yet sexually mature—are culturally conditioned yet derivative functions of natural sex.

To pretend that gender roles can be determined with no regard to sex, and with no regard to the cultural and relational setting of human sexual reproduction, is to be astonishingly deluded. Sexual differences between males and females have objective natural characteristics, and while cultural and community expressions of sex-linked gender roles admit of great variability, it is not endlessly variable because it is tied to natural sexual reproduction, and tied to natural sexual drives and instincts that are there so that the species gets continued. Disrespect those natural realities enough and the species will fail to reproduce. If genocide of the human race is one's objective, then only does it make sense to pretend that sex and gender have got nothing to do with each other, and that there is no need to protect safe and flourishing environments for successful reproductive sex between a male and a female and the long process of the nurture and formation of children. Gender conventions and laws protecting the natural sexual reproduction of humans, and protecting safe and flourishing family environments, is basic for the very survival of humanity.

To deny the natural realities of human sexual reproduction is much the same as pretending that you can make words mean whatever you want them to mean. Words only have meaning at all because there is a real world that they refer to, and because there is conventional agreement about what the various semantic signs mean, and how you meaningfully structure those signs for users of the same language. If language does not link to reality, and if there is no conventional agreement on the meaning and ordering of words, then communication cannot occur. Language is *both* naturally given *and* culturally constructed at the same time. To say that language is *only* culturally constructed is to use language to undermine language. Likewise, cultural gender conventions and natural sexual differences between males and females are integral. Gender is both cultural and natural at the same time.

One is not born either a man or a woman, but in the vast majority of cases, one is unambiguously born either a male or a female. I find it hard to understand why this is considered controversial in any manner. And then, again, obviously, one is culturally socialized into broadly masculine and feminine gender conventions depending on whether one is a male or a female. Is that rocket science? This seems so indisputably obvious, and yet now we are being legally forced to pretend that sex is arbitrarily assigned to babies and that gender identities have nothing to do with conventional sex-linked gender roles that are ultimately related to the realities of human sexual difference, and successful human reproduction and family life.

Contrary to what Judith Butler and other gender theorists assert, gender is not an imponderable and endlessly complicated mystery. Gender is social and broadly normative conventions that accrue around the natural sexual differences between males and females of the human species. Unless you are actively opposed to the social viability of reproductive sex, these conventions are far from rigid and oppressive.

Indeed, the queer in-principle opposition to heteronormative gender conventions *is* actively opposed to the social viability of reproductive sex, because—so the narrative goes—transpeople are profoundly vulnerable and victimized. But this persecution narrative in our very sexually liberal times is a concocted and shameless lie, and queer animus toward the large majority's heteronormativity is entirely unjustified.[3]

Our post-1960s secular societies have largely abandoned sacred definitions of the meaning of sexual difference and religiously framed sexual ethics, so gender nonconformism has never been more socially acceptable. Nobody cares what you do in the privacy of your own relationships; nobody cares (within very broad and non-judgmental conventional reason) what you wear or what gender-nonconforming attitude or interest you have. Nobody gives a toss if you are a gender nonconformist and have a private predilection to kinky yet consenting and legal recreational sex. Nobody is likely to harass you if you are in an openly gay or lesbian relationship. Same-sex relationships are legal and entirely acceptable as an option by our present highly relaxed and liberal gender conventions. Despite relentless propaganda to the contrary by trans activists, there is almost no oppression being visited on heteronormative gender non-conformists of any sort. Indeed, Andrew Doyle correctly notes that,

> Trans-identified people are among the most powerful in society. They are endlessly celebrated by the media and celebrity classes. They are able to enforce speech codes against the will of the

3. Background suspicion and occasional animus will follow any identifiable minority group who deliberately defies broadly accepted public conventions. This is not the same thing as systematic "genocidal" violence toward transpeople. The myth of violent assault vulnerability for transpeople in the liberal West has been deliberately concocted. See Stock, *Material Girls*, 220–24. Stock notes that in 2019 the "Trans Murder Monitoring Project" identified 331 murders of "gender divers" people worldwide; 160 were from Brazil alone (another ninety in other South American countries) with the rest scattered in small concentrations around the world, including nine in all of Europe and not one in Australia. This indeed is shocking and horrifying, but in context, that year there were 63,880 homicides in Brazil. Further, the large majority of South American transpeople who were murdered were sex workers, who, alas, are always vulnerable to violent crime. Stock (p. 223) notes, "when we look at the murder rate of trans people in the UK over a decade it turns out it is . . . around one a year. [Comparing murder rates for the general population with murder rates for the trans population] the murder rate for trans people is lower than for the general population as a whole."

majority of the population in the knowledge that those in authority will support their demands. They are able to call on the police to harass those who dare to refuse to comply. Above all, they enjoy the status of victimhood in spite of being among the safest and least victimized of all demographics.[4]

Largely, no one is going to give a toss if you are trans. Provided, that is, you are not fanatically determined to destroy the majority's heteronormativity gender conventions, and provided you are not determined to force other people to play your performative game about your "sex," that directly defies sex-realism, as if your personal fantasy is an objective truth that we must all believe.

Be as non-conformist as you like in your own private spaces, but public gender conventions as broad guidelines related to the type of committed heterosexual relationships that allow for human reproduction and family nurture and stability remain crucial to a functional society. Public sex-presentation and gender-norm anarchy, and the complete disconnection of personal "sexual fulfillment" from long-term committed reproductive family contexts, is an anti-naturalist attack on the most basic and humanizing institutions: marriage and family. This is an attack that denies the natural linkages between culturally constructed gender norms of the natural reproductive sex binary. These are links that should be respected not destroyed. To destroy them is to war against the natural realities of human sexual reproduction. If we win that war we will destroy ourselves.

Gender theory, which denies the linkages between the natural reproductive sex binary and heteronormative gender conventions, and which treats heteronormative gender conventions as intrinsically oppressive, is wrong. It is wrong in that there really are very important natural purposes (the replication of the species) culturally embedded in broadly heterosexual gender norms, and it is wrong in claiming that one's chosen gender identification is a meaningful determinate of one's sex. This is all obviously wrong, and obviously destructive of human flourishing. Gender theory is not only wrong, it is anti-natural, anti-common-good, and anti-human. Our institutions and law should by no means uphold it.

---

4. Doyle, "Men Do Not Belong in Women's Changing Rooms." Doyle points out the systematic distortion of supposed victimization, violence afflicted, and suicide statistics to promote a narrative of pity for trans activists which is entirely fabricated for political purposes.

QUEER GENDER-IDENTITIES PRESUPPOSE THE GENDER STEREOTYPES THEY ARE SUPPOSED TO SUBVERT

If you read serious feminist thinkers who critically engage with queer gender theory,[5] it becomes clear that both sex-realist radical feminism (TERF)[6] and sex-irrealist trans-inclusionary feminism (TIF) think gender norms are at the root of the oppression of women by men. That there is a certain way of being a *feminine* female that subjugates women to men is something both types of "freedom feminism"[7] find inherently oppressive. TIFs think you will overcome the oppression of women by men by abolishing sex itself, whereas TERFs think you will overcome the oppression of women by men by making sure that women are protected from dominating and invasive men (hence, you need to hold onto the reality of sex to make sure females are not exploited by males).

In this segment, I wish to focus in on the manner in which TIFs and TERFs disagree about gender stereotypes. Because a TERF holds that sex remains objective and fixed, no matter what gender norms you do or do not conform to, one's sex is *not* defined by gender norms or gender stereotypes. Here, a female is a female no matter how atypical they may be as regards culturally normative femininity. And if gender is in some derivative manner sex-linked, though not identical to sex, then if a female is a "butch" lesbian, this is one atypical mode of being feminine; but it is not a mode of being masculine. So a female can express their atypical "gender identity" (if they have a gender identity)[8] and can have whatever sexual orientation feels

---

5. See for example, Lawford-Smith, *Gender-Critical Feminism*.

6. Trans Exclusionary Radical Feminism (TERF) is a descriptor often accusingly hurled against gender-critical feminists by queer trans activists. Gender-critical feminists typically reject this label as they are more than happy to include transmen within the category of "female," though they are indeed not prepared to include transwomen within the category of "female." In this section I will use the term "TERF" not as a term of abuse, but simply as a convenient way of distinguishing gender-critical feminists from TIFs.

7. This is Mary Harrington's phrase. For her critical engagement with "freedom feminism," see Harrington, *Feminism Against Progress*.

8. Notably, Andrew Doyle does not have a gender identity. Some objective facts about him are that he has a sex, he is male, and he has a sexual orientation, which is gay, and there are broadly accepted masculine gender conventions expected in public and impersonal contexts which he is usually comfortable conforming to. But Doyle claims he has no gender identity as he has no idea what that might factually *be*. Indeed, as it cannot factually be anything, but supposedly is a vague subjective feeling about one's own "masculinity" or "femininity" or

natural to them, at the same time that most women will be of heterosexual orientation and be in some manner comfortable with the broad range of feminine self-expressions normative to our liberal culture.

To TERFs, when gender norms presuppose the equality of value between men and women, while respecting sexual difference, and when a culture shows no appreciable difference in power, opportunity, pay, independence, and dignity because of one's sex, then gender will no longer be a form of female oppression. But there is no need for a female who is a gender non-conformist to conform to stereotypical gender norms at all. Non-conformism to gender stereotypes does not change one's sex. Gender non-conformism is a mode of being female (if one is a female); it is not a mode of being some other sex than female.

TIFs are different. Here, because gender identity performatively determines "assigned" sex, if you are a biological female but you don't feel like a female, then you simply change your sex assignment by performing a *male* gender identity. For autism-spectrum, transgender-identifying, magical-thinking-inclined children and young people who believe there is a misalignment between their sex and their gender such that they have unfortunately been "born in the wrongly sexed body," this is a fatal trap. For if one is female but has hairy legs and some facial hair, and one does not like one's non-conformism to culturally perceived feminine gender tropes defined by having no facial hair and having hairless legs, and if, as a tomboyish adolescent girl, you do not like boys and men noticing your breasts, then "obviously" you need to change your sex. If you are an autism-spectrum young woman who is same-sex attracted, but you find this conflicts with heteronormative gender stereotypes, then you change your sex so that you feel no conflict between your sex and the heterosexual gender norm. Though you were "assigned female at birth" you can now performatively (and hence *really*) be a man who is attracted to women, and thus your gender incongruence is fixed and—if you "pass" as someone of the opposite sex—you can now fit the gender norm. In effect, "wrongly sexed" transgender people are *rigid gender conformists* who have reductive and stereotypical conceptions of how biological sex and cultural gender stereotypes must conform to each other. Again, as not a few people in this domain have pointed out, the transgender movement converts young

---

"non-binarinity" or "whatevery" Doyle finds the objectively undefinable "nature" of gender identity makes the notion effectively meaningless. Perhaps, then, no sane person with a respect for objective facts has a gender identity. I am persuaded by Doyle's example and have discovered, now that I think about it, that I also do not have a gender identity.

people who would otherwise grow up to be gay or lesbian into surgically and hormonally altered (and often sterilized) queer straight people. This, effectively, is gay conversion therapy.[9]

"Wrong-body gender essentialists" are not the only types of transpeople. Explicitly queer transpeople who are consciously seeking to subvert any conception of what gender and sex should normatively be—such as Sandy Stone—are fully compatible with gender theory. And indeed, as a strident form of irrealist anti-essentialism as regards all meanings, gender theory should firmly opposed identity politics of *any* sort, as Butler originally did in the 1990s. The "wrong-body" trans essentialist is not actually compatible with gender theory, though the transgender movement is more than happy to use such confused young people in its program to disrupt and undermine sex-realist heteronormativity.

But here is an interesting thing: a male does not *perform* being a man; he simply *is* one. In fact, only a female *could* perform being a man, and only a male *could* perform being a woman. In this context a performance is a studied copying of external conventional gender tropes. So a gender-identity performer treats gender as a real thing and seems to assume that there are right and wrong ways of being gendered, in a way that an actual male being a man or an actual female being a woman does not perform, and may have no particular interest in getting their gender right or having a carefully choreographed gender identity. Only an actor performs being Julius Caesar. Julius Caesar himself—the historical Roman emperor—did not *perform* being himself.

Ironically, gender-identity ideology is fixated with gender stereotypes, treats social constructs as functional essential-identity realities, and treats the actual natural reality of biological sex as a mobile performative convention. This is simply the wrong way around. And as regards liberation from harmful gender stereotypes, this is a serious step *backward* toward hyper-stereotypical and fetishized obsessions with constructed and sexualized gender types.

Gender theory is physically harmful and morally wrong. It encourages harmful gender stereotypes, as the natural body is often irrevocably

---

9. See Hakeem, *DeTrans*. Dr. Hakeem is gay and a psychotherapist who has been working in the transgender space for over twenty years. See his chapter 3, "Trans and Autism" (34–46), and chapter 5, "Trans and Homophobia" (51–56). See Doyle, "New Gay Conversion Therapy." See Barnes, *Time to Think*, 12–13, 35–36, 159–64. There is clear knowledge in the therapeutic field that most "wrongly sexed" autism-spectrum children and young people in gender clinics would grow up to become gay if they were left "untreated."

harmed in order to perform a gendered cross-"sex" identity. Further, the idea that a woman who is uncomfortable with her naturally sexed body must renounce her femaleness and become male is profoundly misogynist. And gender theory simply gets the relationship between cultural gender roles and natural sex back to front. One's natural sex defines the reality of who one is, not cultural gender-identity tropes. Gender theory is both wrong and harmful.

SEX IRREALISM FAILS BECAUSE SEX ACTUALLY IS REAL, AND GENDER IDENTITY IS NOT REAL

As we have seen, the linguistic trickiness of gender theory presupposes that words are entirely human meaning constructs, and that nature itself has no meaning. In other words, we construct nature with our words. This means there is nothing fixed about any natural meaning as all meanings—even scientific meanings—are human poetic glosses on a meaningless brute thereness. Indeed Butler asserts that "if sex is framed within cultural norms, then it is already gender" and "the social *produces* the biological."[10] But these are literal nonsense claims that no sensible person—let alone a scientifically serious or medically responsible person—should believe.

Every human culture—other than postmodern queer university culture—recognizes that there are real and natural human males and real and natural human females, in the real world, and different words for males and females reflect natural realities rather than being simply made up or in any sense socially produced. Why any normal human being would believe an overt denial of factual truth is difficult to grasp. We have seen why our academic culture has got lost deep down in the irrealist and constructivist rabbit hole, but that is an academic game rather than anything continuous with our normal experience of reality.

And here comes pesky bivalent logic again. If—in reality, rather than simply out of conventional conformism—we do *not* actually believe that there is no such thing as objective truth about the natural reality of the human reproductive sex binary (via which we all came into the world) then—in reality—we believe that gender theory is wrong. We can't have it both ways. We *cannot* really believe that, actually, there really are natural males and females in the world, and at the same time maintain that gender theory is true. And indeed we cannot maintain that gender theory (or, indeed, any

---

10. Butler, *Who's Afraid*, 119, 216.

linguistic expression) is either true or false if we are to believe that gender theory is true. Because if it is true, it is neither true nor false! So believing in the truth of gender theory is *a self-defeating contradiction*. And if it is not true, and cannot even be true, why would we believe it? Gender theory is wrong. It makes excellent sense to me that gender identity is an irrealist and fabricated tool of queer political power, but it makes no sense to me at all that sex is an irreal social construct. The natural sex binary is a clear and scientifically verifiable fact.

GENDER THEORY IS ANTI-LIBERAL

We have already looked at this, but it needs re-stating. A modern and liberal public order is grounded in the common respect for true facts, the outlawing of material harms, freedom of belief and expression, and liberal pluralism as regards personal values and beliefs. If we value a liberal public order then we cannot allow the DEI reformation to promote what are effectively public heresy laws prosecuting anyone who disbelieves in gender theory and refuses to use its irrealist and factually false lexicon, or who stands against the objective harms to women that will accompany allowing males to enter female-only spaces and participate in female-only competitions and forums.

Admittedly modern liberalism is in a state of crisis, for after the secularization of the West it now has no horizon of a high qualitative meaning to define the common good other than shopping, and a downside of the liberal experiment is a Hobbesian insistence on the total and arbitrary power of the state when it comes to authorized force. State-backed force is morally arbitrary to Hobbes, and as we have seen with the developments in English law in the late nineteenth century, parliament now has a totally arbitrary sovereignty that overrides all other authorities simply on the grounds of procedural correctness and linguistic construction. Should the state pass irrational and immoral laws, then the state will uphold those laws with total sovereign force. The capture of legislators by gender-theory advocates has put us in the perilous position that natural justice and commonsense morality are being denied by our legal system. Sex-based rights for women and natural justice for parents who do not want to surrender their children to the state-backed genital mutilation and sterilization cult of "gender-affirming care" are now opposed by law. Whether a legal system can long survive a departure from natural justice and factual commonsense truth in domains that directly adversely impact the ordinary lives of all normal people is unlikely. But one thing is very clear: gender theory is *anti-liberal*.

Gender theory legally compels speech that conflicts with factual truth and good conscience when we commonsense sex-realists are compelled to use falsely sexed gender pronouns, and accept falsely sexed identity "assignments." Compelled speech is a direct violation of the freedom of expression that is considered so important for a modern liberal democracy such as the United States. Their First Amendment protects their citizens from compelled speech. This is not the case in Australia. Anti-"sex"-discrimination legislation (without any definition of sex) forces Australians to play along with "gender-identity" categories that commonsense and natural-sex–respecting gender norms know to be false and do not consider to be safe or reasonable.

In a liberal social order, you are free to believe whatever you like about matters of meaning and value, provided you adhere to the laws that do no physical harm to your neighbor. According to Mill's famous tract *On Liberty*, the right to express opinions, even when they offend people you disagree with, is a basic principle of a liberal society. But even though I in good conscience and with good factual reasoning do not believe gender theory to be true (and believe that it cannot be true in its own irrealist terms), not only am I forced to comply with it, I *cannot even debate its faults* without being considered to be performing illegal hate speech! This is *not* liberal. If liberalism is a value we wish to uphold, then it is incompatible with the compelled speech, the enforced agreement, the gagging of vigorous public debate, and the requirement to conform with its anti-sex-realist demands that gender theory is justifying. Thus all supporters of liberalism must recognize that gender theory is wrong.

GENDER THEORY IS ANTI-SCIENCE

As a shamelessly sophistic language game, gender theory has no commitment to truth, other than the supposed truth of the total disbelief in all truth claims. Gender theory maintains that we can know no truths about the actual nature of nature, so science is really just a form of social and cultural governmentality and a means of imposing structures of order and control on others in pursuit of the power, preferences, and freedoms of those who control knowledge construction, funding, and dissemination. Science is simply propaganda. This accounts for how recklessly manipulative the advocates of gender theory are with data and actual science. Truth integrity is not an issue to such linguistic pragmatists; the only issue is effect. The only acceptable data confirms the narrative of the goodness, the importance, the moral imperative of "gender-affirming care." All other data and all other interpretations are excluded in advance by means of the strategic control of the knowledge class.

I am fully aware of the epistemological problems faced by Enlightenment-framed positivism. However, philosophically naïve empiricism—where what you see, as carefully tested and experimentally demonstrated, is really there—is fundamental to the actual practice of modern Western science. A commitment to truthful descriptions of what is actually the case in the natural world—not what we want to be the case, not what we can make to look like it is the case—is the necessary epistemological ethic of the good scientist. As much as modern skeptical, anti-metaphysical, and anti-theological empiricism is unable to justify naïve positivism as truth-revealing, the good scientist knows—as Michael Polanyi put it—more than he or she can tell.[11] One of the things the good scientist knows is that real truths about the natural world do in fact communicate themselves to truth-concerned scientists, even if they do not know how.

In the next chapter we will explore why science requires good faith in the truth-revealing powers of nature, and in the truth-apprehending powers of the humble, and systematically rigorous, and carefully theorizing and testing, and imaginatively open scientist. Approaching science without this faith in truth is exactly what gender theory does, and it is blind to natural truth as a result, and has no appreciation of truth in and through science. But if we are committed to scientific truth, then there is nothing at all controversial or complex about the truth of the natural reproductive sex binary. You need a male father and a female mother to achieve successful human reproduction. There is not a single person alive today that does not have a male father and a female mother. The human reproductive sex binary is the only way you can have human reproduction. This is simply, totally uncontroversially, and obviously true. This basic and demonstrable truth is why there are complex gender norms that have accrued around the natural sex binary, for human reproduction is the nest of human nurture in infant dependence and in childhood formation. Marriage and family are integral with successful human reproduction and the nurture and formation of the next generation of humans. This is not complex. This is not controversial. This is not propaganda. This is simply true.

11. Polanyi, *Tacit Dimension*, 4.

Gender theory is anti-science for it denies the truth of the reproductive sex binary, and it denies the importance of the heterosexual reproductive and humanizing institutions of marriage and the family, as if they have nothing to do with either sex or gender. For the sake of people who will not pay the responsible price for human reproduction (which is anyone who disdains heterosexual committed and reproductive sexual relationships), the people who do not renounce the natural purpose of human sex and who do pay the price for human reproduction are required to throw away all the carefully constructed human institutions that support the very costly, very demanding, and deeply rewarding activities of getting married and having children. So the "play" aspects of sex—the recreation and hedonic aspect—are made central and the "work" aspects of sex—making a marriage work, making a safe and flourishing family environment—are made peripheral. The selfish aspects of being a sexed being—self-actualization, self-identity, self-fulfillment—are made central to human sexuality, and the giving aspects of human sexuality—bearing children, nurturing children, providing for mothers and families as mothers do the hard work of bearing and nurturing infants—is made peripheral.

Men who simply want casual sexual encounters with women, and who have no commitment to the women they impregnate, or their own offspring, are an age-old model of self-centered sexual irresponsibility. Prostitution is an age-old market-driven response to this male repudiation of ongoing responsibility for sexual union with a woman. And marriage and the structures of community and kinship support for spousal and familial fidelity have been the age-old method of containing and limiting this irresponsibility as much as possible. But now, it seems, irresponsibility is upheld as the selfish right of all people—both men and women, and people of all sexual orientations, and all non-reproductive fetishized people—to mastery over their own bodies. Traditionally, of course, having a committed sexual relationship is about the mutual giving over of your body, your substance, and your life to your spouse and family. But in the age of self-gratifying and atomistic consumerism, we seem to believe that all that old-fashioned giving of the self to the other is regressive and oppressive. Sex is, apparently, for the *self*. Once we can do human reproduction outside of the womb, then we can kiss all that old and backward love-based and kinship-committed humanity goodbye. Post-humanity, here we come.

Since the 1960s heteronormative sex and gender conventions have been systematically torn up by individualizing and hedonic market forces, and the casualization of sexual relationships and non-reproductive sexual individualism have been normalized and flourish. This is about as anti-human an ideology as we have ever seen, going with an icepick at the most vulnerable and demanding aspects of human life, without mercy or awareness of the consequences for humanity itself. But this is obviously going to happen if you let queer-sex-and-gender-deviance advocates set the sex and gender terms for the whole of society.

Gender theory is anti-truth, and hence anti-science. But scientific truth is real and gender theory is delusional and self-focused fantasy. Gender theory is not only wrong about the basic scientific facts of human sexuality, it is destructively and dangerously opposed to the central and serious real and natural meanings of human sexuality.

GENDER THEORY IS ANTI-MORAL

Gender theory is anti-essentialist, anti-naturalist, and entirely unconcerned with the destructive impact on our humanity of its concerted assault on the social institution of heterosexual marriage and the kinship-bonded reproductive family. But this, apparently, is all moral.

Morality, at its most basic and uncontroversial definitional level, is broadly understood as social mores defining "good" and "bad" interpersonal and community dynamics. As we are social beings, how we relate to others is the site of conventions and laws that define what is "good" and what is "bad." DEI wishes to define as "bad" all expressions of sex-realism, and any sex-realist conception of heteronormative convention, language, or law. These "bads" are morally undesirable because they filter out diverse gender-identities from being normative; they set up inequalities between good sex and good gender identities, on the one hand, and bad sex and bad gender identities, on the other. And they exclude people formerly considered deviant from the heterosexual norms and conventions of society. DEI wishes to define as "good" total gender-identity and sex-definition anarchy.

Let us drill a little deeper into the so-called morality of the DEI movement.

DEI morality is *anti-essentialist*. That is, there is no intrinsically or essentially good or bad value that is expressed in any belief, motivation, or action. DEI is strictly *immanently framed*, and hence anti-metaphysical and anti-theological. There is no superhuman or divine source of intrinsic values and essential qualitative meanings, hence all values and meanings are human cultural and political artifacts. DEI morality is *pragmatic*. The categories of "good" and "bad" do not express essential moral meanings, rather morals and laws are humanly constructed modes of power; they are modes of achieving the ends you want. You can measure the success or failure of moral pragmatism (where a "good" outcome is the achievement of what you want) in material and quantifiable terms.

So, who else has an anti-essentialist, immanently framed, and pragmatic conception of morality? The obvious answer is political parties and commercial corporations. Electoral success, typically promoted in terms of quantitative econometric outcomes, increasingly defines the inner machine logic of our centrist political parties. Financial success defines the *raison d'être* of the large corporation, which now includes institutions such as universities. The strong uptake of DEI morality by states and corporations is no coincidence. They have the same basic outlook on morality. The matter goes deeper than a harmony of moral philosophy, however, as states and corporations have a morality image problem and DEI morality offers to solve that problem for them.

As much as our cultures of knowledge and power really are anti-essentialist, entirely immanently framed, and ruthlessly pragmatic when it comes to "good" and "bad," the less educated and the less powerful majority of ordinary people are still old-fashioned moral realists in some fashion or another. The relatively uneducated and relatively powerless *hoi polloi* assume moral realism because moral truth is actually real, and one has to be educated out of taking moral reality seriously. But as we live in an at least notional liberal democratic political lifeworld, the legitimacy of power has to be derived in some manner from the consent of the majority. This is a cause of difficulty to our highly educated, very powerful, and often functionally amoral and pragmatic elites. To non-elite moral realists—where there really are qualitative truths that define "good" and "bad," and these truths are not simply made up by us—commercial and political power in our times looks either unsatisfyingly amoral, or actively immoral. It looks like our political and corporate ruling class acts as if they can reduce qualitative moral truth to a function of their own merely instrumental power-advancement. This is seen—by our elite moral pragmatists—as a significant image problem that could have undesirable practical consequences. So some sort of realist-*looking*, but not *actually* realist, moral sheen needs to be painted over raw pragmatic power. DEI morality is perfect for the job!

Token minority presences—a sprinkling of trans, gay, indigenous, disabled people, not selected on qualification and experience merit, but selected for diversity—can make an inherently exploitative organization (like a university) look *really* moral, as if they are acting on intrinsic and essential—perhaps even transcendent—inclusion principles. Crucially, such inclusion does not actually change how the corporation functions in any practically appreciable manner. Ideal! The corporation can now market its moral righteousness and continue with its pragmatic and instrumental wealth- and power-acquisition "bottom line." But actually, this "morality" push fools no one. Pragmatic and marketed morality is no morality at all. The reduction of "the good" to "my wealth and power interests" is a denial of moral value.

We shall explore this further in the next chapter, but unless one is prepared to believe in some essentially qualitative vision of moral truth, it is more honest to say morality is (in the modern and not true sense) a myth. DEI "morality" is as entirely pragmatic, anti-essentialist, and anti-realist as corporate and state power has largely become. In realist terms (and here, I really mean Realist terms, where moral truths have an essentially qualitative meaning) DEI "morality" is an *anti*-morality. It simply uses categories of moral "goodness"—the "liberal" and "tolerant" value of diverse reality and meaning perspectives, the "kind" inclusion of marginal demographics, the "just" compensating victims of oppression—as marketing tools. This is "morality" as a moral-sounding posture that is a useful promotional tool in the pursuit of practical power objectives for their interest base. Gender theory is integral with anti-morality. It is—in any intrinsic sense—morally wrong.

GENDER THEORY IS HARMFUL TO CHILDREN

An obvious and unambiguous harm that arises from the capture of mental health therapeutic norms by gender theory is the sterilization, puberty-blocker-induced sexual dysfunction, and the genital and mammary mutilation of minors. This harm is promoted by mandating that clinicians deploy "gender-affirming care,"[12] heavily pressuring parents to give their

---

12. See LGB Alliance Australia, "Dr Jillian Spencer." Dr. Spencer, who has been suspended by Queensland Health for refusing to comply with a mandated gender-affirming care policy, notes that the Queensland Children's Hospital has "a culture in which clinicians are unable to employ medical discretion or a neutral therapeutic stance and are bound by their employment to affirm children's gender transition." A significant factor in this culture is that government policies are heavily formed by transgender activist organizations such as AusPATH. See Spencer and Clarke, "AusPATH: Activism Influencing Health Policy."

consent to "gender-affirming treatments," and even proceeding with puberty blockers without parental consent for minors in some cases.[13] All of these radical harms have been authorized by the American Psychiatric Association's (APA) fifth edition of the Diagnostic and Statistical Manual of Mental Disorders (DSM-5).

In 2013 the DSM-5 dropped the DSM-4's diagnostic category "Gender Identity Disorder" and replaced it with "Gender Dysphoria." This radical diagnostic recalibration was accompanied by the standard gender theory deliberate confusing of biological sex with psycho-social gender. The DSM-5 had a significant and immediately realized impact in validating what are now called gender-affirming care treatment models around the world, thus facilitating a pandemic of girls and young women with autism spectrum disorder getting onto the gender-transition medicalized conveyer belt.[14]

The APA notes that the DSM-5 changes were made "to avoid stigma ... for individuals who see and feel themselves to be a different gender to their assigned gender." The APA goes on to explain:

> It is important to note that gender nonconformity is not in itself a mental disorder. The critical element of gender dysphoria is the presence of clinically significant distress associated with the condition....

Note the abstract to this journal article: "As a consequence of a membership policy which admits members with lived experience as health experts, AusPATH functions as an activist organization whilst claiming to be a professional association. There is no accreditation or endorsement underpinning AusPATH's influence on health policy in Australia. Its role as an activist organization is demonstrated by a lack of caution in its position statements, which are misleading in circumstances where accurate information has been long available. The considerable influence of AusPATH on health policy in Australia needs to be reconsidered, as well as RANZCP Position Statement 62 which provides insufficient guidance upon balancing research and clinical knowledge, as well as medical ethics, with voices of lived experience."

13. For example, the Honorable Tim Nicholls, minister for health in the Queensland government, issued a media statement on January 28, 2025, regarding the state-funded Cairns Sexual Health Service, noting that the CSHS "delivered an apparently unauthorized pediatric gender service without an agreed model of care. The service was delivered to 42 pediatric [that is, children] gender service clients.... A recent internal review undertaken of the CSHS identified deficiencies relating to credentialling and scope of practice and medicolegal concerns relating to patient and parental consent." Nicholls, "Media Statement."

14. See Shrier, *Irreversible Damage*.

> Gender dysphoria is manifest in a variety of ways, including strong desires to be treated as the other gender or to be rid of one's sex characteristics....
>
> Persons experiencing gender dysphoria need a diagnostic term that protects their access to care and won't be used against them in social, occupational, or legal areas....
>
> Treatment options for this condition include counselling, cross-sex hormones, gender reassignment surgery, and social and legal transition to the desired gender. To get insurance coverage for the medical treatments, individuals need a diagnosis.... Ultimately, the changes regarding gender dysphoria in the DSM-5 respect the individuals identified by offering a diagnostic name that is more appropriate to the symptoms and behaviors they experience without jeopardizing their access to effective treatment options.[15]

Firstly, there is no clear terminological delineation between objective biological sex and subjective gender. Functionally, the APA seems to have accepted a co-constructed sex-gender irrealism. So much for psychiatry as an objective and evidence-based science. In the above APA explanation, biological sex is only directly referred to as "sex characteristics" and it is indirectly referred to as "assigned gender." This is the ideological capture of the APA to non-scientific—indeed anti-science—gender theory.

Secondly, this is an activist justification for a profound diagnostic and treatment regimen change, rather than a clinical justification. Avoiding stigma and making sure that transgender people can get medical insurance for radical sex-presentation-altering treatments are stated reasons for launching the new diagnostic regimen.

A significant key to understanding the therapeutic impact of the shift from the diagnostic categories of the DSM-4 to the diagnostic categories of the DSM-5 is the difference between a *disorder* and a *condition* within the DSM lexicon. If you have a psychiatric *disorder* you have a mental illness. But you can suffer from a psychological *condition* without being mentally ill.

The DSM-4's diagnostic category "Gender Identity *Disorder*" (GID) meant that a physiological male child or youth who believed that he was really female was mentally disturbed. GID is a body morphology disturbance wherein the mentally ill mind rejects, or punishes, or hates, the sufferer's body. Such a sufferer believes—incorrectly—that their natural body is wrongly formed. Back in the DSM-4 day, a psychotherapist did not "treat" the natural body according to the desire of the body-morphology-disturbed

---

15. American Psychiatry Association, "Gender Dysphoria," fact sheet, 2013.

mind. For GID was then seen as a *mental* illness, and it is the mind that is ill, not the natural and healthy body. To this day we do not enable a sufferer from the body-dysmorphic disturbance of Anorexia Nervosa by helping them starve themselves to death.

Prior to 2013 the treatment for sufferers presenting with GID symptoms typically entailed long and non-judgmental listening and talking psychotherapies where the patient could safely explore their gender identity's misalignment with their physical body. In this process the therapist would carefully examine any psychological comorbidities, life traumas, social pressures, and so forth, that might contribute to or even cause GID, in the hope that the patient will, with time, realign their gender identity with their naturally sexed body. Only if, after long attempts, such psychotherapy does not resolve dysphoric anguish for the patient, will reproductive-disabling body-altering accommodations to the mental illness be pursued. Prior to 2013, the large majority of GID juveniles (most of whom were boys) received such talking therapies and grew up to become comfortable with their naturally sexed bodies, with gender dysphoria simply fading away. The large majority of GID boys matured into gay men without undergoing cross-sex hormones or the amputation of their penises and testicles.[16]

The above mental-disturbance-treating therapeutic regimen was largely thrown away by the DSM-5. In the DSM-5 anyone who presents claiming to believe that they are a person of the opposite sex to their natural reproductive physiology is no longer deemed to have a mental health disorder. People, including children, who believe they are transgendered have now been entirely de-pathologized. This, the APA believes, is in aid of de-stigmatizing transgender people and respecting the validity of who queer people believe they are. The APA now firmly asserts that there is no mental illness integral with having a transgender gender identity. But the matter does not rest there, as some transgender people experience their natural and healthy transgender identity (which is, by definition, a non-alignment of their gender identity with their natural sexual physiology) as a cause of severe psychological distress. This is the psychological *condition* of gender dysphoria. Let us unpack a bit further the difference between a

---

16. Dr. Az Hakeem ran the Gender Dysphoria Psychotherapy Service at the Portman Clinic in London from 2000 to 2012 and has been working in this field since in a private capacity. He is a clinical specialist in gender-identity conditions as a psychiatrist and medical psychotherapist. He notes that "studies have repeatedly shown that gender non-conforming children with gender dysphoria, if left alone, will in most cases grow up to be gay adults without gender dysphoria...." Hakeem, *DeTrans*, 55.

condition and a disorder, and why the DSM-5 decided being transgender is not a "disorder," but gender dysphoria *is* a treatable "condition."

If you de-pathologize being transgender then it might seem to follow that gender-identities should not even be mentioned by the DSM. But that would be a problem for transgender lobbyists, because they do not just want to be accepted as normal when they have a different gender to their sex, they also want hormonal and medical treatments so that they can *overcome* the non-alignment of their transgenderism and make their body's sex-presentation comply with their mental gender identity.

For US health insurance purposes, to fund the treatment of gender dysphoria it must be an officially diagnosable condition (or disorder). Thus, the *condition* of gender dysphoria can now be diagnosed, and *non-mental* treatments (for it is no longer a mental health disorder) that socially and cosmetically, but not reproductively, realign one's wrongly sexed body with one's truly gendered identity can now be prescribed.

By discarding the DSM-4 diagnosis of GID, the APA is now sure (on what basis?) that wanting to be a person of the opposite sex is not a mental health disorder. What then causes the distress of gender dysphoria? It *must* be their wrongly sexed bodies. When this outlook is applied to children and youths under the age of majority, puberty can be seen as pathological, and the very possibility of a transgender-identifying child or youth growing to their natural reproductive maturity can be irrevocably removed under the banner of gender-affirming care. But what if these children are just confused? What if their socially situated and mental gender identity is in flux? On what basis can they reasonably be expected to make irrevocable medical decisions that will radically impact their mature adult lives in ways that they cannot properly appreciate as minors?

In the diagnostic categories of the DSM-5, in practice, it is the body of the gender dysphoric sufferer that needs treatment, not their mind. To put it bluntly, it is the naturally sexed body that is the pathogen causing the psychological distress of gender dysphoria. For a transgender-identifying child, puberty itself must here be thought of as pathogenic. This is clearly implied in the treatment recommendations in the DSM-5. Significantly, no other condition in the DSM-5 is caused by having a healthy natural body or undergoing healthy natural maturation. Some of the treatment recommendations for gender dysphoria in the DSM-5 are uniquely strange; who would have thought that chemical and actual castration can cure a boy or young man of anything?

Clearly, the APA is seeking to delicately calibrate its terminology so that transgender people can get insured hormonal and medical "care" for gender dysphoria treatments even though being a transgender person is not a psychiatric disorder. This is a serious conceptual incoherence. For if it is natural and healthy to have a gender identity that is not aligned to the biological realities of one's actual sex, then traumatic psychological distress about the defining feature of that natural and healthy psychological profile is inexplicable in these diagnostic categories. Further, if sex itself is no longer defined by your biological physiology, but is simply assigned, why not simply assign yourself a sex identity that does align with your gender identity, without any medical procedures at all? This entire diagnostic category is astonishingly incoherent in its own terms. Indeed, it seems that highly educated and evidence-based clinical psychiatrists are perfectly happy to accept the idea that mentally healthy transgender people must really have a fixed magical gender spirit that has been born into the wrongly sexed body. Astonishing! What parent in their right mind would trust the APA to wisely treat their gender-confused child when we know that the normal passage of adolescence, youth, and young adulthood can be very rocky and changeable as regards a developing juvenile's sexuality and identity?

Clearly the concerted effort of queer advocates to de-pathologize anyone with a visceral loathing of their naturally sexed body has worked in ideologically capturing the therapeutic profession. And yet, the above astonishing attempt to *associate* clinically significant mental trauma with gender dysphoria, without making gender incongruence itself a mental health *disorder*, is not only glaringly incoherent, it also harmfully obfuscates some very basic facts:

1. Distress about one's sexed body is a reasonably commonplace adolescent experience, and—until very recently—almost everyone who went through it came out the other side into relatively comfortable sexual maturation without sex-mutilating surgeries.

2. Amputating primary and secondary sex organs, particularly for minors, is a drastic and irreversible "treatment" with permanent life-course consequences that minors cannot be expected to fully appreciate.

3. Until recently, those who eventually had sex-presentation reassignment surgeries and cross-sex hormones only proceeded down that pathway after years of psychological therapies seeking to help the individual come to accept their naturally sexed body.

4. The idea that if your mind rejects your healthy and naturally sexed body then your mind is fine and it is your body that should be changed has never been considered a reasonable and essentially automatic therapy model, until very recently.

5. De-pathologizing transgender ideation and replacing "disorder" with "condition" has produced an avalanche of young people who will be permanently sexually disabled for the rest of their lives, most of whom were far too young to really understand what choice they were making.

6. Natural reproductive integrity is a significant natural good. Whether any given child of normal (that is, potentially fertile) reproductive potential will mature into an adult who successfully mates and pairs with their mate to raise their children is not, of course, known when they are a minor. But to exclude that possibility from them is to rob them of the possibility of one of the most essentially human and satisfying life opportunities people get to have. It is a serious harm to rob children of that possibility when they are in a confused and distraught state about their natural nascent sexuality.

7. The integrity of the natural body is a natural good. Of course aids for defects (like glasses) are helpful. Of course cosmetic surgeries that make people feel better about their appearance are often benign, to a point, and satisfying when they work as intended. And technology is increasingly integral with our bodily experiences. But all of this does not discount the intrinsic good of the natural integrity of the human body. We are not post-human yet.

8. Upholding a sacred commitment to the goodness and natural integrity of the human body is integral with the Western medical tradition, as expressed in the Hippocratic Oath. One does no harm to the natural body because the integrity of the natural body is an obvious marker of good health, and good health is a natural good desired by us all.

9. Up until the capture of key therapeutic authorities (like the DSM) by gender theory, anyone who did not want good health for their natural body was considered by therapists to have a mental health problem, even if their patients were convinced that their natural-body-rejecting ideations were perfectly healthy and normal. But now, it seems, the lunatics are running the asylum. Now natural-body integrity for something as integral to human sociality as our natural sex is considered a non-issue, and radically mutilating and dysfunctioning natural

human sexual organs is deemed entirely acceptable, and indeed, mandatory for minors claiming to have a transgender identity.

The supposed hormonal and medical treatments of gender dysphoria for minors is the perpetuation of harm on vulnerable minors, against their best interests, against therapists who are concerned for their best interests, and against parents who must fight the state, the therapeutic authorities, and the relentless online propaganda targeting their child to essentially join a genitally mutilating and sterilization ideology that functions like a cult. This is all of serious harm to children. This harm is ideologically perpetrated by gender theory as aided and abetted by large quantities of state and private funding, to facilitate the strategic capture of law and government. In her forensic exposé of the gender-theory ideological capture of the Gender Identity Development Service (GIDS) for children in the UK, Hannah Barnes's book *Time to Think* opens by noting this deeply worried concern by a therapist working at GIDS: "Are we hurting the children?"[17] Read Barnes' book, read the Cass Review,[18] read brave, outspoken therapeutic voices advocating for a "wait and see"[19] psychotherapeutic approach to gender dysphoria instead of rapid and clinically unproven hormonal and surgical "therapies." The evidence is in: We are hurting the children because we have been duped by gender theory into making ourselves ideologically blind to obvious harms. But getting uncoupled from deep ideological capture is now no easy task, as too many people of power and prestige are invested in the correctness of the gender-affirming care model to back down just because we really are hurting the children. But gender theory *is* harming our children. Gender theory is wrong.

GENDER THEORY IS HARMFUL TO WOMEN

Gender theory is harmful to real, that is naturally sexed, XX chromosomed, women. There are many women who, unfortunately, have had to point this out. I will mention a few of them here, in a brief list, before focusing down on two women—Sandie Peggie and Moira Deeming—in a little more detail.

Women athletes have had to compete against transwomen, such as Riley Gaines swimming against Lia Thomas. Others have had to compete

17. Barnes, *Time to Think*, 1.
18. Cass, "Cass Review."
19. Lane, "New Therapist Group on the Watch."

against XY chromosome DSD athletes, such as Angela Carini boxing against Imane Khelif. Such women have been unfairly, unsafely, and abusively defeated in women's sport by males. As regards traumatizing abuse, Gaines and her teammates had to share women's change rooms with Thomas, a biological male. Some of Gaines's teammates were survivors of rape, and having an undressed male in the female changing room where they themselves were undressed (competitive female swimwear is not a simple fitting process) was unconscionable sexual harassment. But as is routinely the case, it is the woman, not the man, who is considered intolerant, and it is the man, not the women, who will get institutional protection. So-called DEI "equality" is for males, but not for females, certainly not for lesbians.[20] As regards safety, Carini was in a combat sport with a XY chromosomed opponent, where physiological muscle-mass and hormonal differences made this simply not safe for her. Particularly for women who have suffered domestic violence, but also for anyone of traditional sensibilities, watching a male punch a woman in the face on an international platform is itself traumatizing. This is not fair; this is not right. Biological males competing in women's sport is physically, sexually, socially, and competitively harmful to women.

Marian Thompson, J. K. Rowling, Kathleen Stock, Sal Grover, Jean Taylor, Kellie-Jay Keen, Jillian Spencer, Julie Szego, and many other women have found themselves being maligned, deplatformed, fired or suspended, embroiled in costly court cases, physically assaulted, unable to legally hold born-female-only lesbian events, and alienated from the women's services they set up, if they dare to speak up for the preservation of any biological women's only space or forum whatsoever. So much for freedom of association. So much for inclusion for real women. Now fetishizing or opportunist or sexually confused males must be allowed to access women's rape crisis centers, women's change rooms, women's sporting competitions (all Canadian women's weight-lifting records are now held by biological males), breastfeeding services, and gynecological services, and they can often gain access to women's prisons. This makes many women feel unsafe, and not without cause, as they no longer have female-only safe spaces they can rely on. Now calling a maternity ward a *maternity* ward is considered exclusionary and thus not permitted. You put the name "women" on something and there are legally backed and state-supported males who will be determined to be "included" in that space, or to shut it down so that women

---

20. See Szego, "LGBTQ Is Really QTBGL."

cannot have it, or linguistically erase any words and public meanings that exclusively refer to naturally sexed females. How on earth does this advance women's equality, women's dignity, women's safety, or fairness for women? To the contrary, it advances unwanted male intrusions into women's spaces. Janice Raymond's 1979 book *The Transsexual Empire* is proving to be sadly prophetic.[21] Gender theory actively undermines any and every female-only women's space, forum, and category. Gender theory is harmful to biological women, and is seeking to erase the very category of a female sex-defined women.

Sandie Peggie is a Scottish nurse of thirty years' experience with an unblemished record, until 2023. She complained to a transwoman doctor, Dr. Upton, that she was uncomfortable with him being in the staff female changing rooms at the hospital with her.[22] At her workplace tribunal hearing Peggie had to explain: "If I wanted to get changed in front of a man, I would have went to the male changing rooms."[23] At the time she complained to Dr. Upton she was attending to her own menstrual needs. Dr. Upton responded to her expression of discomfort by lodging a harassment complaint against Peggie, which the hospital pursued. The result: *Peggie* was suspended for "harassment," and she was required to apologize to Dr. Upton and undergo a transgender-inclusivity re-education program, both of which she refused to do, and hence she has been under a continuous institutional "misconduct" cloud since Dr. Upton lodged his complaint.[24] Peggie has had to appeal the harassment finding against her in the courts, and this—as I write—is proving to be a costly, time-consuming, and very stressful process for Peggie.

We are at the place where if you are a woman and you expect to be able to undress and attend to intimate personal needs without males being in the female-only safe places set up for such purposes, you have no way of upholding that expectation—which is no longer a right, and no longer legally

21. Raymon, *Transsexual Empire*.
22. Doyle, "Men Do Not Belong in Women's Changing Rooms."
23. Dansky, "Sandie Peggie," n.p.
24. The incident where she asked Dr. Upton to leave the female change rooms was in 2023. As I write, it is early 2025. Peggie has been under a misconduct cloud at her workplace since Dr. Upton's claim of harassment, with new accusations being brought against her for misgendering Dr. Upton—whom she gained legal permission to refer to as male in her tribunal hearing—which she must answer to with her employer in 2025. See British Broadcasting Corporation, "Changing Room Row Nurse Faces Disciplinary Hearing," February 18, 2025.

defensible—if a male decides to enter your female-only space. This is a result of the institutional and legal capture and regulation of public spaces, workspaces, and businesses to gender theory. Gender theory is harmful to the actual need for sexually discriminating safety, fairness, and dignity for women. Gender theory is propagating a huge step *backward* in women's rights.

Peggie's situation is not an isolated case. Wherever there are transwomen and males who for any reason wish to identify as women, natural females (women) no longer have any right to single-sex privacy, safety, or fairness.

Then there is politics.

Australia is perhaps more politically dynamic than people appreciate. March 18, 2023, on the steps of the Victorian Parliament House in Melbourne, was a very busy day. What follows may seem bizarre and unconnected to the relation of gender theory to women's harms to start with, but all will become clear as we go.

On that day, four different groups gathered to make public statements on the steps of Parliament House in Melbourne.

Kellie-Jay Keen was the main speaker at a Let Women Speak (LWS) rally. The central objective of the rally was to advocate for the recovery of sex-based rights for women. A relatively small group of women gathered around the speakers, which included, among others, the gender-critical feminist philosopher from Melbourne University Dr. Holly Lawford-Smith, the Victorian Liberal Party MP the Honorable Moira Deeming, and women's rights advocacy lawyer Katherine Deves. Mrs. Deeming MP had informed her political party that she would participate in the event, without any objection from the party. The LWS rally was non-party-political and single-issue focused advocating for sex-based rights for women.

Opposing LWS was a much larger group of trans-rights activists (TRAs), organized by the Socialist Alternative (SA, a far-left neo-Marxist organization), seeking to drown the LWS women out, waving large red flags, banging objects, chanting TRA slogans, and separated from the LWS rally by a sizable cohort of Victorian police, both on foot and mounted.

Shortly after midday a small group of men dressed in black, who were members of the National Socialist Network (NSN, a far-right neo-Nazi organization), placed themselves opposite the SA protestors, and the NSN then unfurled their banner facing the SA protestors which read "Destroy Paedo Freaks," and they then performed Nazi salutes toward the SA protestors. The police kept the NSN and the SA separated. That day there was also a small group of Freedom Protestors (FP) gathering on the steps, who had been gathering there on Saturday mornings after the heavy lockdowns during the COVID pandemic in Melbourne. At 12:32 p.m., while the LWS speakers were trying to be heard over the SA attempt to drown them out, the NSN joined up with the FP. The FP then unfurled their banner reading "protect our children" directed against the very noisy SA protestors. At 12:47 p.m. it appears that the police asked the NSN to depart. After the NSN and the FP had left, the intensity of the SA attempt to disrupt the LWS increased. By 1 p.m. the SA protesters were becoming very rowdy in seeking to disrupt the LWS rally, and were throwing objects at the police. More police arrived at 1:06 p.m. At 1:15 p.m. MP Deeming spoke for two minutes.[25]

Rukshan Fernando, who recorded these events and submitted a carefully documents affidavit about those events to the Federal Court of Australia, explained the dynamics of that day in this manner:

> Victoria Police stand between two groups that have come to hijack the #LetWomenSpeak women's rights rally in front of Parliament House in Melbourne. The agitators from extreme opposing ideological sides were locked in a stand-off for about 1 hour while guarded by police. At one point the police facilitated the group of men clad in black throwing *Sieg Heil* salutes to drift towards the women's right rally to hold a banner and make gestures to everyone from the steps of Parliament. They were then given a protective police guard when moving out of the Parliament precinct in front of another pro trans rights counter-protest that was trying to drown out the women's rights protest.
>
> In the chaos of multiple protests and counter protests many media and political pundits have taken the opportunity to infer a direct link between the women's rights group and the men clad in black due to the proximity of the groups as well as a shared opposition to other counter protesters. However having been able to observe what happened first-hand it was obvious that both groups agitating had no respect for the women's rights rally, and were mostly there for their own ideological battle and promotion . . . .
>
> A women's rights rally #LetWomenSpeak in Melbourne was disrupted by multiple groups on Saturday afternoon. The women's rights rally had a mix of individuals speaking, and the crowd

---

25. See the May 27, 2024, affidavit of Rukshan Fernando, an independent journalist who took footage of the events, as available through the Victorian Division of the Federal Court of Australia in the Moira Deeming v. John Pesutto defamation case.

listening was made up of a cross section of the community, including members of the LGBTQIA+ community. Trans activists claiming the rally was hateful broke police lines multiple times to try and stop the women from speaking in their designated space, leading to multiple altercations with security and police.[26]

Footage recording the events of March 18 show clearly that the placards and speeches of the LWS rally centered around slogans such as "Let Woman Speak" and "Woman, Adult Human Female," which were about the opposition to free speech and political expression faced by advocates for sex-based rights for women, and showed overt rejection of gender theory's sex-irrealism.[27] They showed no political affiliation, with left or right, either far or center. They had no anti-trans or anti-queer platform, and included lesbian speakers and supporters.[28] The NSN banner had nothing to do with sex-based rights for women, but associated the far-left SA protestors with pedophiles. The target of the NSN actions were clearly directed against the large, loud, and militant (large red flags on pikes) group of SA protestors. The SA protestors were directly and disruptively attacking the LWS event, labeling the woman as bigoted anti-trans Nazis and fascists.

Amazingly, of the three entirely different interpretive narratives, it was the SA far-left narrative that the media and both the center-left and center-right political leaders of Victoria embraced and propagated to the people of Victoria. This clearly illustrates that the far-left interpretive stance on women's rights is also the center-left and center-right interpretive stance. It is because of this interpretive narrative that the two-minute speech of Moira Deeming (though the speech itself was not reported in the mainstream media) very nearly ended her political career.[29]

The media portrayal—strongly promoted by the leader of the Victorian Liberal Party, John Pesutto—was that Kellie-Jay Keen and Moira Deeming were Nazi-aligned anti-trans bigots. This is exactly the same interpretation as the far-left Socialist Alternative pro-trans protestors. The LWS event was portrayed as if advocacy for women's sex-based rights—while refusing to report what they actually said—made these women Nazi sympathizers

---

26. Fernando, May 27, 2024 affidavit, 10, 11.

27. Unshackled, "Let Women Speak 2023 Melbourne Highlights."

28. See the commentary on the event by an anonymous lesbian observer as posted on the LGB Alliance Australia, March 29, 2023: Anonymous, "Déjà Vu."

29. For the actual speeches of the women at the LWS rally, see Keen, "Let Women Speak" (YouTube video).

promoting hatred against vulnerable transpeople. These accusations were entirely false, with Pesutto eventually offering an apology to Keen after she initiated defamation proceedings,[30] but Deeming had to take Pesutto to court for defamation, because he would not settle on terms that were truthful, to clear her name and recover her political career.

The manner activist supporters of gender theory now routinely silence and civically alienate women's sex-based-rights advocates simply by asserting that they are far-right perpetrators of (unreportable) hate speech is exposed in these events. The Let Woman Speak rally profoundly and distressing illustrated that women indeed are *not* permitted to even speak in favor of sex-based women's rights. Distorting optics, shout downs, overt lies, and—for Kellie-Jay Keen in New Zealand a few days later—physical violence against women, were publicly promoted and bipartisan politically endorsed silencing strategies shamefully employed against these peacefully protesting women.

Nazi-alignment accusations against both Keen and Deeming (and every other women who spoke at that rally) were totally groundless and egregiously false, as Deeming's successful defamation action against John Pesutto made incontrovertibly clear. Pesutto was required to pay Deeming AUD $300,000 in damages. The Federal Court of Australia found Mrs. Deeming's case very strong, and the matter very serious.[31]

The brutality and injustice of the way her own political party attacked her, alas, is important to note. Deeming's fifty-seven-page first affidavit outlining the systemic, knowingly false, and very public defamation of her character, in a concerted and calculated attempt to end her political career, by her own political party, is harrowing reading. Deeming illustrates that standing up for women's sex-based rights is a politically dangerous enterprise, as once you cross the line that gender-theory-advocating trans-rights activists draw, you can expect all centrist politicians and the media to turn on you. The total lack of interest in truth in this performative and sophistic enterprise in the pragmatic assertion of normative power is striking.

Moira Deeming is a Māori and Australian-origin woman, who is married to her part-Jewish husband, and she was for some years raised by a

---

30. Willingham, "Victorian Opposition Leader John Pesutto Settles Two Defamation Cases"; Pesutto, "Statement from the Leader of the Opposition."

31. For a detailed fielding of all relevant publicly available documents about this defamation case, see Open Justice with Tribunal Tweets, "Moira Deeming v John Pesutto." See also Open Justice with Tribunal Tweets, "Let Women Speak Melbourne 2023 Press Coverage."

now-deceased and beloved uncle, who was a Jew and Holocaust survivor. Deeming is also a survivor of child sexual abuse who is very aware of the need for safe spaces for vulnerable females. She is unstintingly committed to the safety and integrity of women's-only spaces out of deep and compassionate concern for vulnerable women and girls. Deeming is not in any sense a hate-motivated person.

Deeming is a woman, she is not "white," and she has no association of any manner with neo-Nazi, misogynist, white supremacist, promoters of race-based or any other based categories of hatred.[32] This was all known to John Pesutto, but he deliberately sought to destroy her with defaming Nazi-aligning lies, out of his sense of the political impossibility of seeming to be in any way anti-trans in Victorian politics. Dan Andrews, the then Australian Labor Party premier of Victoria, also denounced Deeming as Nazi-aligned as a means of attacking the Liberal Party in a concurrent bi-election contest (which the ALP won). But this story about Deeming was not one that *he* concocted; this was a story the TRA-aligned mainstream media and the Victorian Liberal Party concocted. The LWS women were used as a political football that both sides of Victorian party politics savagely kicked in order to show how pro-trans-inclusive they both were.

If a woman wants to publicly advocate for sex-based rights for women, she will be accused of being hateful, Nazi, bigoted, and opposed to equality and tolerance. This is what gender theory has done to politics and public debate. Advocating for sex-based rights for women has become reflexively branded as an extremist stance that will not be tolerated by good and kind people. Women can just roll over and have their sex-based rights removed, because advocating for women's sex-based rights has become politically equivalent to being an extremist "far right" enemy of vulnerable gender-non-conforming minorities. Women are often very effectively silenced by brutal personal character and reputation assassinations if they dare to stand up for women's sex-based rights. It takes a very courageous and strong woman indeed to successfully stand against such vociferous and

---

32. From Hon Moira Deeming MP's affidavit in her successful defamation proceedings against former leader of the Victorian Liberal Party Hon John Pesutto MP: "I was partly raised by a Holocaust survivor; my husband is part Jewish; I am part Māori; I am supported publicly by many LGB groups and transgender people; I fostered a Vietnamese asylum seeker. The accusations Mr. Pesutto had made against me [of association with a Nazi organization] go against everything I am and everything I have worked for and have been incredibly distressing and humiliating." Deeming, Affidavit of Moira Deeming, para. 172.

relentlessly defamatory assault. Remarkably, Deeming did not collapse under enormous pressure, but she held her line and was vindicated. Even so, she has made it clear to us all what sort of a fight is involved in even being heard if one is going to stand up for sex-based rights for women in our times. It is the denial of the reality of sexual difference, and the refusal to grant sex-based protections and arenas to women, as promoted by gender theory, that has made women so politically marginalized *as women*. Gender theory is very politically harmful to women.

GENDER THEORY IS WRONG

The willful blindness to obvious natural facts and the genuine harms gender theory perpetrates against women and children show gender theory up as not only *factually* wrong, but as *morally* wrong. Gender theory is wrong in all senses of the word. Any commonsense normal person can see this. But commonsense normal people are now the hapless objects of a deeply invasive top-down social reformation. It is our intellectual, educational, institutional, and political leaders who are imposing gender theory on us all. It is the elites of the knowledge and power structures of our lifeworld who have accepted gender theory.

Alas, it is not enough to appeal to commonsense normal understandings of the facts of human sex and the proper protections of women and children from the types of males who wish to invade female-only spaces, and who wish to entice our children into the cult of queer. We have to go after the elites as well.

The problem for our elites is that gender theory is entirely continuous with the central intellectual developments that have flown out of the Enlightenment purity project. Our elites need to be shown how we can have an Enlightenment lifeworld that does not end up being deeply anti-science, anti-natural facts, and irrationally opposed to age-old familial and public sex-based gender conventions that are actually important for a safe and functioning society. Given where our high culture has taken us over the past few centuries, this is not going to be easy. But we must do our best.

10

Gender Theory Is Wrong: Radical Arguments

(Rebooting the Enlightenment)

As we have seen in the previous chapter, there are obvious enough reasons to find that gender theory is wrong. Further, we have seen that the queer minority attempt to overthrow the heteronormativity majority by means of strategic legal and institutional capture is dangerous to the natural needs and interests of women and children. All we really need to do is elect politicians who will respect scientific facts, ignore elite gender theory, and legislate to protect our women and children from the obvious harms this queer reformation has perpetrated against women and children. By all means, let trans and queer people do whatever they legally want to do in the privacy of their own spaces. By all means, as adults and paying private clients of cosmetic and cross-sex-hormone-providing services, let people do whatever strange and mutilating things they want to do with their own bodies. But in the public domain, we need a return to scientific facts about the male/female reproductive sex binary, and a return to broadly traditional sex-defined public gender norms. And how about we drop artificial victimization gender-identity politics?

Resetting legislation and institutional norms back to how they were in, say, 2010—when queer people had no legal power to force non-queer people to accept their performances as factual truth and a moral necessity—will not harm trans-identifying people, but it will prevent them from harming everyone else. This sort of practical solution is all that is necessary. On the other hand, our knowledge and power elites are going to have to stop believing their own propaganda about the impossibility of distinguishing between a transwoman and a real woman, and that is not going to be easy. And this problem is not simply a matter of hubris either, as high culture has been in a long intellectual spiral down the ever-accelerating vortex of irrealism and narrative poetics.

In the realm of theory, a practical political solution does not go far enough. The problem of brilliant queer advocates capturing our knowledge and power elites will re-occur if we do not address this tendency at its intellectual root.

So, let us go to the root of the matter.

JUST BECAUSE THE ENLIGHTENMENT PROJECT FAILS DOES NOT MEAN POSTMODERN IRREALISM SUCCEEDS

Powerful counter-Enlightenment thinkers from Hamann on have clearly understood that the Enlightenment project, understood as the faith-free and metaphysics-free advancement of liberating science and logic, must fail. And indeed, it does fail. But there are two ways of understanding the meaning of this failure.

The First Path

Firstly, there is the path to sophistic nihilism and irrealism in response to the failure of the Enlightenment project. This pathway shapes postmodern anti-science and irrealist-reason in the manner outlined below.

Trying to establish pure phenomenological scientific truth while refusing to accept anything as a matter of good faith or transcendent truth exceeding our powers of epistemic mastery fails. To those committed to the faith- and transcendence-rejecting method of Enlightenment "purity" put forward by Kant, this must mean that there is no such thing as scientific truth. Science is rather an entirely humanly constructed knowledge discourse that never escapes the context of human language and the poetic interpretive spin of human meaning-construction. Scientific knowledge can thus be useful, but its actual nature is power rather than truth. It has power as regards instrumental usefulness over nature simply because, and if, it works. This does not mean it is true. And as all human discourse is an assertion of political power, so the construction of scientific knowledge is an assertion of political power. Hence, carefully controlling the manner in which "knowledge" is presented, for the sake of advancing political objectives, is simply how things are when it comes to science. Naïve scientists may not understand this, but queer policy advocates certainly do. To queer policy advocates, trying to preserve the false objectivity of "evidence-based" so-called factual knowledge is itself a propaganda enterprise, and the skillful user of pragmatic knowledge-construction will know how to present "evidence" so as to promote their own power interests. To this outlook, everyone uses "evidence" and everyone selects and ignore "evidence" based on what governance objectives they seek to achieve through knowledge-construction. Some people (postmodern sophistic nihilists and irrealists) know they are using knowledge-construction as a tool of power, and hence use it expertly (i.e., without any regard for truth), while other people (naïve scientists) do not know they are using knowledge-construction as a tool of power and believe their own fantasies about objectivity and demonstrated truth. Welcome to the aggressively pragmatic "knowledge" environment of the post-truth world.

When it comes to reason, purged from faith and transcendence, this also is a meaningless construct of human imagination and manipulative genius. Assuming such "pure" reason, reality itself is not seen as structured by cosmic reason. Reason is simply our interpretive means of manipulating the perceived and linguistically signed worlds of our own making. So all arguments—both logically valid and logically invalid, both "true" and "false," are now equal, and the only matter of concern is *effect*. Whether an argument appears *persuasively useful* or not is the only concern when it comes to the use of reason. We are back with the ancient sophist Gorgias, who, for a fee, and by means of slippery linguistic dexterity, could make any weaker argument win.

Thus, accepting the failure of science and reason to be truth-revealing when purged from faith and metaphysics, we end up at pragmatic irrealist nihilism. Needless to say, this is not the destination Kant thought he was heading toward back in the 1780s. Has the Enlightenment project gone off the rails somewhere?

The Second Path

The second path for understanding the failure of the Enlightenment project is not to give up on science and reason as means of understanding truth, but to think carefully about what might have gone wrong with the Enlightenment project such that science and reason become treated as if they are no longer truth-revealing. This path invites us to wonder if we can only still have the science and reason liberationist *aim* of the Enlightenment project if we discard its Kantian faith-and-metaphysics-rejecting *method*.

Bold thinkers have been taking this second approach since Hamann's metacritique of the purism of reason and Kierkegaard's defense of the inescapability of faith. Even so, the determination to purge knowledge from both faith and metaphysics has come to define the Enlightenment project and its collapse into postmodern irrealism. In what follows we shall take this second path again as a means of retrieving the *aim* of the Enlightenment, while abandoning the *method* that has led to its failure.

While it is true that I am a Christian theologian, and deeply influenced by Hamann and Kierkegaard's thinking, I want to make the basic thrust of my argument accessible to our secular age, so I will proceed in a manner that I think will be persuasive both to people of no religious faith and to people of religious faith. To do this I will touch on theology within the thought categories of philosophy.

In a classical manner, I do not accept that there is really a meaningful distinction between theology and philosophy. The great classical sages of the Western tradition—Socrates, Plato, Aristotle—saw divine things as inherently philosophical concerns. I also accept that there are limits to how far a natural-philosophy approach to theology can go, but I think those limits are adequate for the task I have in mind. So, people who are not religious, fear not (too much) for the integrity of your non-believing soul as we proceed. Let us see if we can re-rail the Enlightenment confidence in science and reason as truth-revealing by means of putting faith back into science and metaphysics back into reason.

FAITH IS SENSIBLE, AND FAITH IN SENSORY TRUTH IS A GOOD IDEA

In very simple terms, the word "faith" means "confidence," and it is not a discretely religious or theological word at all. The Christian New Testament lifts the word "faith" (*pistis*) out of its literal marketplace context, where it broadly means "good faith" in the same sense which we mean today when we sell a business.

Confidence is built out of two Latin words, where "con" means "with" and "fide" means "faith." Confidence is a reasonable trust. I sit down on the chair because I am confident the chair will support my weight. I don't have to consciously believe in God to do this. The chair looks sound, it has supported my weight before, hence I don't even think about it, I just confidently sit on the chair. In this sense, confidence is an action. Based on reasonable trust, I act. This is faith.

When I have faith in science, I am not talking about a quasi-religious faith in the all-explaining powers of scientific reductionism (i.e., scient*ism*). Rather, faith in science is a commonplace confidence that science at least usually tells me natural truths about the world, truths which I can actively rely on. I do not need to believe that science tells me *all* truths, or the *complete* truth even about solidly natural and demonstrable physical things, but nonetheless a person with faith in science will be prepared to actively believe that solidly demonstrated scientific knowledge provides one with reasonable and factual truths about the world. As we live in a profoundly technological lifeworld, active faith in science is as second nature to us as using a smartphone. So we do have faith in science, practically, but do we still have faith in science *theoretically*?

There is a fascinating recent field of scholarship broadly called "science studies." Some of the very powerful thinkers that are important to this field are Thomas Kuhn, Michael Polanyi, Paul Feyerabend, and Bruno Latour. It is worth taking a quick look at each of these in order to show how their work can be interpreted in either a broadly modern "faith in science" theoretical direction or in a "science does not give us truth" postmodern theoretical direction.

Thomas Kuhn famously explored the Copernican revolution, and noted how it took over a hundred years for the geocentric model of the heavens to be abandoned after Copernicus put the evidence-based mathematical modeling for a heliocentric[1] solar system forward.[2] This is because the long Western traditions of natural philosophy (what we now call science) use a broadly accepted theoretical system of the meaningful interpretation of natural phenomena, which is a learned, status- and power-supported, authoritative paradigm. People who think outside that broadly accepted paradigm are, by definition, crack-pots. But some crack-pots are actually right, and—if the knowledge systems are not too tightly held together by dogmatic supporters of the prevailing status quo—correct crack-pots will eventually come to be seen as the people who advance great breakthroughs in scientific knowledge. Hence, nurturing your crack-pots seems like a good idea for the advancement of science.

The beautiful thing about Kuhn's work is that it unpicks a key feature of twentieth-century science-loving Western academia, which paints Copernicus and Galileo as great devotees of truth fighting dark-minded religious nut-jobs and eventually winning out for truth. This science-versus-religion mythology was largely invented in the late nineteenth century. But what Kuhn shows us is that there are sociological dynamics integral to the success or failure of competing scientific models, and authority and continuity structures in scientific knowledge are vital for its health and day-to-day work. Further, back in the late medieval and early modern period, the status quo was by no means ignorant and dogmatic, but in fact, the evidence was genuinely hard to interpret and church and university authorities were not persuaded that the heliocentric evidence was strong enough to warrant throwing out the entire basic cosmology of the Middle Ages.

Now, giving close attention to *how* the heliocentric model eventually came to displace the geocentric model gives one optimism that interpretive models indeed are changeable because actual truths about the world eventually break down interpretive paradigms that cannot accommodate observable truth.

But this is not the only way Kuhn's work can be interpreted. By attending to the unavoidable role that institutions, status, money, prevailing belief systems, and power play in how natural knowledge is actually constructed and "advanced," this can lead you to the conclusion that the objective truth about natural reality is—in the final analysis—so inescapably embedded in

---

1. Heliocentrism in solar system cosmology refers to the planets revolving around the sun. Geocentrism, where the planets and the heavenly bodies were believed to revolve around the earth, was its cosmological rival in the time of Copernicus.

2. Kuhn, *Copernican Revolution*; Kuhn, *Structure of Scientific Revolutions*.

the knowledge-production process that the very idea of scientific truth is essentially a con job. If you already believe, for philosophical reasons, that we can only know phenomena, not reality itself, then once you understand the sociological production and propagation dynamics of science, why should you have any confidence in science as truth-revealing at all?

So Kuhn can be interpreted as making a good case for us to have confidence in science as truth-revealing or a good case for us to have no confidence in science as truth-revealing.

Michael Polanyi is harder to interpret in a faithless interpretive direction than is Kuhn, but it is still possible.

Polanyi was a brilliant theoretical chemist who made breakthrough scientific discoveries in his field. He intimately explores how a scientist *actually* discovers scientific truths.[3] This process is inextricably entangled in the fact that we humans are personal beings. We relate to the natural world not as mindless data-crunching machines, but as curious and imaginative, community-embedded persons.

To Polanyi there is an inner and an outer pole to scientific knowledge. The inner pole is the asking person, the outer pole is the telling nature. There are no answers spoken to the mind of the scientist without the asking person. If you are a Humean empirical solipsist, then the asking person is the only reality you can know, and the telling natural reality cannot be assumed to exist independently of your asking. To such a faith-less stance toward the knowledge of nature itself, the asking and the "telling" are really the same thing. Polanyi explicitly rejects this outlook from the grounds of the actual experience of scientific knowledge-production. To Polanyi we only ask because there is a nature willing to tell already there.

Paul Feyerabend was deeply engaged with the problems and paradigm-destabilizing features of quantum physics, was a powerful philosophical thinker, and had a keen interest in the historical context of scientific thinking.[4] He destroyed positivist methodological certainties and derided the epistemically tyrannical claim that science gives us a decisive and reductive set of firm positive truths. He delighted in pointing out how scientists actually pragmatically construct useful fairy tales in their attempts to know nature.[5]

---

3. Polanyi, *Personal Knowledge*; Polanyi, *Tacit Dimension*.
4. Feyerabend, *Against Method*.
5. Feyerabend, *Tyranny of Science*.

Feyerabend has always been a controversial figure to interpret. Some find him a firm ally of the postmodern opposition to the metanarrative of scientific truth and a rude affront to any serious positivist and empirical philosophy of science. Others find him deeply sensitive to the wonders, mysteries, and inherent humilities of the scientific enterprise and no enemy of scientific truth, even if our best tools of grasping after it are indeed imaginative and poetic myths. Personally, I am with this second approach and find Feyerabend a delight to read, as his approach has strong and overt resonances with Kierkegaard's concern with not crushing existential truth by an abstracted commitment to some supposedly pure objective truth.[6] But clearly, if you are looking to make any sort of "pure" Enlightenment claim about reductively positivist scientific truth, Feyerabend is a ruthless and powerful enemy, and he is going to look like an advocate of postmodern epistemic anarchy.

Bruno Latour looks sociologically at the practices of scientists. There is often a soft dissonance between, on the one hand, the "fairy tales" of rigorous scientific objectivity and decisive demonstrations of facts and theories, and, on the other, the *actual realities* of scientific work. Scientists themselves seem to live quite happily with this dissonance, and when it comes to it, some level of background lifeworld dissonance is simply unavoidable for any of us. But Latour notices that the modern conception of a tight demarcation between a meaningless and objective domain of material facts and the subjective and personal domain of meaning is a cultural fiction. In fact, in practice, "we have never been modern."[7]

Latour's work can be interpreted to mean that one can have no confidence in the truth-revealing powers of science because human knowledge is intrinsically contingently situated in its interpretive structure. Or Latour's work can be interpreted to point to the astonishing wonder that while science really is a contingent medium of human knowledge-construction, it can—in some manner—transmit real natural truths to us.[8] We have a choice as to how we interpret the field of science studies. But let me argue as to why we should interpret science to be truth-revealing, provided we have good faith in our partial abilities to receive real natural truths about the world through our senses.

6. Feyerabend, *Against Method*, 156.
7. Latour, *We Have Never Been Modern*.
8. See Tyson, *Astonishment and Science*.

Early modern science—and indeed modern science up until Huxley's agnostic separation of science from religion in the late nineteenth century—was theologically warranted by Judeo-Christian monotheism. That is, because nature has a single Creator, it is a unified, ordered, and purposeful reality. Because the Divine Mind is the grounds of order and meaning in nature, our minds can detect aspects of real meaning and real order in nature. Assuming this high theological warrant for human sense and reason to be truth-revealing as regards the natural world, modern science lifts off. The question of whether you can believe in the truth-revealing powers of modern science and in the existence of a unified and ordered cosmos that is inherently intelligible without assuming this undergirding theological warrant is an interesting theoretical question. But as a matter of historical fact, Western culture *did* assume divine warrants for the knowability of real natural order and meaning, and this *was* integral with the very invention of modern Western science. Further, after the de-Christianization of Western intellectual culture (1870s to 1970s) I would say the evidence is pretty clear in that if one abandons this cosmic theological warrant, then there is no philosophical reason why nature should be inherently unified, ordered, and available to our perceiving minds as truth-revealing. If this is the case then we may still need some sort of minimalist theological warrant to underpin our conception of nature as truth-revealing.

Thinking philosophically, the sort of theological warrant I am here advocating is not that hard or costly to have. Any non-committed but open-minded member of the secular scientific age can believe in such a religiously low-maintenance "God."

Paul Davies is a physical cosmologist, and he is not in any practicing sense religious. His book *The Mind of God* is a fascinating argument as to how, without any religious faith, a scientist is more or less compelled to respect the staggering complexity and yet ordered and finely tuned unity of the physical cosmos.[9] But be not disturbed, scientific agnostic readers. The "God" of Davies (which is Pascal's "God of the philosophers") makes no religious demands on anyone. This "God" is very theologically thin. All "God" means to Davies is something like "the unified intelligibility of the cosmos." Any non-religious person, as well as persons of sincere religious conviction, can at least intellectually acknowledge such a minimal cosmic architect "God" without any religious or moral consequence. You can believe in that "God" and disbelieve that "God" has any interest in you

---

9. Davies, *Mind of God*.

personally at all. You can believe in Davies's "God" and disbelieve—like Davies—that there is an afterlife or judgment, and you can believe that human religions are nothing but imaginative fabrications. This was, after all, Aristotle's basic outlook on "God" and "religion." But even so, Davies's very thin and non-religious "God" makes a difference to how you think about scientific truth.

This takes us back to the primary parting of the ways in the Western intellectual story—the parting of Plato from the sophists. If you believe that the uncertainties and contingencies of human knowledge make the pursuit of truth impossible, then words are merely human poetic constructions and their only real use is as tools of power. This is the sophist trajectory. If you believe that truth is a divine reality that we can in some manner at least partially know, then the aim of words is to understand truth. And here is the problem: If our culture does not prioritize truth over power when it comes to the meaning of words, pragmatic power freaks will crush anyone committed to the search for truth, because a pragmatic power freak does not play fair when it comes to the true meaning of words. This is exactly the problem that sex-realists face when confronted by sex-irrealists who are only interested in capturing law and institutional and educational governance structure to promote the fantasies that suit them over any commonsense realist categories of what men and women simply are.

So if a culture upholds good faith in "God"—as the sacred and true principle of real order and meaning undergirding the physical cosmos, and as also undergirding our powers to at least partially apprehend real truths about that physical cosmos—then one's culture will respect the truth of scientific facts. Without such a common respect for the divine source of truth itself, one's culture will only respect power and will not understand truth.

Note well, the warrants of the truth of science cannot be scientific knowledge itself. Our science studies scholars make it very clear that *science itself provides no ultimate warrant for its own truth*, as it really is a profoundly contingent, imaginatively constructed, political, and inherently human knowledge enterprise. One cannot give to science the honor that only belongs to "God." The warrant for the truth of science cannot be human knowledge itself; it must be some First Principle—in Aristotle's sense—on which the human pursuit of truth itself is premised. Truth itself is a horizon above human knowledge which all our poetic meanings and contingent interpretive constructions need to be overshadowed by if they are to be good-faith enterprises in truth-seeking.

The faith-purging "purity" of the Enlightenment method not only made science anti-realist, it made it irrealist, and it made scientific truth itself an impossible horizon for human meaning. That faith-purging purity was a terrible mistake that ultimately destroyed the Enlightenment aim of using science to liberate ourselves from ignorance. We can only retain that high Enlightenment hope for science as a truth-seeking discourse about the natural world if we recover good faith in science as truth-revealing. To recover that good faith, we need to be prepared to hold as sacred the very principle of well demonstrated scientific evidence, and evidence that is not sophistically, linguistically, and legalistically tweaked so as to make the "facts" say whatever we want them to say. And for goodness sake, that human sexual reproduction is premised on the sex binary of male and female humans is no difficult feat of scientific gymnastics. Let us go back to obvious scientific truth, please! But to do so is to recover the dignity, even the necessity of good faith in truth itself. This is something gender theory sophistically rejects. And the choice is stark. Recover faith in scientific truth or embrace postmodern and sophistic irrealism. Save or destroy the Enlightenment aim of liberating ourselves from ignorance via science.

METAPHYSICS IS REASONABLE, AND THE METAPHYSICS OF REASON IS A GOOD IDEA

What the broadly modern and Western philosophical mind does not like about faith is also what it does not like about metaphysics. There are two problems. Firstly, faith and metaphysics presuppose that we have to acknowledge a horizon of meaning that is above our own minds. This is considered an affront to our "grown-up" intellectual dignity. Secondly, we cannot use "pure" reason or "pure" empirical knowledge to prove any truth of faith or metaphysics—faith and metaphysical commitments remain inherently speculative. This is an affront to our epistemic mastery. "Speculative"—which became a term of derision in the Enlightenment—traditionally means "seen from afar." The Latin word *speculare* (the root of the modern English word "speculative") means "watch" or "look out," as in look at something from a lookout, from a high point that provides an overview perspective.

Demonstrating everything and believing nothing we cannot prove within the domain of human epistemic mastery are the Enlightenment drivers that have delivered postmodern sophistry to us. For if you are not interested in (supposedly unattainable) truth, you need accept no meaning horizon above your own mind and desires. And if you find that all proofs constructed with purely rational and empirical parameters are either circular or cannot be made indubitably secure from skeptical attack—and hence proof is not obtainable either—then you can feel justified in holding a totally skeptical unbelief, not only toward rational and empirical proofs, but especially toward meaning speculation about any transcendent or essential reality.

But here I want to look at the metaphysics of reason. For another term for the Enlightenment is "the Age of Reason."

The Greek philosophical concept of Logos is a big deal to Plato, to stoics, and to Jewish and Christian philosophy,[10] and it is "one of the central terms of classical Greek culture."[11] In many regards the Age of Reason is a modern expression of the ancient radiance of Logos lingering, perhaps before the fall of the night, on the life of the early modern Western mind.

You can translate Logos into English as "word," as "meaning," as "argument," as "logic," as "reason." It is a big idea carrying a great deal of metaphysical weight in the West's intellectual history. At least it *was* a big idea, until we cut ourselves "free" from metaphysical speculation.

The basic classical idea of Logos is that there is a divine and intelligible order to the cosmos, and this order is communicated (spoken to us) via the connection between the Mind that speaks order and meaning into reality, and our own tiny minds, which, via the use of reason, can in some measure hear the divine song of meaning that is sung to us through the cosmos. So the beauty of natural ratios (Latin *ratio* is one translation of Greek *logos*), the harmonies of the heavenly spheres, the natural order that provides flourishing for living beings and that expresses natural goodness, this is divine Logos at work within nature. Logos itself originates from beyond nature in some traditions and from within nature in other traditions, and it connects with our own rational capacities so that we can grasp traces of real meaning and truth in our minds. This is, if you will, an enchanted cosmos, enchanted by intrinsic and essential meanings that are gifted to natural reality from a divine source. There is no firm separation of the natural from the supernatural here, as the natural is the medium of the divine.

The Greek, Roman, Jewish, Christian, and Islamic love of reason is a *theological* love. It is a love between the human and the divine. It is initiated

---

10. See the "logos" entry in Peters, *Greek Philosophical Terms*.
11. Hornblower and Spawforth, *Oxford Classical Dictionary*, 882.

from the divine as a seductive wooing in Plato, and those human souls open to divine things are drawn by the intelligibility of Beauty, Goodness, and Truth to the Goodness Beyond Being (God), which is the Source of this divine communication from the ever-speaking Logos. This is no cold rationalism. This is the highest eroticism of the mind and the quest of the soul for its divine Source in the Western metaphysical traditions.

Now, as we have already seen, the metaphysical cosmic horizon of reason was bashed out of Western philosophy by Kant, and by the train of developments that followed him. By the twentieth century Anglophone philosophy has a purely formal and deflationary linguistic conception of reason, which carries precisely no cosmic meaning at all. Philosophy itself has ceased to be a spiritually nourishing quest of the mind for transcendent meaning and has become the dry logical bones of "conceptual engineering." Words have become human constructions that formal legal definitions have made authoritative by the black box of a process we have entirely constructed, or they are simply tools of manipulative power. Reason itself has no meaning.

When I studied philosophy as an undergraduate, being good at the equations of logic, I did well in philosophy. But—I vividly recall—it was killing my soul. The deflation of all significance to a flatly materialist positivism, the reduction of reasoning to the dry formalism of well-engineered argumentative constructs, gave me no spiritual nourishment. Indeed, it was spiritually toxic. And, frankly, it is a very abstract form of speculative idealism, entirely disconnected from the realities of my actual experience of the world. For I experienced the world as richly meaningful. In the ordinary relationships of my life, I experienced the reality of moral qualities. Largely though beauty and music, I experienced flashes of astonishing revelation. In dreams and worship, I experienced traces of transcendence that cannot be captured by the abstract reductions of flat materialist and overtly pragmatic cosmic nihilism. The philosophy I was being taught simply did not connect to the reality I experienced. At some point I had to choose: Am I going to persist with the reductions, deflations, and abstractions of philosophy and forget the world as I actually experience it or am I going to need to find a different sort of philosophy that does connect with my experience of the world? Plato and Kierkegaard came to my aid (thank God!).

Kierkegaard talks about a leap of faith. And to be clear, the philosophical commitments underpinning a reductive and deflationary view of a flatly material, qualitatively meaningless, and transcendentally vacuous view of the world are *just as much a leap of faith* as those underpinning a more classical, Logos-framed view. But if you leap away from Logos, then there is really nothing special or sacred about reason. Leaping away from Logos is to end the Enlightenment vision of the Age of Reason.

As with the above argument about the theological warrant of scientific truth, the theological warrant for a metaphysics of reason is not that hard for the non-religious person to accept either. The basic question is, does reason itself mean anything? If no, leap through reductive positivism and linguistic deflation to the complete postmodern fabrication of all linguistic meanings. If yes, then leap back to some sort of notion—however theologically minimalist—of divine Reason. Let us look at this second possibility.

For reason to be more than simply the manipulation of grammatical sums to get whatever answer you irrationally predetermine that you want,[12] reason itself has to have a meaning grain running through it that you need to cut with. That is, for reason to be meaningful you can't simply use linguistic tricks to say whatever you want to say. Saying anything you want to say without the imposition of any essential meaning is actually speaking gibberish. For words to have meanings that are connected to a meaningful and intelligible reality, there needs to be a structure of intelligence and meaning underpinning reality itself, and our words need to have some sort of connection to that meaning. Faith in that sort of reason is to leap into the metaphysics of divine Logos. Without metaphysical confidence in reason itself, all arguments, all words, are ultimately sound and fury signifying nothing. Trying to bring about an Age of Reason once you have denounced any metaphysical commitment to the transcendent reality of Reason is not going to work. In the name of reason you will produce sophisticated justifications for the entirely irrational. This is exactly what Judith Butler has achieved with her brilliance.

A metaphysical commitment to a meaningful cosmos grants two things to the use of human language. Firstly, it allows us to find partially adequate gestures of meaning to the high and intrinsic meanings that are shot through our ordinary experience of reality. Secondly, it limits the game functions of language. Language is not simply *our* game if it is overshadowed by high meanings. A certain sacred respect for truthful reasoning, not simply factually truthful (as with science) but also truthful as regards meanings and values, can overshadow our clever linguistic constructions if we approach those constructions with a reverence for divine Reason itself.

12. To David Hume, famously, reason is the purely instrumental slave of the passions.

If we hubristically presume to be the source and destiny of all linguistic meaning, our reasoning is simply an imaginative trick, and ultimately nonsense, if meaning and value are not themselves prior to human language.

So yet again, as with a faith in the truth-revealing powers of science, a metaphysical confidence in reason is no terribly demanding thing to ask of anyone. It is not a difficult ask, even though it is, in the final analysis, theologically premised, but it is the theology of the philosophers, of Plato and Aristotle, not the theology of religion of which I speak here.

If science and reason mean something to us, they need to mean something to us for reasons that are *beyond* science and reason themselves. The Enlightenment experiment has shown us that if we try to justify science and reason only *within* the limits of human knowledge, as defined by entirely humanly constructed science and reason, we will lose both. But we do not need to know *much* about the high warrants of science and reason, we just need to show good faith to those warrants as a commitment to truth before power, philosophy rather than sophistry, intrinsic meaning and essential value rather than nihilism and "pure" performative *poesis*. Such commitments are necessary to save the Enlightenment from death at its own hands. And, of course, if "pure" science cannot tell us about natural reality, and if "pure" reason is meaningless linguistic poetics, then for what *reason* could we embrace absurdist sophistic nonsense? And what *reason* could there be why we should negate our actual experience of finding ourselves in an intrinsically valuable, transcendently traced, and inherently meaningful cosmos? The Enlightenment can only be salvaged by a return to faith and metaphysics—even if just a very minimalist return—but equally there is no *reason* why we should disbelieve in faith and metaphysics if the failed Enlightenment project leads—as it does—to the collapse of science and meaningful reason.

DISCARDING A REASONABLE NATURALISM IS A MISTAKE

The rejection of sex-realism is the rejection of a reasonable naturalism. A reasonable naturalism is not a construction of pure science or pure reason, and it is not the rejection of science and reason themselves, where language is just a poetic game and our bodies are just performative texts that we can play and write however we choose. A reasonable naturalism accepts commonsense scientific facts as truth-carrying, and expects of reasoning that it reaches toward real meanings and real values. Neither of these features of reasonable naturalism are unreasonable, complicated, or contentious. There really is male and female human sex, and these are not in any sense difficult to scientifically identify in the vast majority of cases. The conventional meaning of women as adult human females and men as adult human males is not complicated or debatable in any scientific or reasonable sense. A male cannot become female and a female cannot become a male. No one is born in the wrongly sexed body. These things are simple but valid truths of reasonable naturalism. There really should be nothing controversial about these truths at all. In fact, there *is* nothing controversial about these truths, and you have to deny science and reason to sophistically "argue" that a transwoman "really is" a woman.

We discarded a reasonable naturalism because we wanted a faith-free and metaphysics-free naturalism that we have now discovered we could not have. By the late twentieth century, this enterprise had produced an academic environment where all forms of naturalism are giving way to irrealism and performative linguistic constructivism. Nature is still there, is still factually and meaningfully available in some sense to our knowledge, and respecting natural truths is still important. So clearly, this collapse of a reasonable naturalism is a mistake. If the Age of Reason ends in an anti-science and linguistic poetic constructivism, unfettered by reality itself, something has gone badly wrong.

Peter Harrison is a historian of science. Indeed, Harrison is one of the best historians of science presently writing. His 2024 book, *Some New World*, is an exploration of how we got to decouple scientific naturalism from Christian theology.[13] Scholars familiar with early modern science understand the intimate connections between natural theology and natural philosophy from the beginning of the new experimental approach to what we now call "science" in the seventeenth century, up to the late nineteenth century when "science" and "religion" were separated out as discrete territories.[14] Harrison's *Some New World* is a monument to scholarly rigor with, frankly, far more density of references to each sentence than you are likely to find in similar highly regarded historical explorations. I know Peter well, academically, as I have worked closely with him at the University of Queensland on an international science and religion project. My sense is that Peter feels he needs to make his argument absolutely bulletproof,

---

13. Harrison, *Some New World*.
14. See Harrison, *Territories of Science and Religion*.

not simply because he is an extremely rigorous scholar (which he is), but because though his argument is quite simple, and really, quite obvious, it is leaning strongly against the dominant mythologies about naturalism and modern science that have been both upheld by positivists and anti-realists of various modern hues, and rejected by postmodernists in recent times.

Our contemporary problem is, we only have three narratives about naturalism. Firstly, there is the positivist narrative where "pure" empirical objectivity gives you truth about reality. Second, there is the anti-realist narrative where nature is a phenomenological construct, a function of our own epistemic categories and meanings, and is not actually "Truth"-revealing (being about phenomena, not noumena), though it is pragmatically "truth" revealing (if it works, it is functionally "true"). Thirdly, there is the postmodern narrative. Here positivism is flatly rejected and anti-realism is released from pragmatic "truth" categories that still presuppose largely positivist but skeptically framed conceptions of nature. Thus we have an irrealist "naturalism" where nature (singular) does not exist, but rather there is an infinite poetic sea of natures that are all (in the end) private linguistic, performative, and pragmatic constructs. All three of these narratives are premised on the validity of one move in the nineteenth century: the uncoupling of natural philosophy from natural theology. This uncoupling is what Harrison looks at closely, and he finds it is something of an incredible confidence trick, and our three dominant naturalisms thereafter are all bound to fail—which they do.

There is a switch that happens between Isaac Newton and Bertrand Russell. To Newton and other influential seventeenth- and eighteenth-century natural philosophers, the laws of nature are things we can observe, and although we cannot observe God, the causal regularities of nature are the direct action of God. This is particularly so when it comes to gravity, which is an incompressible force at a distance (there is no mechanical means whereby the force can be accounted for), which we can describe but not explain. To Newton, gravity is the finger of God, as are all causal regularities in nature.

Newton is what is called, in the jargon, an occasionalist. That is, an occasionalist holds that all actions in nature are ultimately caused by God, thus natural events are simply the "occasion" wherein God acts. The "laws of nature" to Newton are, thus, the regular actions of God in the physical cosmos. God, being the Super Rationalist, acts so regularly that we can model his actions precisely with mathematical expressions (the language that God has written the "book of nature" in). Newton is a fine exponent of what Harrison calls early modern scientific supernaturalism.[15]

Speaking for myself, I find early modern occasionalism to imply a frighteningly mechanical, determinate, and tyrannical set of theological notions, and the entire stance also seems preposterous. But here is the thing. It is Newton's conception of the laws of nature that really gets modern science into the air. And however strange it may seem to us, the "laws of nature" are directly *theological* to Newton.

Backing away from the particular matrix of problematic voluntarist and determinist theological assumptions common to the early modern West, what we are seeing here is a distinctive expression of a Logos theology of creation. The natural world as God's creation can be understood with reason because nature itself is a direct and active expression of the Reason of God. The relation between our capacity for reason and the Reason of God is why natural philosophy (science) can be done. So early modern *science* is—as everyone who was doing it understood—a natural *theology*. And the fact is, to this day, why there is order in the natural cosmos, and what—say—makes gravity work, remains entirely unknown to us. But it is the secularization of the "laws of nature" that flips early modern scientific supernaturalism to Victorian anti-supernaturalism in the name of a new type of science, a science that is totally *autonomous from* (and *in conflict with*) religion. Thomas Huxley is a key player in the invention of late nineteenth-century anti-supernatural scientific naturalism.

It is helpful to cite Harrison at some length on this remarkable flip from early modern scientific supernaturalism to late nineteenth-century anti-supernaturalism, which Harrison also calls metaphysical naturalism:[16]

> The common assumption of a scientific revolution premised on a break with the theological understanding of nature cherished by the medieval "age of faith" is at best half-true. It is not that theological understandings were replaced by secular ones. Rather, a different set of theological understandings came to the fore. In an important sense, nature become more thoroughly "supernatural" than it had ever been in the medieval period . . . , [for in early

---

15. Harrison, *Some New World*, 238.

16. Harrison thinks of "*methodological* naturalism" as an approach to observing and describing nature without reference to miracles or God, which nonetheless has no negative connotation about miracles and God. In contrast, "*metaphysical* naturalism" refers to the stance where only nature really exists, and God and miracles are ruled out of reality *a priori*. Metaphysical naturalism and materialist atheism are integral.

modern science, e]very "natural" event was directly produced by God.

... Medieval science was relatively independent of theology; early modern science is deeply entangled with it, complicating any neat linear trajectory towards modern naturalism.

For all this, the scientific supernaturalism of the early modern period was an indispensable way station on the path towards a thoroughgoing metaphysical naturalism. The reduction of the complex, multi-layered, causal economy of the Middle Ages to a divine monopoly was susceptible to a hostile take-over in which God's immediate action could simply be redescribed in purely naturalistic terms. All that was required was for God's ongoing but immutable activity to be given a new label: "nature." This option was not fully realized until the nineteenth century when habituation to the notion of laws of nature led to amnesia regarding its theological origin.[17]

All of which is to say that there is an anti-theology, and hence an anti-Logos inclination, embedded in post-nineteenth-century scientific naturalism, which makes its "methodological atheism"[18] in no sense theologically or metaphysically neutral, but spirals science itself away from cosmic Reason and away from any real categories of natural meaning and value.

I am not trying to twist anyone's intellectual arm behind their back about God or religion here, but I am pointing out that twentieth-century scientific naturalism is deeply anti-theological, as it is not only methodologically atheist, it is metaphysically anti-supernaturalist, and this has the effect of untying the long Western connection between human reason and divine and cosmic Logos. And, as Harrison points out, we only have modern Western science because of its theological conception of the laws of nature, and its Baconian pragmatic reading of a biblical imprimatur to "rule the earth" with better technological power. Experimental, utilitarian, demonstrable scientific knowledge—with its distinctive baggage of blessings and curses—only arises out of the modern Christian West. Throwing away the theological ladder by which science was achieved ends up throwing away the Western conception of Logos as well. But then we can no longer reason about nature, taking seriously its commonsense meanings and purposes and its transcendently overshadowed horizon of unreachable

---

17. Harrison, *Some New World*, 237–38.

18. See Milbank, *Theology and Social Theory*, 253. Milbank here looks at methodological atheism in the social sciences.

cosmic meaning. At least, our *scholars* cannot take it seriously. We have a high culture bereft of Logos now. No wonder we are susceptible to absurdist irrealism.

As mentioned, the three sorts of naturalism available to our educated knowledge class are positivist, anti-realist, and irrealist. None of these allows for cosmic Logos. None of these can either sustain or allow for knowable natural truths. We need *a fourth type* of naturalism displaying a commonsense and humble openness to natural truths, cosmic meanings, and intrinsic values. We do not currently have that fourth option in our knowledge class.

But the reality is, there really are males and females in the world, and customary gendered norms respecting their differences and upholding functional complementary relations between males and females, particularly centered around marriage and the reproductive family, and respecting female vulnerabilities in relation to male power, are integral with human flourishing. This is all very easy to grasp through sense and reason if sense is understood as truth-revealing and if reason is, in some culturally mediated sense, integral with cosmic natural meanings, values, and purposes. The way we actually live is embedded in the fourth naturalism whatever our knowledge elites think (and most of their lives are embedded in this fourth naturalism too).

Provided we politically ignore our knowledge class, there is nothing to worry about. But when we make laws and shape institutions to crush natural truths and natural meanings out of normal human life, then we are in serious trouble. And we now *are* in serious trouble for this very reason. We need to recover a reasonable naturalism that respects scientific truth and that respects the embedding of customs and sex-relation norms in natural meanings and natural purposes. These natural meanings need to be understood as in some sense overshadowed by *real* cosmic meanings that we must uphold as in some sense sacred and as demanding non-negotiable respect. Every other civilization in human history has been able to do this in the domain of recognizing the natural reality of men and women, treating familial relations as sacred, and acknowledging the sexual vulnerabilities and maternal needs of women as requiring protection. Why are we so special that we can't do this?

THE ENLIGHTENMENT WE CAN STILL HAVE

The aim of the Enlightenment is somewhere between failing and failed. That aim was liberation. The Enlightenment was going to liberate us from ignorance and superstition by means of science and reason. But science no longer gives us even the most basic truths, such as distinguishing the difference between a human male and a human female. And reason has no relation to cosmic truth, but all meanings are simply poetically and performatively constructed in whatever self-creating fantasy one wishes. So much for the Light of Reason driving away superstition and ignorance!

The reason the Enlightenment project failed is its methodology rather than its aim. The method of removing faith and transcendence from science and reason has destroyed the truth of science and the meaning of reason. So we find ourselves at a moment of crisis and decision.

If we push forward down the post-truth road the Enlightenment's method has delivered us at, then we can forget any sort of natural truth and any sort of natural meaning and value, and this will impact human sexual behavior and the humanizing impact of natural familial formation, and we will travel in uncharted post-human waters. This is a sophistic journey where all meanings are constructs of power, and where there is no natural truth or conventional value one can appeal to if one feels one's very humanity is being crushed.

If, on the other hand, we think, "well something must have gone wrong," then we need to wind back along the pathways we have taken, which have brought us to this post-human juncture, and find where the mistake was. The mistake of the Enlightenment is its methodology. Its determination to excise science from faith and reason from high meaning is the wrecking ball for the most basic and essential truth, meaning, and value categories of the human condition in Western civilization. High culture thinkers concerned about the human viability of Western civilization need to go back and fix these methodological problems. We need an Enlightenment where scientific truth really matters, and where reason has substantive meaning again. There is no reason why we should not have a good Enlightenment provided we can recover faith in the truth-revealing powers of science and an openness to reality being intrinsically meaningful, however much that meaning might escape anything like human epistemic mastery.

11

Recovering a Lifeworld Without Gender Theory

IN THIS BOOK I have given a genealogy of how gender theory arises. It arises out of the misguided "purity" methodology of the Enlightenment. The core driver for the present collapse of the Age of Reason is, as is usual with civilizations, hubris. We, in some supposed "adulthood of humanity" now look down on all our forefathers and foremothers as childishly ignorant and superstitious about truth and reason. From our lofty heights we can no longer see the male/female natural sex binary. From here all traditional customary modes of respecting the differences between men and women, and all the traditional organic human institutions integral with sexual reproduction (marriage and family), are now seen by us as oppressive. Some maturity!

Gender theory is wrong. By its own irrealist categories, it cannot make any sense as true, and using slippery sophistic performativity, its DEI "morality" is an entirely pragmatic grab for queer power. Furthermore, it is destructive: it is destructive of women's hard-won sex-based rights; it is destructive of the safety of vulnerable women and children; it is destructive of the very meaning of scientific truth; it is destructive of policies and laws that respect scientific truth; and it uses vulnerable and confused young people to advance its queer ideology at the cost of their sterilization and genital and mammary mutilation. Gender theory is both *wrong* and *bad*. It is an attack on the safety, fairness, dignity, and the very bodily integrity of women and children.

To conclude this book we shall now briefly spin though what we need for our lifeworld if we are to cleanse ourselves from this wrong, bad, and destructive gender theory.

THE CHOICE BETWEEN SOPHISTRY AND PHILOSOPHY

The ancient struggle between those who only see words as tools of power (the sophists) and those who see words as fragile but nonetheless serviceable means for seeking truth (the philosophers) has reached a point of crisis. Sophistry is decisively winning in our academies and state-regulated contexts. It has always been pretty popular in unscrupulous commercial and political contexts.

Sophistry can only really gain the sort of influence it now has in the context of mass compulsory state-controlled education. There are, of course, many good things about the way we have increasingly done education since the late nineteenth century, but the industrial-scale formation of minds has never been possible before, nor more subject to the strange excesses of university fashion as it now is. Compulsory state-regulated education has risen at the very same time that the church has fallen as a former of children's basic human values and belief commitments. The slack in high meaning formation produced by the departure of the church has been taken up by the market, and this century, by online algorithms. Education that is not simply secular—here meaning non-sectarian—but anti-supernaturalist in a flatly materialist sense, sits happily with the consumer-formation technologies that really shape our children's values and beliefs. Our children now learn what it means to be human—about the social, relational, and sexual worlds, and about the strange lands of postmodern identity politics—with no high horizon of meaning to bother them at all. Sophistry has never had it so good. Gender theory fits into this sophistic lifeworld as comfortably as a fish swims in water.

As parents, as scholars, as politicians, as *humans*, we have to choose between sophistry and philosophy. A lifeworld seeking to leave gender theory behind will need to choose philosophy over sophistry.

Philosophy is not rigid and dogmatic, but it *is* concerned with truth. But it is now the case that factual truths and reasonable moral values, and reasonable natural meanings, need to be actively chosen. If you are required to call someone by a wrongly sexed pronoun, if you are required to accept males in a female changing room, if you are professionally required to "affirm" the sterilization and mutilation of children, then you have a responsibility to reject sophistry and stand up for philosophy. If we all do it, it will stop. If we all lose our jobs, all have to go through the courts, all cause trouble at the schools of our children, all support women's sex-based rights, the power of sophistry can be broken. If we leave it to a brave few, sophistry has gained control of power, and those brave few will be defeated. The time has come to stand up for basic truths and sensible sex-based gender norms. This requires the rejection of the "validity" of sophistic power games and a return to truth and natural meanings.

SCIENCE

Modern science has its problems, and I have written several books about that.[1] But the scientific commitment to truth is very important and it is under serious threat. State-funded "blue sky" scientific research at our universities—the pursuit of truths about nature for the sake of truth—has been systemically eroded, and increasing replaced with "industry-link" financially interested power. The bureaucratic pressure academics in the neoliberal (i.e., sophistic) university are now under to publish or perish is producing a "replication and fraud crisis" in research. The careful ideological filtering of what can and cannot be said, and even what can and cannot be known as regards anything to do with gender dysphoria, transgenderism, or detransitioning, heavily filters both the gathering and dissemination of public information. Scientific truth is under threat. Faith in science as truth-revealing, and a strong re-commitment to an open, truth-seeking, academically and ideologically unfettered, and carefully scrutinized scientific research culture, must be upheld. If we cannot uphold truthful and open scientific epistemic ethics then science will descend into a branch of sorcery—a tool of power—where the inner secrets of what is really happening are carefully guarded from public knowledge.

Gender theory directly opposes scientific truth as regards the human sex binary. But gender theory is objectively false, and the obvious facts of bio-medical science are true. No amount of sophistic language games can conceal this basic reality. But are we going to stand up for scientific truth, or will we allow the anti-science of gender theory to dictate terms to us?

1. Tyson, *Seven Brief Lessons on Magic*; Tyson, *Christian Theology of Science*; Tyson, *Theology and Climate Change*.

MEDICINE AND THERAPY

The logic of saying that gender incongruence is not a mental disorder but is "natural" and hence mentally "healthy" can only be achieved by taking irrealist sophistic trickery seriously (which is itself incoherent). But then, going on to assert a moral imperative to supposedly "treat" a natural and mentally healthy sex-gender misalignment by permanently disabling the actual sex of children and young adults is about as far from the Hippocratic Oath as it seems possible to get. It is a serious strain to science and reason to assert that sex-gender misalignment is natural and healthy, but it makes no scientific or reasonable sense at all to imply that one's healthy naturally sexed body is a treatable mental illness.

So-called gender-affirming care is a set of medical practices that assumes that gender incongruence is mentally healthy, and that one's naturally sexed body is in fact the "wrong" body for a gender-incongruent person. Both the above assumptions are offenses against science and reason. But the incoherence of this stance is even more staggering than this. For by its own logic, if being transgendered is a natural and psychologically healthy non-alignment of one's sex with one's gender identity, then it must be transphobic to perform hormonal and surgical interventions that attempt to *align* the social and performative appearance of a transgendered person's sex with their gender identity. And if being trans means that one's gender does not align with one's sex, and if this is natural and healthy, how then does one account for gender dysphoria as a profound psychological distress caused by gender-to-sex non-alignment? Everything is being fudged here to hide radical natural-health-damaging hormonal and medical practices passed off as the legitimate therapy of gender-affirming care. But the basic reality is that you cannot treat a psychological anguish with a medical therapy. You treat medical illnesses with medical treatments, and you treat psychological illnesses with psychological treatments.

What these astonishing conceptual incoherences demonstrate is that therapeutic authorities have been fabulously gamed by queer activists. For the point of being queer, as activists like Sandy Stone understand it, is to use hormonal and medical technologies to do fundamentally *unnatural* things to your body, so as to disrupt and subvert "natural" and "normal" sex and gender categories. How therapeutic authorities were ever convinced that being trans is natural defies explanation.

Delusional and disturbed Autism Spectrum Disorder children and youths, who have been groomed to believe that they have an opposite-sex gender-essence, and that their naturally sexed body is loathsome and foreign to them, are being used by queer activists. "Wrong body" gender-essentialist minors are being used to advance the subversion and disruption of natural and healthy sex and gender categories in the larger society. These unscrupulous activists are gaming therapeutic authorities and legislators to the real and terrible harm of vulnerable children and youths.

Let us return to basics. The fact is, however much you may want to be a person of the opposite sex, that is a delusional desire that medical science *cannot* achieve for you.

Does anyone deny this? Does anyone really maintain that taking cross-sex hormones, surgically removing one's natural genitals and natural secondary sex characteristics, then having prosthetic cosmetic sex-organ substitutes carved into and constructed upon your body *actually changes a person's sex* from being, say, male to being female? This is not how the sophistic game is played. The game is that all "sex" (either of both "cis" and "trans" people) is a cultural and individual poetic gender-identity construction, so there is no such thing as a naturally sexed person at all. This is an obvious and preposterous falsehood, somehow accepted by our medical and therapeutic professionals. Giving in eventually to people's delusional desires may indeed be a final course of action if they cannot find a psychologically sustainable path out of their "wrong-body" delusion, but going straight to affirming a delusion—as if it is not a delusion—at the cost of the real integrity of the healthy naturally sexed body is ideologically driven *malpractice*, particularly for children. This is not mental health *care*.

We have looked at this already. But essentially, medical science and psychological and psychiatric therapies are ignoring evidence-based knowledge and are illustrating ideological and institutional capture to gender ideology in the present climate. It is time for more psychologists, psychiatrists, endocrinologists, and surgeons to lose their jobs because they will not cooperate with the anti-science and physically harmful ideological capture of their professions.

LIBERALISM

Compelled speech requiring the acceptance of anti-science gender theory as truth is now becoming legally mandated in many jurisdictions. This is not liberal. There is *no* argument based on empirical evidence that does or could reasonably demonstrate that a man who identifies as a woman is *in fact* female. Being required to speak as if the legal fiction of "gender identity" defines a person's "real" sex is being required to performatively and linguistically participate in a falsehood. Being required to act as if the legal fiction of "gender identity" defines a person's "real" sex is making females compete with men in sport, housing male sex offenders in women's jails, giving men access to women's rape crisis centers, and requiring women to "include" men in female toilets, changing rooms, breastfeeding groups, and other places that have always been single-sex spaces for the protection, modest, and dignity of women. This is not liberal. Rather, this is an abnegation of people's freedoms of speech and belief, and an invasion of female safe spaces very much against the will and desire of vulnerable and/or traditional women. Liberalism allows individuals to believe whatever they like about their own identity, and allows people to behave sexually however they like privately, within the boundaries of mutual and informed consent and the law. But it does *not* require the public affirmation of other people's sexual practices, non-sex-defined gender-identities, or verbal fantasy performances.

Gender theory is *profoundly anti-liberal*. It has no regard for individual belief and conscience on the matter of gender identity but requires non-queer, non-gender-theory-believing people to conform to opposite-sex-presentation queer gender-identity performances that are empirically false and deluded. People cannot be compelled to profess religious beliefs, and just because I am a Christian does not mean you are required to agree with my very serious high truth beliefs when you talk with me. The same should apply to the gender religion. People should be free to have a gender identity as believers in the gender theory belief system, but no one should be compelled to agree that any person's personal gender-identity beliefs that are sex-incongruent are actually true when it comes to a person's sex.

CONCLUSION: WHY GENDER THEORY FAILS AND WHAT WE CAN DO ABOUT IT

Most fundamentally, gender theory fails because it is false. Unsurprisingly, gender theory has only succeeded politically because we have lost the ability to recognize the difference between truth and falsehood in our high culture. This is because we have lost faith in science and abandoned any high metaphysical vision of reasonable natural meanings. Our knowledge elites are the most lost, for they are most tied to the irrealist and sophistic embracing of power over truth promoted in the West by a deeply flawed Enlightenment "purity" methodology.

I am a member of the knowledge elites. I know what the intellectual engines are that have formed the truth-skeptical and meaning-nihilist cultural ethos of the prevailing progressive orthodoxies. I would be surprised if that ship can turn itself around at this point. But as a Western lifeworld we need to turn around. The turners of the ship are not going to be intellectual elites. They are going to be the common people who still have common sense. They are going to be mothers and father who still understand what their children really need. They are going to be professionals who refuse to play along with the removal of sex-based rights and dignities for women. They are going to be the healthcare professionals who stop believing obviously harmful ideologies and insist on upholding the real interests of the children and youth they are there to help.

But there certainly is a job to be done by knowledge elites. The recovery of faith in science and the recovery of meaningful reason need powerful and courageous thinkers to come forward and save the West from its present intellectual and moral malaise. We need thinkers who can recover the Enlightenment aim, but without accepting the impossible Enlightenment methodology that has led us to where we now are.

Light and Truth, that is what we need to recover now.

Bibliography

American Psychiatry Association. "Gender Dysphoria." Fact Sheet, 2013. https://www.psychiatry.org/File%20Library/Psychiatrists/Practice/DSM/APA_DSM-5-Gender-Dysphoria.pdf.
Anonymous. "Déjà Vu: Attending the 'Let Women Speak' Rally." March 29, 2023. LGB Alliance Australia. https://www.lgballiance.org.au/ourstories/deja-vu.
Aristotle. *Metaphysics*. Translated by Hugh Tredennick. Loeb Classical Library 287. Cambridge, MA: Harvard University Press, 2006.
Austin, J. L. *How to Do Things with Words*. Reprint, London: Martino, 2018.
Bacon, Francis. *New Atlantis and the Great Instauration*. Reprint, Oxford: Wiley-Blackwell, 1989.
———. *The New Organon*. Reprint, Cambridge: Cambridge University Press, 2000.
Baines, Emma. "Nurses Threaten to Sue Trust over Behaviour of Trans Colleague." *Nursing Times*, May 29, 2024. https://www.nursingtimes.net/policies-and-guidance/nurses-threaten-to-sue-trust-over-behaviour-of-trans-colleague-29-05-2024/.
Barker, Sarah. "Did Mara Yamauchi's Question Scare Imane Khelif Off?" *The Female Category*, November 19, 2024. https://www.thefemalecategory.com/p/did-mara-yamauchis-questions-scare.
———."Lavender League Creates a Safe Space for Queer Women, Nonbinary, and Trans People." *The Female Category*, March 20, 2025. https://www.thefemalecategory.com/p/lavender-league-creates-a-safe-space.
Barnes, Hannah. *Time to Think*. London: Swift, 2023.
Bartlett, Robert. *The Natural and the Supernatural in the Middle Ages*. Cambridge: Cambridge University Press, 2008.
Bauman, Zygmunt. *Liquid Modernity*. Cambridge: Polity, 2012.
Beauvoir, Simone de. *The Second Sex*. London: Vintage, 1977.
Berger, Peter L., and Thomas Luckmann. *The Social Construction of Reality*. New York: Anchor, 1967.
Betz, John. *Christ the Logos of Creation*. Steubenville, OH: Emmaus Academic, 2023.
Blackburn, Simon. *Plato's Republic: A Biography*. New York: Grove, 2006.
———. *Think*. Oxford: Oxford University Press, 1999.
Blondel, Maurice. *Action*. South Bend, IN: University of Notre Dame Press, 1984.
British Broadcasting Corporation. "Changing Room Row Nurse Faces Disciplinary Hearing." February 18, 2025. https://www.bbc.com/news/articles/c3d5d0x97vy0.
Bromwich, Robert. "Federal Court of Australia. Tickle v Giggle for Girls." Federal Court of Australia 960, Summary, August 23, 2024. https://www.fedcourt.gov.au/__data/

assets/pdf_file/0013/120622/Summary-Tickle-v-Giggle-for-Girls-Pty-Ltd-No-2-2024-FCA-960.pdf.
Buber, Martin. *I and Thou*. Translated by Ronald Gregor Smith. Edinburgh: T&T Clark, 1937.
Butler, Judith. *Who's Afraid of Gender?* Dublin: Allen Lane, 2024.
Butterfield, Herbert. *The Whig Interpretation of History*. New York: Norton, 1965.
Cahill, Thomas. *How the Irish Saved Civilization*. New York: Anchor, 1995.
Calvin, John. *The Institutes of the Christian Religion*. Reprint, Peabody, MA: Hendrickson, 2008.
Cass, Hilary. "The Cass Review. Independent Review of Gender Identity Services for Children and Young People: Final Report." April 2024. https://cass.independent-review.uk/home/publications/final-report/.
Council of Europe. "Sex and Gender." 2025. https://www.coe.int/en/web/gender-matters/sex-and-gender#.
Currah, Paisley. *Sex Is as Sex Does*. New York: New York University Press, 2022.
Dansky, Kara. "Sandie Peggie." *The TERF Report*, February 15, 2025. https://karadansky.substack.com/p/ffs-friday-sandie-peggie.
Davies, Paul. *The Mind of God*. London: Penguin, 1992.
Dawkins, Richard. *The God Delusion*. Boston: Houghton Mifflin, 2006.
———. "Race Is a Spectrum. Sex Is Pretty Damn Binary." *Areo Magazine*, January 5, 2022. https://richarddawkins.com/articles/article/race-is-a-spectrum-sex-is-pretty-damn-binary.
Deeming, Moira. Affidavit of Moira Deeming. Victorian Registry of the Federal Court of Australia. Lodged 27/05/2024. Moira Deeming v John Pesutto. https://www.fedcourt.gov.au/__data/assets/pdf_file/0020/121484/First-affidavit-of-Moira-Deeming-27-May-2024.pdf.
de Lubac, Henri. *The Mystery of the Supernatural*. New York: Herder & Herder, 2018.
Desmond, William. *Hegel's God*. Aldershot, UK: Ashgate, 2003.
Dicey, A V. *An Introduction to the Study of the Law of the Constitution*. 8th ed. 1915. Reprint, Indianapolis: Liberty Classics, 1982.
Doyle, Andrew. "Men Do Not Belong in Women's Changing Rooms: The Tribunal of Sandie Peggie Has Exposed the Bullying and Entitlement of the Trans Activist Movement." *Andrew Doyle* Substack, February 13, 2025. https://www.andrewdoyle.org/p/men-do-not-belong-in-womens-changing.
———. "The New Gay Conversion Therapy." *Triggernometry*, podcast, March 30, 2024. https://podcasts.apple.com/gb/podcast/the-new-gay-conversion-therapy-andrew-doyle/id1375568988?i=1000650877119.
———. "The WPATH Files: 'One of the Biggest Medical Scandals of the Century.' Free Speech Nation." GBNews, March 10, 2024. https://www.youtube.com/watch?v=90QdwKxtqaA&t=129s.
Draper, John William. *History of the Conflict Between Science and Religion*. 1876. Gutenberg eBook 1185: https://www.gutenberg.org/files/1185/1185-h/1185-h.htm.
Durkheim, Émile. *The Elementary Forms of Religious Life*. Oxford: Oxford University Press, 2008.
Empiricus, Sextus. *Outline of Pyrrhonism*. New York: Prometheus, 1990.
Fausto-Sterling, Anne. *Sexing the Body: Gender Politics and the Construction of Sexuality*. New York: Basic, 2020.

BIBLIOGRAPHY

Fernando, Rukshan. May 27, 2024, affidavit of Rukshan Fernando, Federal Court of Australia. https://www.fedcourt.gov.au/__data/assets/pdf_file/0020/121448/Affidavit-of-Rukshan-Fernando-27-May-2024.pdf.

Feuerbach, Ludwig. *The Essence of Christianity*. Reprint, New York: Prometheus, 2013.

Feyerabend, Paul. *Against Method*. London: Verso, 1988.

———. *The Tyranny of Science*. Cambridge: Polity, 2011.

Flood, Alison. "Richard Dawkins Loses 'Humanist of the Year' Title over Trans Comments." *The Guardian*, April 20, 2021. https://www.theguardian.com/books/2021/apr/20/richard-dawkins-loses-humanist-of-the-year-trans-comments.

Frankfurt, Harry. *The Reasons of Love*. Princeton, NJ: Princeton University Press, 2004.

Franklin, James. *Corrupting the Youth: A History of Philosophy in Australia*. Sydney: Macleay, 2003.

Funkenstein, Amos. *Theology and the Scientific Imagination*. Princeton, NJ: Princeton University Press, 1986.

Gawkroger, Stephen. *The Emergence of a Scientific Culture*. Oxford: Oxford University Press, 2006.

Gerson, Lloyd P. *Ancient Epistemology*. Cambridge: Cambridge University Press, 2009.

Goodman, Nelson. *Ways of Worldmaking*. Indianapolis: Hackett, 1978.

Greiner, Nick. "Australian Liberalism in a Post-Ideological Age." Alfred Deakin Lecture 24. Melbourne University, 1990.

Guesmi, Haythem. "Reckoning with Foucault's Alleged Sexual Abuse of Boys in Tunisia." Aljazeera, April 16, 2021. https://www.aljazeera.com/opinions/2021/4/16/reckoning-with-foucaults-sexual-abuse-of-boys-in-tunisia.

Haidt, Jonathan. *The Anxious Generation: How the Great Rewiring of Childhood Is Causing an Epidemic of Mental Illness*. Dublin: Allen Lane, 2024.

Hakeem, Az. *DeTrans*. Sydney: Independently Published (Amazon), 2023.

Harrington, Mary. *Feminism Against Progress*. Washington, DC: Regnery, 2023.

Harrison, Peter. *The Fall of Man and the Foundations of Science*. Cambridge: Cambridge University Press, 2007.

———. *Some New World*. Cambridge: Cambridge University Press, 2024.

———. *The Territories of Science and Religion*. Chicago: Chicago University Press, 2015.

Harrison, Peter, and John Milbank, with Paul Tyson, eds. *After Science and Religion*. Cambridge: Cambridge University Press, 2022.

Harrison, Peter, and Paul Tyson, eds. *New Directions in Theology and Science*. London: Routledge, 2022.

Hart, David Bentley. *The Experience of God*. New Haven, CT: Yale University Press, 2013.

Haynes, Kenneth, ed. *Hamann: Writings on Philosophy and Language*. Cambridge: Cambridge University Press, 2007.

Henry, John. *Knowledge Is Power. How Magic, the Government and Apocalyptic Vision Helped Francis Bacon Create Modern Science*. London: Icon, 2003.

Hornblower, Simon, and Antony Spawforth, eds. *The Oxford Classical Dictionary*. 3rd ed. Oxford: Oxford University Press, 2003.

Horton, Jonathan. "Limits of Legislation as a Source of Law: An Historical and Comparative Analysis." PhD diss., University of Edinburgh, 2015.

Hughes, Mia. "The WPATH Files." Environmental Progress, March 4, 2024. https://environmentalprogress.org/big-news/wpath-files.

Johnson, Daniel. "Michel Foucault: The Prophet of Pederasty." *The Critic*, April 2021. https://thecritic.co.uk/issues/april-2021/michel-foucault-the-prophet-of-pederasty/.

BIBLIOGRAPHY

Kant, Immanuel. *Critique of Pure Reason*. London: Everyman, 1991.

Keen, Kellie-Jay. "Let Women Speak Australia—Melbourne." March 18, 2023. https://www.youtube.com/watch?v=9047VZvDgAA&list=PLgSfHNWm4FOrumOR2OlYUsIhWhtMiJQ3c&index=6&t=4417s.

Kierkegaard, Søren. *Concluding Unscientific Postscript to the Philosophical Fragments*. Princeton, NJ: Princeton University Press, 1992.

———. *Philosophical Fragments* and *Johannes Climacus*. Princeton, NJ: Princeton University Press, 1985.

King, Peter, ed. *The Cambridge Companion to Peter Abelard*. Cambridge: Cambridge University Press, 2004.

Kingsnorth, Paul. "The Neon God." *Abbey of Misrule*, April 26, 2023. https://paulkingsnorth.substack.com/p/the-neon-god?.

———. "The Universal." *Abbey of Misrule*, April 14, 2023. https://paulkingsnorth.substack.com/p/the-universal.

Klima, Gyula. "The Medieval Problem of Universals." *Stanford Encyclopedia of Philosophy*, 2022. https://plato.stanford.edu/entries/universals-medieval/#UnivViaAnti.

Kuhn, Thomas. *The Copernican Revolution*. Cambridge, MA: Harvard University Press, 1957.

———. *The Structure of Scientific Revolutions*. Chicago: Chicago University Press, 1962.

Lane, Bernard. "New Therapist Group on the Watch: The 'Affirmation-Only' Mindset Is Coming Under Increasing Challenge from Health Professionals." *Gender Clinic News*, May 27, 2022. https://www.genderclinicnews.com/p/new-therapist-group-on-the-watch.

Latour, Bruno. *We Have Never Been Modern*. Cambridge, MA: Harvard University Press, 1993.

Lawford-Smith, Holly. *Gender-Critical Feminism*. Oxford: Oxford University Press, 2022.

LGB Alliance Australia. "Dr Jillian Spencer, Queensland Child Psychiatrist, Advocates for Caution in Treatment of Gender Care." July 31, 2023. https://www.lgballiance.org.au/news/dr-jillian-spencer.

Lightman, Bernard, ed. *Rethinking History, Science, and Religion*. Pittsburgh: University of Pittsburgh Press, 2019.

Llach, Laura, and Johan Bodinier. "'A Cavity Is Not a Vagina': Transwoman Refused Healthcare in France." *Euro News*, September 15, 2023. https://www.euronews.com/2023/09/15/a-cavity-is-not-a-vagina-trans-woman-refused-healthcare-in-france.

Lyotard, Jean-François. *The Postmodern Condition: A Report on Knowledge*. Manchester: Manchester University Press, 1986.

Marx, Karl. "Contribution to the Critique of Hegel's Philosophy of Right: Introduction (1844)." In *The Marx-Engels Reader*, edited by Robert C. Tucker, 53–65. 2nd ed. New York: Norton, 1978.

McNeill, J. R., and Peter Engelke. *The Great Acceleration: An Environmental History of the Anthropocene Since 1945*. Cambridge, MA: Harvard University Press, 2014.

Milbank, John. *Theology and Social Theory*. 2nd ed. Oxford: Blackwell, 2006.

Mill, John Stuart. *On Liberty, Utilitarianism and Other Essays*. Reprint, Oxford: Oxford World's Classics, 2015.

Nagel, Thomas. *Mind and Cosmos*. Oxford: Oxford University Press, 2012.

Nicholls, Tim. "Media Statement: Investigation into Paediatric Gender Health Services Provided in Cairns." January 28, 2025. https://statements.qld.gov.au/statements/101904.

Nietzsche, Friedrich. *Human, All Too Human*. Reprint, London: Penguin, 1994.

Numbers, Ronald L. *The Creationists*. Cambridge, MA: Harvard University Press, 2006.

Nussbaum, Martha. "The Professor of Parody: The Hip Defeatism of Judith Butler." *The New Republic*, February 23, 1999. https://newrepublic.com/article/150687/professor-parody.

Open Justice with Tribunal Tweets. "Let Women Speak Melbourne 2023 Press Coverage." September 23, 2024. https://tribunaltweets.substack.com/p/let-women-speak-melbourne-2023-press.

———. "Moira Deeming v John Pesutto: A Case Resource. Former Parliamentary Liberal MP Sues Liberal Leader for Defamation." September 23, 2024. https://tribunaltweets.substack.com/p/moira-deeming-v-john-pesutto-a-case?r=9mutz&utm_campaign=post&utm_medium=web&triedRedirect=true.

Pabst, Adrian. *Story of Our Country: Labor's Vision for Australia*. Brisbane: Connor Court, 2019.

Pasnau, Robert. *After Certainty*. Oxford: Oxford University Press, 2017.

Pesutto, John. "Statement from the Leader of the Opposition." May 17, 2024. https://www.johnpesutto.com.au/media-releases/2024-05-17-statement-from-the-leader-of-the-opposition.

Peters, F. E. *Greek Philosophical Terms*. New York: New York University Press, 1967.

Pieper, Josef. *Scholasticism: Personalities and Problems of Medieval Philosophy*. South Bend, IN: St Augustine's Press, 2001.

———. *What Does "Academic" Mean?* Reprint, South Bend, IN: Saint Augustine's Press, 2015.

Polanyi, Michael. *Personal Knowledge*. Chicago: University of Chicago Press, 1958.

———. *The Tacit Dimension*. Chicago: University of Chicago Press, 1966.

Przywara, Erich. *Analogia Entis*. Translated by David Bentley Hart and John Betz. Grand Rapids: Eerdmans, 2014.

Raymon, Janice G. *The Transsexual Empire: The Making of the She Man*. Boston: Beacon, 1979.

Schopenhauer, Arthur. *The Horrors and Absurdities of Religion*. London: Penguin, 2009.

Scruton, Roger. *Kant: A Very Short Introduction*. Oxford: Oxford University Press, 2001.

Shapin, Steven. *Never Pure: Historical Studies of Science as If It Was Produced by People with Bodies, Situated in Time, Space, Culture and Society, and Credibility and Authority*. Baltimore: Johns Hopkins University Press, 2010.

Shrier, Abigail. *Irreversible Damage: Teenage Girls and the Transgender Craze*. London: Swift, 2020.

Simpson, Christopher Ben. *The Truth Is the Way: Kierkegaard's Theologia Viatorum*. Eugene, OR: Cascade, 2011.

Singer, Peter. *Hegel: A Very Short Introduction*. Oxford: Oxford University Press, 2001.

———. *Marx: A Very Short Introduction*. Oxford: Oxford University Press, 2018.

Smith, Ronald Gregor. *J. G. Hamann*. London: Collins, 1960.

Soh, Debra. *The End of Gender*. New York: Threshold, 2020.

Sorman, Guy. "Was Michel Foucault a Pedophile?" Nicholas Marshall, March 13, 2021. https://www.youtube.com/watch?v=oCuhpjS3oCo.

Spencer, Jillian, and Patrick Clarke. "AusPATH: Activism Influencing Health Policy." *Australasian Psychiatry* 33 (January 5, 2025) 273–77. doi: 10.1177/10398562241312867.
Spencer, Nick. *Atheists: The Origin of the Species.* London: Bloomsbury, 2014.
Stanley, Matthew. *Huxley's Church and Maxwell's Demon: From Theistic Science to Naturalistic Science.* Chicago: University of Chicago Press, 2015.
Stock, Kathleen. *Material Girls: Why Reality Matters for Feminism.* London: Swift, 2021.
Strauss, David. *The Life of Jesus Critically Examined.* Reprint, Cambridge: Cambridge University Press, 2010.
Szego, Julie. "LGBTQ Is Really QTBGL." *Szego Unplugged*, September 2, 2023. https://szegounplugged.substack.com/p/lgbtq-is-really-qtbgl.
Taylor, Charles. *The Language Animal: The Full Shape of the Human Linguistic Capacity.* Cambridge, MA: Harvard University Press, 2016.
———. *A Secular Age.* Cambridge, MA: Harvard University Press, 2007.
Tyson, Paul, ed. *Astonishment and Science: Engagements with William Desmond.* Veritas. Eugene, OR: Cascade, 2023.
———. *A Christian Theology of Science.* Grand Rapids: Baker Academic, 2022.
———. *Returning to Reality.* Kalos. Eugene, OR: Cascade, 2014.
———. *Seven Brief Lessons on Magic.* Eugene, OR: Cascade, 2019.
———. *Theology and Climate Change.* Routledge: London, 2021.
UnHerd. "Richard Dawkins vs Ayaan Hirsi Ali: The God Debate." June 3, 2024. https://www.youtube.com/watch?v=DBsHdHMvucs.
The Unshackled. "Let Women Speak 2023 Melbourne Highlights." Rumble. https://rumble.com/v2dr1pq-let-women-speak-melbourne-2023-highlights.html.
Varoufakis, Yanis. *Economic Indeterminacy: A Personal Encounter with the Economists' Peculiar Nemesis.* London: Routledge, 2014.
Virilio, Paul. *The Great Accelerator.* Cambridge: Polity, 2012.
Walker, Angelina. "Nurse Wins Right to Call Female-Identifying Transgender Doctor a Man in Tribunal Case." Nurse.org, January 29, 2025. https://nurse.org/news/nurse-wins-transgender-tribunal-case/.
White, Andrew Dixon. *A History of the Warfare of Science with Theology.* Sydney: Wentworth, 2019.
Willingham, Richard. "Victorian Opposition Leader John Pesutto Settles Two Defamation Cases." Australian Broadcasting Corporation, May 16, 2024. https://www.abc.net.au/news/2024-05-16/john-pesutto-defamation-case-settled-anti-trans-rights-protest/103858502.
Wintgens, Luc J. *Legisprudence: Practical Reason in Legislation.* London: Routledge, 2012.

www.ingramcontent.com/pod-product-compliance
Lightning Source LLC
Chambersburg PA
CBHW031429150426
43191CB00006B/457